# DAVID BREARLEY

### AND THE
### MAKING OF THE

# UNITED STATES
# CONSTITUTION

---

## DONALD SCARINCI

*First Edition*

Published by

An imprint of the Public Policy Center of New Jersey
Trenton, New Jersey
*www.njheritage.org*

Printed in the United States of America
2005

ISBN 0-943136-36-9

# Foreword

## Rediscovering David Brearley
### By Mark J. Magyar

I have a confession to make: Three years ago, at the annual New Jersey Legislative Correspondents Club Dinner, when Michael Murphy, co-chair of the Public Policy Center of New Jersey's Board, introduced me to Donald Scarinci, I did not know — or did not remember — who David Brearley was. Like anyone who has spent any time with Donald since December of 2001, I quickly found out.

While serving as counsel to incoming Governor McGreevey's transition team, Donald spent his off-hours scouring the State Archives, the State Library and the Trenton Public Library for information about David Brearley, the least famous of New Jersey's four signers of the U.S. Constitution.

After his first two months of wading through both original and secondary sources, Donald's political and legal instincts convinced him that Brearley had made major contributions to the development of the early republic that had been overlooked by historians. He was right.

David Brearley deserves a biography, and Donald Scarinci has delivered a well-researched volume that adds both new knowledge and invaluable perspective to New Jersey history, to judicial history, and particularly to our understanding of the development of the U.S. Constitution.

Brearley's brilliance at the Constitutional Convention has been obscured by William Livingston's reputation, by William Paterson's greater skill as an orator, and by the understandable tendency of many Constitutional scholars to view the Convention through the eyes of James Madison, whose record of the daily debates is so much more complete than the notes taken by the Convention's official secretary. Madison was a co-author and champion of the "Virginia Plan" that was on the fast track to adoption before Brearley, Paterson, and the "New Jersey Plan" got in the way.

The battle between the Virginia Plan and the New Jersey Plan is usually viewed through the prism of the large-state/small-state rivalry that ultimately produced a U.S. Senate in which each state has equal representation. But there was an underlying struggle as well over separation of powers.

Like the Articles of Confederation and the various state constitutions in existence at the time, the Virginia Plan accorded primacy in every area to the legislative branch. The New Jersey Plan was developed by a delegation drawn from the executive and judicial branches of the New Jersey state government — including a Supreme Court chief justice (Brearley), a former state attorney-general (Paterson), a governor (Livingston), and a Supreme Court clerk (William Churchill Houston) — who had chafed under a New Jersey Constitution that made them subservient to the Legislature. Their New Jersey Plan provided an alternative vision that strengthened the independence of both the executive and judicial branches.

Most significantly, Brearley, who as New Jersey's chief justice had been the first in the nation to declare a law unconstitutional, fought to ensure that the power to judge the constitutionality of laws was lodged in an independent judiciary.

The high respect that Brearley earned from his fellow delegates was demonstrated when he was chosen to chair the critical Committee on Postponed Matters that was created after a day of desperate debate in which it seemed that three months of difficult compromises might very well unravel. In just five days, "the faithful Judge Brearley ... [and] his admirable committee moved in as a rescue party to make up the Convention's mind," historian Clinton Rossiter notes.

What Brearley presented to the convention for the first time on Tuesday, September 4, 1787, was the Electoral College, which was designed not only as a small-state/large-state compromise for the selection of a president, but also to make the president independent of the powerful Senate that had been created. Brearley's committee also developed the office of the vice-presidency, and resolved impeachment procedures and a dozen other politically sensitive issues that the full convention had been unable to resolve.

Brearley made another major contribution to the Constitution he had worked so hard to create by personally guiding New Jersey's Ratification Convention to a much-touted unanimous vote. His success came at a critical point after Pennsylvania had ratified the Constitution during a bitterly divided convention and approval in the upcoming Massachusetts convention did not seem assured.

Livingston, who had trusted Brearley to steer the Ratification Convention, made him the leading member of the first New Jersey Electoral College delegation in 1788, and newly elected President Washington made him New Jersey's first federal district judge the following year. But in 1789, at the age of forty-five, Brearley's promising career was cut short when he died after a lingering illness.

It was Paterson, not Brearley, who went on to serve on the U.S. Supreme Court, where he sat beside Chief Justice John Marshall as he delivered his landmark ruling in *Marbury vs. Madison* that established in federal precedent the prerogative of judicial review over the constitutionality of laws that Brearley had pioneered on the state level twenty-three years before.

Good history requires serious detective work, especially when it comes to the Colonial and Revolutionary eras, from which so much wrong information has found its way into encyclopedias, local histories and other secondary sources.

No, David Brearley was not a delegate to the New Jersey Constitutional Convention of 1776: Convention records, Brearley's letters and the almanac in which Brearley recorded occasional entries show he was chasing Tories in Monmouth County at the time in his capacity as colonel of the Monmouth County Militia.

No, he never attended Princeton University, although he did read law with a local lawyer and later received an honorary degree.

And no, David Brearley was not jailed for treason and freed by a mob of neighbors on the eve of the American Revolution. It was his father, David Brearley Sr., a leader during the anti-proprietary Land Riots of the 1740s, who was broken out of jail by a cudgel-wielding crowd in 1747, when the future judge was just two years old.

While dispelling long-held myths, Donald Scarinci fills in some of the human side of this very public man, including his courtship of the beautiful Elizabeth Luttrell, who was raising a six-year-old daughter she bore out of wedlock after a teen-age affair with a British soldier of noble birth stationed at the Old Barracks in Trenton.

Donald traces Brearley's military career as a colonel in the Monmouth County Militia, a lieutenant colonel in the Continental Army, and a judge over court martials at Valley Forge. He explores the development of Brearley's personal relationships with Livingston, Paterson and Houston that were so important to the development of New Jersey state government in the 1780s and the shaping of the New Jersey Plan.

Donald's book is a remarkable accomplishment, and we are proud to publish it.

# TABLE OF CONTENTS

# Preface

This book owes it origins to the weeks I spent in Trenton working as counsel to Governor James E. McGreevey's transition team. The governor's contagious respect for the history of his office inspired me to continue this project and bring it to a conclusion.

I want to thank Congressman Robert Menendez, who "discovered" the painting that became the cover to this book in the halls of Congress near the House Gallery. His love and dedication to public service would have made the titans who framed our Constitution feel proud of their achievement and justified for their sacrifices. He will surely be pleased to no longer have to listen to my stories about the life of David Brearley as if they were current events.

I would like to thank my wife, Lisa, for sharing her love of history with our family and for offering her many thoughts about this book. My daughter, Elizabeth, and my son, Paul, have listened to my stories about Colonial and Federal-era America, and I hope that they have become inspired to learn more and to continue in the footsteps of the great patriots who risked everything for their ideals.

I would like to thank my friend, Ken Hollenbeck, who encouraged me to write this book and who supported me through its publication. I thank my partners, Robert E. Levy, Victor E. Kinon, Patrick J. McNamara, Andrew L. Indeck, John M. Scagnelli, Joel R. Glucksman, Joseph A. Ferriero, Richard M. Salsberg, Matthew J. Giacobbe, Joseph M. Donegan, Fred D. Zemel, Theodore A. Schwartz, and Thomas J. Cafferty, who never once complained that so much of my time was consumed with historical research rather than more contemporary business pursuits.

There were so many people who have contributed to this book that it is impossible to adequately express my gratitude. Special thanks go to Dawn Josephson, Jean La Corte, Claire Pappas, Sean Hughes, Theresa Consoli, Larry Kraft, and Assemblywoman Bonnie Watson-Coleman. I would also like to thank Bob and Dorothy Shubert of Triart Graphics and Eric Bielawski of White Eagle Printing for their extraordinary efforts.

The staffs of the New Jersey State Library, the New Jersey State Archives, the Special Collections and Archives room of Rutgers University's Alexander Library, the Monmouth County Historical Association, and the Trenton Public Library provided extensive assistance. Dr. Katherine Ludwig, Associate Librarian for the David Library of the American Revolution, Washington's Crossing, Pa., and Christine Kitto of the Seeley G. Mudd Manuscript Library at Princeton University guided us through their collections.

I am grateful to Mary Nelson Tanner, the Lawrence Township historian who has researched the Brearley family and provided fifteen pages of helpful comments on an early draft of this book, and to John Fabiano, the president of the Allentown-Upper Freehold Historical Society, who shared his research not only on the Brearley and Rogers Families, but also on William C. Houston, whose biography I am sure he will write someday.

Like any historian, I am indebted to those who have gone before, most notably Richard McCormick of Rutgers University, whose books provided a much-needed historical framework on the evolution of colonial and revolutionary New Jersey; 19th Century historian William S. Stryker for his military research and the careful copy he made of the notations in David Brearley's almanac, and Brendan McConville for his ground-breaking work on the New Jersey land riots. I relied heavily on the original sources pulled together in Max Farrand's three-volume collection of the papers of the Constitutional Convention and Merrill Jensen's multi-volume collection of the papers of the ratification debates in New Jersey and other states. Mark Edward Lender shared an early draft of his history of the federal court system in New Jersey.

Fabiano, Lender, Professor Robert Williams of Rutgers University Law School, Camden, and Sharon L. Naeole read various drafts of the book and provided valuable suggestions. Ms. Naeole also provided important research expertise and editing.

Finally, I would like to thank Mark Magyar, president of the Public Policy Center of New Jersey, for having the confidence in me to publish this book and for the endless hours over the last year that he has spent on edits, additional research, and rewrites. Without his efforts, this book in its present form would not have been possible.

For most people, the name David Brearley holds little historical significance. He was not a United States President, nor did he gallantly lead troops into a defining Colonial-era battle. There are no statues constructed in his honor and no monuments depicting his actions. He made no eloquent speeches, and he did not attain great wealth or fame.

Yet David Brearley was one of the most progressive legal

minds in the history of New Jersey and in the history of the United States of America. His contributions to our democratic system shaped our current society, and his bravery and wisdom on the Revolutionary War battlefields helped secure our country's future.

David Brearley lived during the mid-to-late eighteenth century — a time when our nation was still young and struggling for independence from England. As a young adult, Brearley enrolled in the Continental Army not long after the Declaration of Independence was read in New Jersey. He had a fiery passion for the revolutionary cause, even long before he read Thomas Paine's *Common Sense.*

Brearley also had a passion for people's rights, and as such he pursued a career in law. He served as a colonel of the New Jersey Militia and as a lieutenant colonel in the New Jersey Brigade in the Continental Army. He presided over courts martial at Valley Forge, where he came to the attention of General Washington.

But it was along the streets of Allentown, New Jersey, the place where he lived much of his adult life, that Brearley developed his interest in politics. Years later, the State Legislature of New Jersey would recognize Brearley's political zeal by   selecting him as the chief justice of the Supreme Court. Even though this post took him from military service, it allowed Brearley to travel the land and resolve disputes throughout the future state. The relationships he established and the reputation he developed helped Brearley become a credible representative for New Jersey.

Brearley later brought this credibility with him to Philadelphia in 1787 when he helped shape the United States Constitution. When he returned home to New Jersey after the Constitution's forming, he was one of the leaders of ratification.

His fellow New Jersey leaders certainly recognized his contributions, and as such they later elected him as one of New

Jersey's first presidential electors in 1789. It was then that Brearley gave his vote for George Washington to become the first President of the United States. Washington later reciprocated the political gesture by appointing Brearley first federal judge for the district of New Jersey.

Despite all his accomplishments and affiliations with political leaders of his day, Brearley himself never attained the historical status that his revolutionary counterparts had. Unlike his fellow New Jersey Constitutional delegates — William Livingston, William Paterson, and Jonathan Dayton — David Brearley has no city named after him, no college or university as his namesake, and no formal remembrance of his accomplishments. The history books are largely devoid of his name, except for brief mentions of his appearance at the Constitutional Convention in Philadelphia in 1787.

Why has David Brearley been so overlooked for so long? Perhaps his untimely death at the age of forty-five is to blame. Surely, based on Brearley's past, had he lived a long life he would have attained much greater political success. Perhaps Brearley's lack of memorabilia is part of the challenge. He left few writings for the future generations to read, and much of what he had in his early life was destroyed in a home fire.

Whatever the reason, it is time for David Brearley to become known to New Jersey and to the nation.

*Donald Scarinci*
*Lyndhurst, New Jersey*
*May 10, 2005*

## CHAPTER ONE

# Saving the Constitution

## David Brearley and the Creation of the Electoral College

*"Each State shall appoint in such manner as its Legislature may direct, a number of electors equal to the whole number of Senators and members of the House of Representatives, to which the State may be entitled in the Legislature. The Electors shall meet in their respective States, and vote by ballot for two persons, of whom one at least shall not be an inhabitant of the same State with themselves ..."*

— David Brearley, chairman of the Committee on
Postponed Matters, reporting to the Constitutional
Convention, September 4, 1787[1]

Like most days during the summer of 1787, the large second-floor windows of the Pennsylvania Statehouse collected the sunlight and distributed it across a sea of papers on top of tables covered with green cloth. But on Friday, August 31, most delegates to the Constitutional Convention did not notice the sunlight. Inside the room, few were smiling.

For the second time in three months, the convention was in

danger of collapse, and this time David Brearley was worried. The first time, in June, it had been different.

In June, Brearley and fellow New Jersey delegate William Paterson had personally precipitated the first crisis with their obstinate challenge to a "Virginia Plan" that would have created a national Congress based entirely on population. Under Madison's scheme, they knew, large states like Virginia and Pennsylvania would run roughshod over the interests of smaller states like New Jersey and Delaware.

The forty-two-year-old lawyers made an effective team. Paterson, the eloquent Princeton-educated orator who parlayed his position as the state's first attorney general into a lucrative law practice representing the rich and powerful, was "one of those kind of Men whose powers break in upon you, and create wonder and astonishment."[2] Brearley, New Jersey's stern-visaged Supreme Court chief justice, could not rival Paterson as an orator, but his "perspicuity of argument and persuasive eloquence which carried conviction with it"[3] was particularly effective in small groups and committees, where his steadfast commitment and attention to detail invariably thrust him into a leadership role.

Buttonholing their fellow delegates for weeks in the backrooms of Philadelphia's taverns and eating houses, Brearley and Paterson deftly put together a makeshift coalition of small-state delegates from Delaware, Maryland and Connecticut, and anti-Federalists from New York to oppose the Virginia Plan. They lost every important procedural and substantive vote, every important debating point, but by mid-July, they wore down the prestigious Virginia and Pennsylvania delegations. Roger Sherman's "Connecticut Compromise" — which would give every state an equal voice in the Senate, in exchange for a House of Representatives based on population — was a clear victory for New Jersey, one that might not be achievable again if the compromises of the preceding three months fell apart.

On August 21, Brearley wrote to Paterson, who had returned to his law practice after the "Connecticut Compromise," to warn that the new Constitution they had fought so hard to create was in danger of collapse: "Every article is again argued over, with as much earnestness and obstinacy as before it was committed."[4] But Paterson had not returned, and now, the last day of August threatened to be the last day of the convention.

From the opening gavel, the debate in Philadelphia that day was marked by despair and doubt. Could the convention reach final agreement on the remaining difficult issues, including how to elect a chief executive? Did the Constitution on which they had worked so hard and so long for the past three months have any chance for adoption, no matter how low they set the number of states required for ratification? Was the Constitution before them worth signing? Or should a new convention be established to start all over again?

Madison and Sherman argued over how many states should have to ratify the new Constitution. Madison pessimistically proposed a bare majority — any seven states with a majority of the population — while Sherman, ever the optimist, said it would be "a breach of faith" to require ratification by fewer than all thirteen. Unlike New Jersey, most state delegations were bitterly divided. Maryland's Luther Martin predicted his state would oppose the Constitution. The influential George Mason of Virginia declared that "he would sooner chop off his right hand than put it to the Constitution as it now stands." And Virginia Governor Edmund Randolph, still angry after losing the battle over representation asserted that the various state ratification conventions should feel free to propose changes to be submitted to another "General Convention" — a proposal that raised the possibility that a new convention could undo all the work of the current convention, even if the states somehow ratified the Constitution.[5]

At the end of the day, after voting to allow ratification by conventions of nine states, the exhausted delegates agreed to a suggestion by Sherman to refer all remaining unresolved issues, including how to elect a President, to a new Committee on Postponed Matters, made up, like all other committees, of one delegate from each state.[6]

The day's debate had underscored the fragility of the compromises worked out so far and the importance of the compromises to come, and that was reflected in the choice the various state delegations made. This new committee would be made up of proponents of a strong Constitution who were capable of — and were committed to — reaching the difficult compromises needed to avert another convention.

The committee included such stellar delegates as Madison, Sherman, Gouverneur Morris, and John Dickinson of Delaware, but the chairman of the committee appointed to save the Constitution would be David Brearley.

Brearley's selection as chairman was a mark of the respect he had earned during the preceding three months for his ability to work with others and to develop alternative solutions to complex problems. He had worked closely with delegates from four other states with very different interests in developing the New Jersey Plan, and his fellow delegates knew that he was the one who ran the numbers used to determine representation under various models. He was a good listener, and his judicial precision would be needed in drafting the compromises to be presented to the full Convention. His leadership in the Masons and the Society of the Cincinnati provided important fraternal ties in almost every delegation. Finally, Brearley's willingness to carry out his duties quietly and without braggadocio — which he demonstrated throughout his career — made him well-liked in a convention filled with giant egos.

"As a man, he has every virtue to recommend him," Georgia

delegate William Pierce wrote.[7] Brearley was almost literally born to revolution: His father, David Brearley Sr., was charged with high treason and jailed for his leadership role in the land riots against Crown and Proprietary interests that swept New Jersey in the mid-to-late 1740s. He served three years as a lieutenant colonel in Washington's army, from Long Island to Brandywine, Valley Forge to Monmouth. In his first year as New Jersey's chief justice, he became the first judge in the nation to declare a law unconstitutional, setting a precedent for judicial review that would ultimately be established as a bedrock of the American constitutional system in *Marbury vs. Madison.*

Brearley, like Livingston and Paterson, bridled under the system of legislative dominance created under the New Jersey Constitution of 1776, which was regarded as one of the worst state constitutions in the nation. He favored greater independence and stronger powers for the executive and judicial branches of government than Madison's Virginia Plan originally contemplated. Now, as chairman of the Committee on Postponed Matters, he was in a strong position to fight for those beliefs.

The list of "Postponed Matters" referred to the Brearley committee was daunting. After more than three months of debate, the Constitutional Convention had yet to decide how to elect a chief executive, or what the powers and duties of the chief executive or executives might be. No decision had been made on how long the chief executive would serve, or how an executive who exceeded his authority or committed a crime could be removed from office — critical points for men who had fought a revolution challenging the absolute power of the monarchy. No decision had been made on the appointment of government ministers, ambassadors, or judges. Nor had the convention decided whether to give the new national government the power to tax and regulate trade, which had been the original issue Madison and

Randolph had brought before the Annapolis Convention the year before and which led directly to the Constitutional Convention.

At the usual pace of debate and deliberations, it would have taken the convention weeks, or even months, to reach agreement on these issues. As Brearley and Madison knew, the convention was at a fateful juncture. Based on the tenor of the August 31 session, the convention might not hold together another month. Understanding the need to reach solutions, the Brearley Committee "moved in as a rescue party to make up the Convention's mind."[8]

On Tuesday morning, September 4, David Brearley rose from his chair and read a report to the assembled delegates that was stunning in its scope and originality. In a remarkably productive four days, Brearley and his committee had reached agreement on a series of compromises that would shape American government and politics for centuries.

The new nation would have a powerful president with the authority to make treaties and to appoint all of his cabinet members and senior government officials, Supreme Court justices and federal judges, and ambassadors, subject only to the advice and consent of the Senate. The president, vice president and independent judiciary would be subject to impeachment and removal only for treason or official misconduct.

The president and the vice president — a new concept never even discussed in the previous three months of debate — would be selected by an electoral college. An ingenious and ultimately controversial mechanism, the electoral college built on the Connecticut Compromise in balancing large-state and small-state interests in its apportionment of votes. Just as important, the electoral college ensured that each state would have a role in the selection of the president of a new federal system of government, which itself represented a compromise between the national government that Madison had originally wanted and the loose confederation of states that had proved inadequate for the previous nine years.

Congress would have the power to tax and regulate trade, providing the new federal government with the ability to raise its own budget, and would no longer have to beg state governments to pay the taxes requested by Congress.[9]

For five days, the full convention debated the Brearley committee recommendations with great passion, but made only a few minor changes in the resolutions.

On Monday, September 17 — seventeen short days after the Constitutional Convention had teetered on the edge of dissolution — David Brearley walked to the front of the room, signed the Constitution he had done so much to shape, and disappeared into historical obscurity.

This is his story.

CHAPTER TWO

# Prelude to Revolution

## The Brearleys of Maidenhead, the Anti-Proprietary Committees, and the New Jersey Land Riots

*"Sir, I think it is my duty to inform your Exc'y that yesterday about 4 in the afternoon a number of men came to Trenton in a riotous manner armed with Clubs and Cudgells and breaking open the prison took away with them one David Brierly, a prisoner under my care and keeping."*

— Hunterdon County Sheriff David Martin, in a
letter to Governor Jonathan Belcher, December 7, 1747[1]

D avid Brearley's grandfather, John Brearley, was about thirty-five years old when he emigrated to the New World on *Friend's Adventure*, which sailed up the Delaware River and anchored off Bucks County, Pennsylvania, on September 28, 1682, across the narrow river from the New Jersey lands where he would make his fortune.

John Brearley paid for his passage by agreeing to serve four years as an indentured servant to the George Pownall family.

While indentured servitude was relatively common in the late seventeenth century, Brearley's lack of resources to pay for his passage at the age of thirty-five certainly indicates that neither he nor his family were wealthy, or perhaps that a business had failed.

John Brearley's poverty was most likely recent. Just two generations before, James Brearley — who was probably John Brearley's grandfather — had been sufficiently prominent to be granted a coat of arms and crest by James I, founder of the House of Stuart, in 1615; as a young lawyer, David Brearley wrote to the Herald's College of London to obtain the coat of arms, which bears the motto *Honor virtutis praemium*.[2] Another Brearley relative, Christopher Brearly, served as governor of York Castle in 1640, just five years before John Brearley was born.[3] The Brearley — or Brearly or Brerelay or Brereleye — family name goes back in York another 250 years, and included not only the distinguished Sir John Brereleye, who lived in York in 1488, but also the notorious highwayman Richard de Brerelay, who was hanged for the armed robbery of Geoffrey Chaucer, author of the *Canterbury Tales*, and his guards in 1390.[4]

The *Book of Arrival for Philadelphia and Bucks County* records the entry of John Brearley as one of three indentured servants brought over by the Pownall family:

> *George Pownal and Ellenor his wife of Lostock in the County of Chester yeoman Came in the afforesd Ship Calld the friends adventure of Liver poole & arrived at the afforementioned day in this River Delaware — with their Children Ruben, Ellizabeth, Sarah, Rachel, Abigall pownal And theire servants John Brearele, Thomas Leister & Martha Worrell. To serve foure years a peice, wages passage dyett & apparel dureing the Said terme & Land accustomed — free from their Servitude the 29 day of the 7th mo 1686.[5]*

During his indentured servitude, John Brearley presumably lived on Pownall's 560-acre farm in what is now Makefield Township in Bucks County. He had married, and a daughter, Mary was born about 1694; his wife, whose name is unknown, died sometime between 1694 and early 1697.[6]

By then, John Brearley had moved to West Jersey; Township of Nottingham records report him as a resident on January 25, 1695.[7] He had also acquired some wealth, enough to purchase 200 acres of land on June 22, 1695, in the forks of the Shabakunk creek in Hopewell Township[8] and another 600 on the Delaware River in Hopewell (now West Amwell Township) the following year.[9]

A year later, he made another acquisition — a second wife.

David Brearley's grandmother, Sarah Wood, was a child when she arrived in New Jersey in December 1678 from Hull, England, on the *Shield,* which was the first ship to anchor in Burlington, the future capital of West Jersey. Political involvement was in the Brearley blood on both sides of the family. Sarah's father, John Wood, a widower who arrived "with his Children John, Joseph, ester, mary, Sarah Wood," and settled on 478 acres along the Delaware River in Falls Township, represented Bucks County in the Pennsylvania Assembly in 1682 and 1683.[10]

Sarah's first husband, Charles Biles, arrived in Burlington himself in 1679 from Dorchester, England, on the appropriately named *Elizabeth & Sarah.* Biles purchased a 200-acre farm that straddled the Princeton Pike in Maidenhead from Joseph English on November 5, 1695, the same year that Brearley moved to the new settlement. Biles died in 1696, leaving Sarah with two sons, John and Alexander, and a daughter, Sarah, ranging in age from about three to no more than eight years old.[11]

Referring to the relatively quick courtship and marriage of John Brearley and Sarah Biles, Lawrence Township's official history suggests that "A widow with four children, in such a wilderness, needs a protector; a widower, in such a wilderness, needs a wife."[12]

By March 9, 1697, within a year of her husband's death, Sarah Biles and John Brearley were already married.

Under existing law, the Biles family farm would pass on to her oldest son, John, so Sarah purchased a 100-acre tract just to the north for her second son, Alexander. Brearley bought the farm to the south of the Biles homestead for his new wife and family, and that is where they raised their family, which now included his three-year-old daughter Mary, and her two sons and daughter. The Biles-Brearley plantations ran from Franklin Corner Road to Meadow Road along both sides of what would become the Princeton Pike.[13]

With their combined estates, the Brearleys were a leading family in the new and fast-growing Township of Maidenhead, whose creation was authorized by the Colonial Supreme Court in Burlington in 1697, the year they were married.[14] (The municipality would be known as Maidenhead until 1816, when the New Jersey Legislature voted unanimously that Maidenhead was "an indecent and improper name for a public body or place" and changed it to Lawrence Township in honor of Captain James Lawrence, the naval captain from Burlington who died in the War of 1812 after giving the U.S. Navy its motto, "Don't give up the ship.")[15]

John Brearley already was playing an important role in the new community, serving as its first constable — a position that also included other duties. Shortly after Maidenhead was formed, the Colonial Supreme Court ordered Brearley, as constable, to select twelve men to lay out the new town's main road:

*Beginning on ye ad line at Yorke Old Road at ye corner of Joseph Worth's land, thence to ye eight mile*

# David Brearley Family Tree

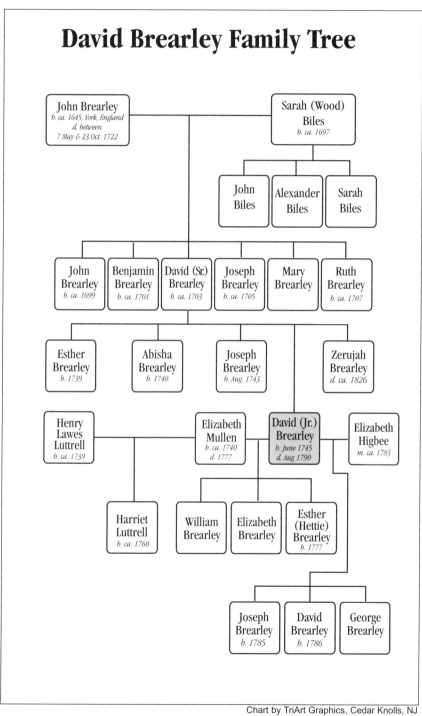

*Runne thence through Jonathan Davis's his land*
*Improved & Inclosed, thence over ye six mile Runn*
*through Theophilus Phillips land, thence over several*
*mens lands & over Thomas Smiths land to ye five mile*
*Runne thence over Mahlon Stacy's land to Assunpink*
*Creeks near ye mill of Mahlon Stacy.*[16]

John Brearley was described as a miller on the 1695 deed, but he also was "quite a land speculator."[17] He sold the Shabakunk land in 1701, later sold off four hundred of the six hundred acres along on the Delaware, and "acquired 30 shares of a proprietary tract in Sussex County" that stayed in the family for at least three generations.

His family grew as rapidly as his estate. Sarah gave birth to John in about 1699, Benjamin in 1701, David (the father of the future chief justice) on May 14, 1703, Joseph about 1705, and Ruth about 1707, giving them a family of nine children, all of whom lived to adulthood, which was unusual in the colonial period.[18]

In 1712, Maidenhead's citizens voted at a town meeting to tax themselves "for the promoting of a County in the upper parts of the province above Assunpinke" Creek. John Brearley was named along with Joshua Anderson and John Bainbridge as one of three trustees for the account set up for that purpose. Brearley's relative wealth can be seen by his agreement to pay a tax of one pound, ten shillings — an amount that was second only to John Bainbridge's tax of two pounds. Of thirty-six landowners who agreed to be taxed, only eleven paid taxes of one pound or more; the others paid six to fifteen shillings.[19] One year later, Brearley and Bainbridge were designated by the Town Meeting to represent Maidenhead at a January 8, 1713, meeting in Burlington "to procure a County."[20]

On March 11, 1714, the efforts of the citizens of Maidenhead and other towns would bear fruit, when the General Assembly voted to create the new County of Hunterdon[21] (which actually included what is both Mercer and Hunterdon counties today) from the northern part of Burlington County. Brearley's grandson, David, would represent the county he helped create at New Jersey's ratification convention for the Constitution.

Brearley was appointed overseer of the poor at the 1712 Town Meeting,[22] the first that appears in the *Minutes of Lawrence (Maidenhead) Township*, and his name and the name of his sons and grandsons would appear frequently throughout the book for the following century under a variety of spellings, including Brearly, Brearley, Braly, Brairly, Brailey, Braily and Brareley. Brearley would serve as assisting freeholder in 1718 and hold his final office as commissioner in 1719.[23]

John Brearley also was one of the landowners who signed the deed providing land for the construction of the Presbyterian Church of Lawrenceville.[24]

When John Brearley died in 1722, at about sixty-seven years of age, he was able to leave the family's mansion house, plantation and another thirty acres to his son John; another recently purchased plantation and an additional thirty-five acres to son Benjamin; a large plantation overlooking the Delaware River, near the spot where Washington's troops would cross more than a half-century later, to be divided by sons David and Joseph; forty-five pounds each to daughters Mary Olden and Ruth Brearley; and evenly divided shares of his proprietary tract in Sussex County among the six children. His stepsons, John and Alexander Biles, previously had inherited their own farms, his stepdaughter Sarah was included in her mother's will, and his son David would receive his mother's river plantation when she died. Sarah Wood Brearley survived her husband by nine years, dying in 1731.[25]

Not all of the land in Maidenhead was free and clear in title, however. It would be up to John Brearley's sons and the sons of his fellow settlers to sort out the dispute.

David Brearley Sr., father of the future chief justice, shared his father John's appetite for land. His first appearance in the *Minutes of Lawrence (Maidenhead) Township* is his appointment in 1737 to one of two township "survaior" positions, and his second in 1742 is as one of two "survaiors for the highways."[26]

His third, on March 12, 1745, is as one of Maidenhead's two freeholders — the township's highest elected positions. The preeminence of the Brearley family in Maidenhead can be seen from the election of his eldest brother John as collector and his next-oldest brother Benjamin as one of two surveyors — giving the family three out of ten positions in the township government that year.[27]

What is not known for certain is where David Brearley Sr. and his wife, Mary Clark, were living. While the land along the Delaware River that David Brearley Sr. inherited from his father and mother is located in Hopewell Township, he was clearly a resident of Maidenhead from 1737 onward when he was first elected surveyor. The five Brearley children, including the future signer of the Constitution, were all born at Spring Grove Farm in Maidenhead.[28]

Spring Grove Farm was made up of the 100-acre farm that David Brearley Sr. purchased from his stepbrother, Alexander Biles, in 1746 and the adjacent original 200-acre Charles Biles farm that he acquired three years later from the children of his other stepbrother, John Biles, who had died. However, it was "not unusual for someone to live in a house prior to its purchase," Winona D. Nash, the Lawrence Township historian, noted in a 1999 commentary on W.H. Brearley's research in which she concluded that it was indeed possible that the five

Brearley children were born at Spring Grove Farm, as W.H. Brearley contends.[29]

Esther's birth in 1739 was followed by those of sister Abisha on August 13, 1740; Joseph on August 6, 1743; David, the future chief justice on June 11, 1745, and sister Zerujah, for whom no date of birth is recorded.[30]

While David Brearley Sr. possessed deeds to his lands from his father and later his stepbrother and his stepbrother's family, a longstanding dispute over land titles resumed in the 1740s that evidently threatened his holdings, which stretched along both sides of the present-day Princeton Pike from Franklin Corner Road to Meadow Road.[31]

The land that John Brearley, Charles Biles and other early settlers purchased in Maidenhead was part of a 15,000-acre tract that Dr. Daniel Coxe of London acquired in 1680 and conveyed to the Quakers of The West Jersey Society, who sold it through their agents.

But in 1702, Coxe's son, also named Daniel, arrived in West Jersey and informed Maidenhead's citizenry that they had paid only for the right to use the land, and that they would have to pay additional sums to him to obtain clear title to the land they had cleared and the homes they had built.

Maidenhead's furious citizens met with Coxe and Thomas Revell, one of the West Jersey Society's original land agents. At the meeting, a price of twelve pounds per one hundred acres was agreed upon, but only thirty-eight families agreed to pay.[32]

Similar situations prevailed in East Jersey, where colonists who had purchased land from local Indian tribes balked at paying additional quit-rents of a half penny per acre to the original Proprietors who had received East Jersey as a land grant from the Crown.

In the 1740s, these longstanding grievances over property rights came to a head, as land riots broke out throughout New

Jersey — one of the first outbreaks of violence in what would be three decades of growing confrontation between colonists and their Royal rulers that would ultimately lead to revolution.

Nothing underscored where the Crown's interests lay more than the 1738 appointment of Lewis Morris as the first separate Royal governor for the newly consolidated colony of New Jersey. Morris had spent his entire career serving powerful London land interests in both business and government.

Morris was not only the American agent for the West Jersey Society, Daniel Coxe's land agent, from 1703 to 1736, but also the president of the powerful Board of Proprietors of East Jersey from 1725 to 1730. Furthermore, from 1702 until his official appointment as governor, Morris was a dominant figure in New Jersey government, serving continuously on the provincial Council or in the colonial Assembly, plus three separate stints as acting governor.

When Morris died in 1746, he left a province "aflame with riot." Farmers in Elizabethtown and Newark were in open revolt over unresolved litigation challenging their property rights by the Proprietors of East Jersey that Morris had represented.[33]

In Maidenhead and other towns where the West Jersey Society had sold land once, then tried to sell it again, the dissent reached treasonous levels, and David Brearley Sr. was in the thick of the dispute.

To the Royal Governor and his Crown-appointed twelve-member ruling Council, Brearley and his associates were "rioters." But the word "rioters" underestimated their level of organization, ideological cohesion, respectability, and popular support that the Brearleys and other leaders of the revolt enjoyed throughout the disputed tracts.

The forty-two-year-old Brearley and his friends Edmund

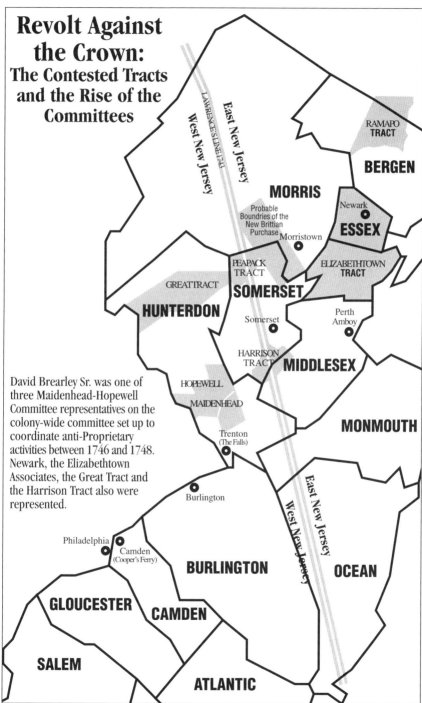

# Revolt Against the Crown:
## The Contested Tracts and the Rise of the Committees

LAWRENCE'S LINE 1743

West New Jersey

East New Jersey

West New Jersey

RAMAPO TRACT

BERGEN

MORRIS

Probable Boundries of the New Brittian Purchase

Newark

ESSEX

Morristown

PEAPACK TRACT

ELIZABETHTOWN TRACT

GREAT TRACT

SOMERSET

HUNTERDON

Somerset

Perth Amboy

HARRISON TRACT

MIDDLESEX

HOPEWELL

MAIDENHEAD

MONMOUTH

David Brearley Sr. was one of three Maidenhead-Hopewell Committee representatives on the colony-wide committee set up to coordinate anti-Proprietary activities between 1746 and 1748. Newark, the Elizabethtown Associates, the Great Tract and the Harrison Tract also were represented.

Trenton (The Falls)

Burlington

East New Jersey

West New Jersey

Philadelphia

Camden (Cooper's Ferry)

BURLINGTON

OCEAN

GLOUCESTER

CAMDEN

SALEM

ATLANTIC

Map by TriArt Graphics adapted from maps and charts in Brendan McConville's
*Those Daring Disturbers of the Public Peace*

Bainbridge and John Anderson, all duly elected town officials and scions of the three largest land-owning families in Maidenhead, represented their town on a colony-wide Committee that anticipated the Committees of Correspondence that John Hancock and Samuel Adams would create in another challenge to the Crown twenty years later.

The local Committees formed a shadow government that stretched across the colony from Newark and Elizabethtown to Peapack in Somerset County, the Harrison Tract in Middlesex, across the Great Tract in Hunterdon, and south to Hopewell and Brearley's own hometown of Maidenhead.[34]

Brearley and other leaders felt that they had been forced into open rebellion by a government that represented only the most privileged. The Brearley, Bainbridge, and Anderson families all had addressed petitions of grievance to the King, the Governor, the Council and the Assembly,[35] but they held out little hope for justice. While the popularly elected Assembly was sympathetic or at least neutral, the ruling Council was made up of men like Robert Lewis Morris, the lawyer who represented both the East and West Jersey Proprietors in their claims to royal title over 600,000 acres of disputed lands; James Alexander, the leader of the East Jersey Proprietors; and John Coxe, heir to the Coxe family's claims over the land Brearley and his neighbors had purchased in the 1690s.

The Committees set up their own courts, chose their own militia officers, and, as the ruling Council well knew, "had joined in firm Engagements to Stand by one another to Death" and "Should they be Opposed by Fire arms, to take up Fire arms to Defend themselves."[36] Nor would they allow their leaders to stand trial. For two years, whenever a Committee member was arrested, contingents from the various Committees would join together to break down the doors of the jail to set him free. Not even the jail in Perth Amboy, home to the royal governor, was safe.

On July 20, 1747, in a particularly brazen and deliberate challenge to royal authority, Brearley and the Committees orchestrated an assault on the jail in Perth Amboy to free his neighbor and fellow Committee leader John Bainbridge.

More than 200 rebels, including representatives of every Committee from Hunterdon's Great Tract to Ramapo in Bergen County, gathered in Perth Amboy at a prearranged time. As a symbolic challenge to the Proprietors' authority, the crowd tied their horses to the fence of Andrew Johnston, an East Jersey Proprietor who served on the ruling Council, and then marched on foot under their own flag with two fiddlers playing. In the lead were Edmund Bainbridge, son of the imprisoned leader, Simon Wyckoff, and Amos Roberts, the captains of the Maidenhead, Harrison Tract, and Newark anti-Proprietary militias.[37]

When the Sheriff of Middlesex tried to read King George I's proclamation against riots, one of the crowd "knocked him down, and Gave him a Wound on the head of three Inches Long." Another "struck the Mayor" and beat up several others. They warned the authorities that "if they had been Shott at, they would have Sent to a party they had Left out of town and Gott Arms, Ammunition and provisions and Levelled Amboy with the Ground, and Destroyed the Authority and drove them into the Sea."[38]

The ruling Council launched an extensive investigation. After numerous interviews with witnesses, Brearley and thirty-one others were charged with "High Treason in Levying Warr" against King George II.[39] The indictment was issued in August by the colony's Supreme Court chief justice, John Coxe, whose family was the largest shareholder of the West Jersey Proprietors who were demanding the payment of large sums from Brearley, his brothers and neighbors in Maidenhead and Hopewell, and residents of the Great Tract in Hunterdon County.

It was not until November 25, three months after the

indictment was issued, that the Sheriff of Hunterdon arrested the first of the thirty-two men charged with high treason. It was David Brearley.

Brearley had no doubt that his fellow Committee leaders would mount an assault in sufficient numbers to free him from the jail in Trenton, where he as being held, just five miles south of his home. Nor did the colony's ruling Council.

When new Governor Jonathan Belcher asked the Council's "Advice on the News and Proofs of the intention of the Rioters to break open Hunterdon Gaol and rescue Brierly," the Council urged him to direct "the Colonel of the Trenton Regiment to set a Guard" on the jail.[40] But when the popularly elected Assembly, whose leaders included John Low, a member of the anti-Proprietary Committee in Newark, made it clear they would not sanction and, more important, would not pay for the increased guard, Belcher backed off.

It would not take a crowd of 200 to free Brearley, and the Committees knew it.

About four o'clock in the afternoon on December 4 — nine days after Brearley's arrest — a small contingent of twenty riders armed with clubs arrived at the jail in Trenton. Among the contingent were at least six of the leading citizens of Maidenhead: John and Abraham Anderson, Edmund and John Bainbridge Jr., Jonathan Pierson, and Samuel Price.[41] Abraham Anderson had been freed from the Somerset jail the previous December, and all but Pierson were already under indictment for treason. Without troops from the Trenton garrison, Hunterdon Sheriff David Martin knew defense of the jail was "impracticable," and so did the riders. Martin reported:

> *I contented myself with meeting them in the street*
> *near the prison door, and Enquiring what they came for*
> *in such a riotous manner. They answered they Came for*

David Brierly, whom I detained in prison and whom they must have out.

I Expostulated with them about the <u>Seriousness</u> of the Crime they were going to Commit; that the repeating of this Crime so often was a Great aggravation of their Guilt... (W)hatever Constructions the Law might put on what they had done before in breaking Gaols, ... as the prisoner whom they now Came to rescue was committed at the suit of the King by Virtue of a writt on an Indictment for High Treason by the Law, ... the doing of it as this particular Junction was a Great Insult and an open defiance to the whole Body of the Legislature of this province now Sitting and Deliberating how to Quiet the Disturbances they had occasioned.[42]

The riders listened attentively, but unmoved. John Anderson and Edmund Bainbridge threatened to ride to Burlington themselves the following week to give a full account of their activities to the governor and the Assembly, presumably at the head of another armed band.

Sheriff Martin recognized Bainbridge and pointed out that he was already wanted on the same indictment for high treason as Brearley. In what he knew to be a futile act, Martin said, "I arrested him in the midst of them, and told them it was equally Criminal to rescue Bainbridge as Brayley, but all to no purpose."[43]

While the Sheriff watched helplessly, the crowd broke down the door to the jail and freed David Brearley.

A chagrined Sheriff Martin reported Brearley's escape in a letter to new Governor Belcher three days later: "Sir, I think it is my duty to inform your Exc'y that yesterday about 4 in the afternoon a number of men came to Trenton in a riotous manner armed with Clubs and Cudgells and breaking open the prison took away with them one David Brierly, a prisoner under my care and keeping."[44]

Belcher delivered Martin's report on Brearley's escape and other issues "relative to the Riots" to eight members of the Council of New Jersey who gathered for a meeting in Burlington on December 9.[45]

Brearley was rearrested, and this time he, John Anderson, and Edmund Bainbridge were taken for trial to Somerset County, away from the base of their home support. While they languished in prison, town ledger books and colonial legislative records critical for establishing land ownership disappeared and presumably were destroyed.[46]

Putting down a land riot that enjoyed popular support was not what the sixty-five-year-old Belcher had in mind when the former governor of Massachusetts and New Hampshire lobbied so hard in London to win Crown approval for a final sinecure in New Jersey.

Belcher "translated his predisposition to avoid the burdens of office into a principle of statesmanlike aloofness," trying to distance himself from the actions of the rioters while resisting pressure from the Council for a crackdown that would require money and troops he did not have.

With Belcher unwilling to exercise leadership, the Council and the Assembly reached their own compromise, which included a measure for the "preventing of riots," balanced by an amnesty law that required rioters to swear an oath of allegiance and post bond in money or land as a guarantee that they would not engage in further violence.

When rioters in Morris and Essex counties refused the amnesty offer, the Council urged Belcher to ask King George II to send troops, which the Hanoverian king would do two decades later in response to protests throughout the colonies against the

Sugar Act and the Stamp Act. Belcher's refusal to call in the troops, coupled with the perception that he was closer to the "ploughmen" than to the moneyed interests now led by Robert Morris, the son of former Governor Lewis Morris, led to his official reprimand and the appointment of Morris' allies to Council vacancies. Nevertheless, the politically weakened Belcher would continue to serve as governor until his death in 1759.[47]

Coxe's land claims in Maidenhead were ultimately upheld by the courts, but the amount his descendants collected was negotiated on a case-by-case basis. Some of the original buyers who "left their farms preferred to sell out rather than pay so much as a shilling more than the original price for clear titles to their land," the town's official history asserted.[48]

David Brearley Sr. and the men who freed him from prison, including John Anderson and Edmund Bainbridge, and their families, all stayed in Maidenhead. The rebels suffered no loss of political power or prestige as a result of their civil disobedience. The Brearley family, in particular, gained in prominence.

David Brearley Sr. was elected a town commissioner again in 1751 and 1752, a surveyor of highways in 1756, surveyor in 1759, and somewhat ironically, constable in 1761. He served as overseer of roads for the western end of Maidenhead in 1765 and 1766, and as a member of the town committee from 1769 until 1771, when he finally stepped down from his last elective office at the age of seventy. David's brothers John, Benjamin, and James all served for many years in elective positions.[49]

In retrospect, the David Brearley Sr. jailbreak and the threat by Bainbridge and Anderson to take their case directly to the governor, Council and Assembly at the head of an armed band represented the high-water mark of the most significant challenge to the Crown's authority in the colonies since Bacon's Rebellion flashed across Virginia in 1676. While Bacon marched on the Virginia Statehouse at the head of armed troops and burned Jamestown to the ground, the Maidenhead rebels acceded to the pleas of their allies in the Assembly and did not ride on Burlington.

While Bacon's Rebellion is more famous, New Jersey's less-known land riots arguably were just as important, particularly in their ramifications for the Revolution that lay ahead. Armed resistance to efforts by Proprietors exercising royal authority to seize lands tilled by New Jersey farmers began in Hopewell, a few miles from Brearley's Maidenhead home, in 1735 and lasted well into the 1750s. What the New Jersey Committees learned was that Crown government was weak, and could be resisted by a united citizenry organized into a sophisticated political network and willing to take up arms.

It was a lesson they passed along to their sons.

The anti-Proprietary Committees of the 1740s were succeeded in the 1760s and 1770s by the Committees of Correspondence and Sons of Liberty organizations. Cities and towns where the Committees were strong and where land riots took place proved to be hotbeds of Revolutionary fervor. Abraham Clark, a member of the Elizabeth Town Associates in 1744 at the age of eighteen and the leader of an armed raid during the struggle over Morgan's Mine in 1755,[50] was one of New Jersey's dominant political leaders during the Revolution and a signer of the Declaration of Independence. Clark's Presbyterian Church in Elizabethtown also produced Governor Livingston; Elias Boudinot, who rose to president of the Continental Congress; Matthias Ogden and Elias Dayton, the colonels of the First and Third New Jersey Regiments; and Jonathan Dayton, who would serve with David Brearley Jr. as a delegate to the Constitutional Convention in 1787.[51]

David Brearley Sr. would watch with pride as his sons,

steeped in the tradition of the anti-Proprietary struggle, proved to be equally fervent patriots.

The old rebel would live until October 4, 1785 — long enough to see his sons, Joseph and David Jr., lead New Jersey troops against the British, and long enough to see David Jr. named as chief justice of the New Jersey Supreme Court, the same position that had been held under the Crown by the hated John Coxe, the blue blood who had ordered his arrest for high treason. Truly, for David Brearley Sr., "the world turn'd upside down."

# Chapter Three

# Son of Treason

## Law, Romance, and Revolution

*"On Tuesday Night, the 26th, ult., the House of David Brailow, Esq.;*
*Attorney at Law, at Allentown in New Jersey, was entirely consumed*
*by Fire, together with all his Books and Furniture; the Family with*
*Difficulty escaped with their Lives."*

— Pennsylvania Gazette, March 7, 1771[1]

Politics, government and public affairs were a constant in the David Brearley Sr. household, and not surprisingly, both of his sons, Joseph and David, followed their father into public life, growing up to become early and outspoken advocates of independence.

"Information about David's childhood and youth is virtually nonexistent," Mary C. Tanner, a local historian who has researched the Brearley family extensively, wrote in Lawrence Township's tercentenary history in 1997.[2]

David grew up on the 300-acre Spring Grove Farm with his father, David, and mother, Mary; two older sisters, Esther and

Abisha, who were six and five years old when he was born; his brother, Joseph, who was two years older, and a younger sister, Zerujah.

Zerujah reportedly bore a striking resemblance to her brother, David. According to one family story, "once a small child who knew her [Zerujah] but not him [David], on seeing Col. David Brearley, said, 'Oh, mother, here comes Aunt [Zerujah] Pearson, in cocked hat and breeches." Zerujah would raise one of her brother David's grandsons.[3]

In addition to his own large family, David grew up with dozens of relatives nearby, including five branches of Brearley aunts, uncles, and cousins, and three branches of relatives from his mother's first marriage to Charles Biles.

The family homestead that Brearley's Uncle John inherited was located just east of Spring Grove Farm on the edge of the Great Meadow where Maidenhead's early settlers put their livestock to pasture.[4] In 1761, when David was sixteen, he watched — and undoubtedly was called upon to help — when his Uncle John and Cousin James built a Georgian brick farmhouse on the property for James to live in. This house, known locally as "the Brearley House," was preserved and is now home to the Lawrence Township Historical Society.[5]

Secondary sources insist that Brearley attended Princeton University, then called The College of New Jersey. The National Archives and Records Association, for example, in its 2001 Web biographies of signers of the Constitution, states that Brearley "attended but did not graduate from the nearby College of New Jersey (later Princeton)."[6] Princeton University's extensive records, however, show that he was never a student at the college. The original confusion, no doubt, stems from Brearley's later receipt of an honorary Master of Arts degree from the college and from mistaken assumptions concerning biographical reports stating that Brearley "read law" at Princeton.[7]

While many famous lawyers of Brearley's generation attended college, even those who did subsequently studied law under the tutelage of an established lawyer, for whom they would perform duties similar to those performed by law clerks in the nineteenth and twentieth centuries. William Churchill Houston and William Paterson, Brearley's fellow delegates to the Constitutional Convention, both graduated from The College of New Jersey and then read law in Princeton with Richard Stockton, one of New Jersey's signers of the Declaration of Independence.

While it is not known with whom Brearley read law, there is no reason to disbelieve the assertion that he did so in Princeton, just five miles north of the family's Spring Grove Farm in Maidenhead.

Brearley's decision to read law would make him the first of John Brearley's descendants to seek a career beyond farming and land-owning in the Maidenhead area, and it is evidence of an intellectual curiosity and most likely a desire for a career in public life beyond the local offices his grandfather and father had held.

The months Brearley spent reading law around Princeton would have exposed him to the intellectual ferment of a unique college town. While colleges like William & Mary, Harvard, Yale and Kings College (now Columbia) drew students almost exclusively from their home states of Virginia, Massachusetts, Connecticut and New York, the College of New Jersey drew students from throughout the colonies, including a significant share of future delegates to the Constitutional Convention.

Brearley was admitted to the Bar in 1767, so he most likely would have read law in Princeton between 1765 and 1767. Princeton's student body in 1766 included two future New Jersey delegates to the Constitutional Convention, William Paterson and William Churchill Houston, as well as future

Maryland delegate Luther Martin. Connecticut delegate Oliver Ellsworth, who had transferred from Yale, graduated three years before. Making the educational journey north would be James Madison, who would arrive from Virginia in 1769 and complete the demanding four-year curriculum in just two years, and future North Carolina delegate William Richardson Davie, who would graduate in 1776 with New Jersey delegate Jonathan Dayton. Another North Carolina delegate, Alexander Martin, had graduated in 1756.[8] The college's president during the Revolution, the Reverend John Witherspoon, would become the only clergyman to sign the Declaration of Independence.

Professors at The College of New Jersey taught the ideas of Enlightenment philosophers, including the concept that citizens possessed inherent individual rights that had been encapsulated in English Common Law. The college would become a hotbed of student protest leading up to the Revolution.

The years that David Brearley Jr. spent reading law undoubtedly reinforced the emphasis on the need to stand up for individual rights that his father set with his leadership of the Maidenhead community during the Land Riots when David was a child. During the 1765 furor over the Stamp Act, a tax imposed by the British government on letters and legal documents, it was Princeton lawyer Richard Stockton who urged New Jersey's General Assembly to send delegates to the Stamp Act Congress that would meet the following month in New York; not doing so would make New Jersey "look like a speckled bird among our sister Colonies," Stockton asserted.[9]

On November 1, as a twenty-year-old law student, Brearley would have watched with special interest as New Jersey's lawyers ceased all legal work as a protest against the Stamp Act. By the end of the month, New Jersey's General Assembly would officially denounce the tax.

The British government's repeal of the Stamp Act in 1766

was followed in 1767 with its replacement with the Townshend duties imposing taxes on paper, tea, lead, and other commodities imported by the colonies, but for Brearley, those years were eventful for other reasons.

In a span of just over a year, Brearley was married, inherited a stepdaughter, was licensed as an attorney, purchased a house in Allen's Town (present-day Allentown) in Monmouth County, and opened his law practice there.


Brearley's future wife, Elizabeth Mullen, was born in the village of Amwell in Hunterdon County and was a child when her father, John, an immigrant of Irish descent, died in 1749. Her mother, Elizabeth, married a man named Stevenson and the family moved into a "large old brick mansion known as the Clay Hill property" on what is now Pennington Avenue in Trenton.[10]

Elizabeth was about eighteen years old, "a young woman of rare beauty," when she met and fell in love with Henry Lawes Luttrell, the eldest son of the Earl of Carhampton, "in society" in Trenton.[11] An Irish nobleman of "short stature and dark complexion," Luttrell was not quite twenty years old, serving as an Ensign with His Majesty's 48th Regiment of Infantry, which was temporarily quartered at the Barracks in Trenton during the French and Indian War.

One family account says that Elizabeth's mother "never suspected any strong attachment between" her daughter and the young ensign; another says that her Quaker family "strongly opposed their intimacy." In any case, "a mutual and ardent attachment between them resulted." A "crisis in the affair of the lovers" was created when Luttrell's father procured a commission for him as captain of the 16th Regiment of the Light Dragoons that Colonel Burgoyne was raising, requiring his son to leave for

England. Elizabeth and Henry decided to elope. The marriage ceremony was either "performed by the chaplain of the Regiment, as it has always been believed by the family," or, "as is said by others, by another officer who personated the chaplain." No records of any marriage were found.[12]

Elizabeth went with Henry to New York and had already embarked on board the ship for passage to England when her mother arrived to reclaim her:

> Mrs. Mullen was convinced that Luttrell had deceived her daughter. Elizabeth was scarcely 18 at the time. There was no public marriage.... Mrs. Mullen went on board the ship herself, in disguise, accompanied by an officer, reclaimed her daughter as a fugitive, and brought her back to Trenton.[13]

Luttrell protested, but the marriage contract was not considered legal because both he and Elizabeth were under age. He had no choice but to sail with his regiment to England.

The marriage contract may not have been legal, but the marriage had been consummated. Elizabeth was pregnant, and gave birth to a daughter, Harriet Luttrell, at her father John Mullen's homestead in Amwell, fifteen miles removed from the gossip of Trenton society.

The heartbroken Luttrell "wrote to Elizabeth repeatedly, and endeavored to get her to go over to Ireland." But his "letters were intercepted, and she was eventually persuaded that she had been deserted by him. Under this impression, and through the influence of her family, she finally married" David Brearley.[14]

By the 1880s, Brearley family lore passed down through three generations told how Brearley had met the beautiful Elizabeth in 1759 when he served as "the legal adviser of her Mrs. Mullen in the affair" of reclaiming her from the ship.[15] It would be yet another twist to this highly romantic tale, if it were true. David Brearley, however, was five years' Elizabeth's junior and just thirteen years old at the time that Luttrell sailed to England.

Again, according to family lore, Brearley believed Elizabeth to be "wholly without blame in regard to the affair with Luttrell. He was a man of a very high sense of honor, and would not have married her had he not considered her to be morally innocent of fault in the matter, and the victim of some strategem."[16] But perhaps the serious-minded young lawyer was just as smitten as the noble ensign had been and did not care; he is described as "most tenderly attached" to her.[17]

Brearley was about twenty-one years old when he married the beautiful twenty-six-year-old Elizabeth in 1766, according to one account, or 1767, according to W.H. Brearley's genealogical research in the 1880s, which relied upon a deed signed by Brearley and "Elizabeth, his wife" and "witnessed by Harriet Luttrell" that was in the possession of Louisa Brearley, David Brearley's grand-niece, at the time.[18] Harriet was about six years old at the time.

By then, Luttrell was serving with his regiment in Portugal. He would not marry until 1776 and would not inherit his father's title until 1787. He never forgot Elizabeth or their young daughter. "Mr. Ryall," who studied law in Brearley's office, recalled how "Luttrell constantly remitted funds for the maintenance and education of his daughter, Harriett."[19] Two letters from Brearley to William Montgomery in Dublin requesting payment of "fifty pounds British Sterling" from the "account of the Honourable Colonel Luttrell" are in the Monmouth County Historical Association's archives.[20]

Brearley chose Allen's Town, a village east of Trenton that served as a stagecoach stop on the Lower York Road that connected New York to Philadelphia, to settle his new family and open a law practice. In May of 1767, he moved into a low, old-fashioned house at 5 York Road, near the intersection of Paine (now Church) Street, and hung his out his shingle.

An established agrarian village, Allen's Town already contained approximately eighty buildings, farms, and homes, as well as two churches, two cemeteries, and stables. Along York Road stood three taverns, several blacksmiths, a cooper, a brew house, two mills, a farmer's market house, a general store, a tannery, and a pork-processing business. Brearley was one of several lawyers, and there was at least one doctor.

Brearley's house was located next to Isaac and Hannah Rogers, who had been married for almost ten years and whose family history would become closely entwined with the Brearleys in the years ahead. Isaac Rogers was thirty-nine years old with two boys, Benjamin, seven, and James, four, and a two-year-old daughter, Elisabeth,[21] when the Brearleys and seven-year-old Harriet moved in next-door. Over the next decade, Hannah and Elizabeth each would have four more children, who would grow up together.

Isaac Rogers was the second son of the late Samuel Rogers Sr., who immigrated from Ireland in the 1730s. Settling in Allen's Town, Samuel Rogers Sr. "became an extensive land-owner, carried on a prosperous mercantile employment, and lived in a style corresponding with his abundant means."

Isaac inherited his father's mercantile business, along with his magnificent house, whose "front door was elegant mahogany, with a large knocker of Brass, with a Lions head thereon," and a large spring house with an elegant second-floor ballroom "with a large looking glass affixed in the wall & seats around the walls with cushions thereon."[22] His growing tannery complex, which eventually contained fifteen vats, a large barkhouse, millhouse, currying and shoemakers shops, stood just behind the Brearley home.[23]

Brearley and Rogers shared an interest in the law; Rogers' obituary would extol his "sound and clear judgement, which enabled him to execute the important trust of a magistrate with a becoming dignity, and a steady and impartial administration of justice."[24] Like Brearley, Isaac and his older brother, Samuel Rogers Jr., also would prove to be fervent patriots.

The Brearleys were in Allen's Town less than four years when, on February 26, 1771, fire swept through the home they shared with Harriet, now about ten years old, and one or two children of their own, depending upon when William and Elizabeth were born. As the *Pennsylvania Gazette* reported in its March 7 edition:

> *On Tuesday Night, the 26th, ult., the House of David Brailow, Esq.; Attorney at Law, at Allentown in New Jersey, was entirely consumed by Fire, together with all his Books and Furniture; the Family with Difficulty escaped with their Lives.*[25]

Brearley built a new home on the same site.

By 1771, the year of the near-fatal fire, Brearley was serving as Monmouth County surrogate, handling wills and probate cases under an appointment from William Franklin, New Jersey's royal governor, who was the son of Benjamin Franklin. He "appears to have executed the business of that office, at Allentown, not only for Monmouth County but also for Burlington, for in that year the will of William Montgomery of Upper Freehold, and that of Mary Cubberly of Nottingham, were both proved at Allentown before David Brearley, Jun[r], Surrogate, and there are later instances of the same kind."[26] The appointment as surrogate gave Brearley the opportunity to demonstrate his competence to hundreds of his fellow citizens as they came to him to disperse the possessions of deceased family members and adjudicate probate cases. It also gave him ample opportunity to discuss the events of the day with a wide range of citizens.

The 1770 repeal of all of the Townshend acts except for the tax on tea, coupled with the British government's decision not to force tea upon the colonies over the next several years, resulted in three years of relative calm. But Parliament's passage of the Tea Act in May 1773 giving the British East India Company the right to sell tea directly to the colonies led to the Boston Tea Party that December, and New Jersey and the other colonies erupted.

In January 1774, students at The College of New Jersey broke into the steward's storage room and burned the college's supply of tea in protest. The following month, the New Jersey General Assembly created a Committee of Correspondence to share information with other colonies about any British actions affecting their "Liberties and Privileges."[27]

On June 1, New Jersey's Committee of Correspondence denounced Parliament's decision to close the Port of Boston in retaliation for the Boston Tea Party, and five days later, the "Freeholders and Inhabitants of the Township of Lower Freehold" in Monmouth County set up the first local Committee of Correspondence.[28] Within six weeks, Monmouth and ten other counties had set up county Committees of Correspondence.[29]

A three-day general meeting of seventy-two delegates representing the county Committees of Correspondence, held in New Brunswick in late July, pledged support to the rebellious citizens of Boston and elected William Livingston and four other delegates to represent New Jersey at the First Continental Congress in Philadelphia. This first national assemblage since the

Stamp Act Congress of 1765 declared taxation without representation to be unconstitutional and endorsed a non-importation, non-exportation boycott against Britain.

New Jersey's counties began forming Committees of Observation to monitor compliance with the boycott, and on December 22nd, just one year and six days after the Boston Tea Party, New Jersey had its own "tea party." In Greenwich, men dressed as Indians broke into a storehouse containing tea from the British ship *Greyhound* and burned the tea in an open field.

Royal Governor William Franklin appealed to the New Jersey Legislature on January 13th, arguing that the Committees of Correspondence were trying to usurp their power. But the Assembly responded by endorsing the Continental Congress' actions and by appointing the same five delegates to represent New Jersey at the Second Continental Congress.

Monmouth County, Brearley's adopted home, was the first to form militia companies in preparation for potential hostilities with British troops: On March 6, 1775, the Freehold Committee of Observation and Inspection announced publicly that "A very considerable number of the inhabitants of Freehold have formed themselves into companies and chosen military instructors under whose tuition they have been making rapid improvement."[30]

Six weeks later, the clash between British troops and Massachusetts militia at Lexington and Concord put the colonies clearly on the road to revolution.

While New Jersey had been relatively united in its opposition to the Stamp Act, the Townshend duties, the Tea Act and the Intolerable Acts, the prospect of outright revolution quickly divided the state and its leaders.

Most men who held top offices in the state government, including the speaker of the Assembly, the Supreme Court chief justice, and most members of Royal Governor Franklin's Council were Loyalist or neutral, as were the sheriffs of Monmouth,

Hunterdon, Gloucester, and Burlington. The East Jersey Board of Proprietors, the large landowners whose fathers had battled the Elizabethtown and Newark farmers during the land riots of the 1740s, were also largely Loyalists.[31]

Some prominent citizens did join the rebel cause, including two members of the Royal Governor's Council, Richard Stockton and Francis Hopkinson, who would later sign the Declaration of Independence, and John Stevens Sr., who would chair the New Jersey convention that would ratify the new U.S. Constitution in 1787. But, as historian Richard P. McCormick noted,

> ... with the departure of many men who had formerly wielded great power an unusual opportunity existed for new men, many of them of little note before the war to come into prominence. Such men, for example, as Abraham Clark, William Paterson, David Brearly, Elias Boudinot, and Andrew Sinnickson — all of relatively humble origins — attained high positions chiefly because of the revolutionary overturn of the new order.
>
> For what ends were these men contending? In brief they were struggling to maintain the independence of the new state and nation. More fundamental, they wanted to preserve their rights as they understood them...[32]

Little is known of Brearley's early Revolutionary activities, and the principal story that has been passed down through the years in various short biographical sketches in books, on the Web,and in other secondary sources is evidently incorrect.

"At the outbreak of the Revolution," as one typical account put it, "Brearley was arrested by the British on grounds of treason but was freed by a mob sympathetic to the patriot movement." No original source can be found for this story, which clearly appears to be a matter of confusion with his father being arrested for treason and freed by a mob during the 1747 land riots. But the confusion goes back at least to 1886, when W.H. Brearley's genealogical report stated that Brearley "became early and prominently identified with colonial resistance to the British, and was arrested for high treason, but liberated by a mob of his fellow citizens."[33]

Another story passed down through the years is that Brearley had a reward on his head because he served as a delegate to New Jersey's first constitutional convention. The official Allentown history says of Brearley: "In 1776 he was a member of the first constitutional convention, for which he was outlawed by the British government and a reward of £500 was offered for his apprehension."[34] W. H. Brearley reports the amount of the reward as £100 for any member of that constitutional convention, and adds that David "and his brother used to come to the old homestead like hares to a burrow, watched by their Tory neighbors and relatives, eager for the reward." Once again, the story is false. Brearley did not even attend the New Jersey Constitutional Convention in June 1776; he spent the month helping to suppress Tory opposition in western Monmouth County.

Nevertheless, it is clear both David Brearley and his older brother Joseph, who was still living in Maidenhead, were fervent and early patriots, judging from the military ranks they attained so early in the war.

# CHAPTER FOUR

# The Brearley Brothers
# Go to War

### Retreat from Quebec,
### Retreat from Long Island,
### Victory in Trenton

*"Colonel Brearley is just now arrived from Allentown, which is in the
neighborhood of the Monmouth insurgents. ... They had confederated under oath — at least part of them. About thirty are flying on
board the enemy fleet, our militia in pursuit. ... The leaders, if they
can be apprehended, will be punished."*

— Samuel Tucker, President of the New Jersey
Provincial Congress, to John Hancock, President
of the Continental Congress, July 6, 1776 [1]

Two weeks after Lexington, New Jersey's Provincial
Committee of Correspondence called upon New
Jersey's thirteen counties to send delegates to a
Provincial Congress. The eighty-five delegates convened in

Trenton on May 23, 1775, and concluded their first session on June 3 by calling upon the counties to raise £10,000 and urging the Committees of Observation to:

> ... acquaint themselves with the number of male inhabitants in their respective districts, from the age of sixteen to fifty, who are capable of bearing arms; and thereupon form them into companies consisting, as near may be, of eight men each; which companies shall so formed shall, each by itself, assemble and choose, by plurality of voices, four persons among themselves, of sufficient substance and capacity for its officers, — namely one captain, two lieutenants, and an ensign.
>
> 2d. That the officers so chosen, appoint for their respective companies fit persons to be sergeants, corporals and drummers.
>
> 3d. That as soon as the companies are so formed the officers of such a number of companies as shall by them be judged proper to form a regiment do assemble and choose one colonel, one lieutenant-colonel, a major and an adjutant for each regiment.[2]

Two months later, the Provincial Congress would reverse this democratic process under which militia companies elected their own officers; as of August 16, all officers were to be commissioned by the Provincial Congress or the Committee of Safety.[3]

David Brearley Jr., now thirty-one, quickly attained the rank of lieutenant colonel in the Monmouth militia, and his brother Joseph, at age thirty-three, was commissioned on November 20 as captain of the 2nd Company, Second Battalion of the Jersey Line in the Continental Army.[4]

It was Joseph who would see action first, and his letters

would give David insight into the difficulties facing the new Continental Army in the field.

In late January 1776, General Washington asked Congress to request each state to send troops to Canada to reinforce Benedict Arnold's small force. Arnold still hoped to capture Quebec despite the disastrous New Year's Eve defeat in which General Richard Montgomery had been killed.

Colonel William Maxwell's 2nd Battalion was ordered to Canada, and on February 4, Captain Joseph Brearley led the first company north. He wrote to his brother David from Albany on February 18:

> We have arrived here after a Tollerable march of eleven days. I have nothing memorable to acquaint you of in regard to our Journey. Only, we was agreeably disappointed in travelling near ninety miles in slays [sleighs] & chiefly on the North River — I cannot conclude without giving you Some Description of the place we are now in which realy by no means answers my Expectations. It is a City Situated upon a Tollerable pleasant River, but it is fixt in a nasty sunken hole the houses huddled up in a confused manner. It contains three times the No. of houses Trentown does there is a few good house but their churches & the chief of these houses are of the Ugly out of the way dutch construction I ever saw. Upon the whole, I think the place is like a Dm'd Hog Sty & the people who are in it is not much better than Hoggs. I hope I shall be able to leave it in 3 days, as I have no Inclination to long stay in such a place.
>
> I am Dr. Brother Yrs tr Jos Brearley
>
> P.S. I have the pleasure to inform you that I have

brot *All my Company to Albany to a man being the fifth Company from the Westward — there is no more Coms yet arrived tho Col Lowrie & the Pennsylva Comp is expected every hour — from every circumstance I can learn Quebec must be taken ere Long. We learn there is now abt. 13 hundred troops there. Which with our reinforcements will Efectually I think settle the matter.*[5]

On March 7, Joseph wrote again to his brother David from Montreal in a letter notable not only for its vivid description of the rigors and hazards of a long late-winter march, but also for insights it offers into the patriotic fervor that the Brearley brothers shared:

*I have now the pleasure of an opportunity to inform you of our arrival at this place after a very fatiguing March of 27 days with the loss only of 8 men left sick on the Road. Our arrival was Sunday night last. 6 days we lay at Albany are included in the 27 — ... Montreal is distant from Trenton about 500 miles, all which way out men performed with the greatest Spirit Imaginable.*

*We were obliged to lay out in the woods & on the lakes three nights, the weather being extremely Inclement we suffered much. Eight or nine days were were crossing the Lakes Champlain & George which at the crossing places are about 180 miles from Land to Land. Two days of the nine, we waded through water and slush half leg deep, occasioned by a Southwest Storm of Rain. the last of these two days in the afternoon the wind shifted round to the North & brought a most Dreadfull Cold Storm of Snow there which came directly in our faces. Here we was all near perishing had it not been for a few hardy fellows who pushed on to an*

Island at about a distance of 12 miles where they kindled a fire & then returned for them left scattered on the Lake, Many of whom when they were taken up was helpless but with care they were brought to and seem now as hardy as the next except one who at this time lays poorly. Having plenty of Provisions it seemed in some measure to mitigate their distress — I doubt if History can furnish us with greater performance in marching. One day with another average nearly 24 miles as for the Small lift we got in Sleds was verry Tryfling — I hope our countrymen will now be convinced that although we are inexperienced & Young Soldiers, we are determined to persevere with firmness unto the end & that they who think us Poltroons will Cheat themselves — What but the Glorious cause of <u>Liberty</u> could induce us & our men to expose ourselves to the many dificulties they have already surmounted.

I have now given you a Sketch of our March & in all probability this will be the last acct youl have from me untill my adventure will afford you something more agreeable. I will therefore give you notice of what is expected we are going about — General Lee who is to take the Command of the Department is hourly expected, his disposition & great Spirit, will I presume erelong prove the Valour of our Troops. God grant they may acquit themselves like Soldiers & more especially the Jersey Blues. May they return Crownd with Fresh Laurels to add to their former greatness — there is not the most distant prospect of the Garrison of Quebeck Surrendering. Preparation for Storming is daily making Ladders for Scaling the wall which carry Twelve men about are now ready. Nothing delays our attack but a parcell more Troops. The Garrison consists of about

*1200 or 1400 men. We are yet only 1400 strong but expect 3 times that number very soon — Ere another month depart expect to hear of the Reduction or at least Seige of Quebeck. Our men are animated with the pleasing thought of plunder which make them like so many Ceasors — We being fired with a Thirst after Honor & the welfare of our country hope to acquit ourselves like Noble Sons of Freedom & show the dogs of Tyranny we dare fight for Liberty — Next Monday is the day we propose to Set off for Quebeck — please give my kind respects to our family. Mr. Phillips (Second Lt. Jonathan Dickinson Phillips) joins in compliments to you all & hope youl remember him to Major Phillips. Remember me to all Enquiring friends Adue*

*Joseph Brearley, Capt*

*P.S. Please to give my particular respects to Major Brearley [presumably David Brearly Sr., father of Joseph and David]. Mr. Phillips likewise desires to present his respects to him & will write you both at first convenient opportunity — Major Rhea is just now arrived in good health, Capts Lowry & Stout are likewise arrived with Adjutant Anderson & Quartermaster Shreve.*[6]

David Brearley's letter of February 18 to his brother in Canada has not been found,[7] but his May 22 response to Joseph's letter shows that his first months of service were much less stressful than his brother's:

*Dr Brother*
*I have recd your favour of 7th of March from Montreal giving an account of your March which must*

*have been a most dreadfull one. It was what your friends dreaded before you went, tho we did not choose to discourage so necessary & laudable an undertaking. hope your dificultys are now over & that you are in possession of Quebeck an account of what I anxiously expect to receive every day — we are in tollerable quiet here tho we are obliged to keep up a constant guard of Militia at Sandy Hook to prevent the marines from plundering the Inhabitants as the men of war have been obliged to sail down there from New York which they left through fear of the Batteries lately erected there. I have been to New York (with) General Dickinson & have had the Honour of viewing the works in company with the Generals Putnam Thomson & many of the fortifications are complete & the others in great forwardness so that they are in no apprehension of danger of a fleet should venture in. — I have no news to make you acquainted with. Major Brearley has lately moved down to Newport & joined Billy Anderson in a mill. Your friends are all very well here — I take the opportunity of sending this by Lieut Lloyd who you are acquainted with a very worthy young fellow who youd please to introduce to the officers of your comp. I am with kindest compliments to the gentleness of my acquaintance with you.*

*Dr Brother Yours Affectionately*[8]

David Brearley had written a letter on January 31 to Samuel Tucker, President of the New Jersey Provincial Congress, then meeting in New Brunswick, recommending Richard Lloyd for a lieutenancy. "He will offer a good recommendation which among others I have signed, but from my long acquaintance with him and knowledge of his good Character, think it a duty to mention him in particular to you, he served his apprenticeship with Mr. Rogers in Allen Town since which he has been in the West Indies for sometime."[9] Brearley's recommendation was accepted, and Lloyd's appointment came through in time for him to personally deliver Brearley's May 22 letter.

Brearley was mixing his militia duties with what was evidently still a busy law practice. On January 16, 1776, he began keeping entries in a *Gaine's New York Pocket Almanac 1776-1777*. The entries in the almanac are generally laconic — the first two entries record "Middlesex Court" under January 16 and "Monmouth Court" for January 23 — but the book provides a reliable, if intermittent, record of Brearley's itinerary and significant events of his life through December 1786. Brearley carried the almanac with him for eleven years.

General William Scudder Stryker, the Union Army veteran best-known for his 1898 book *The Battles of Trenton and Princeton*, had access to Brearley's almanac. In his article "The New Jersey Continental Line in the Indian Campaign of 1779," Stryker reported that Brearley's "diary, still extant, is a curious mingling, for months, of drilling his regiment to-day, brisk skirmish with the red-coats the next day, and the third day opening some Court of Oyer and Terminer."[10]

Stryker's papers included eleven neatly handwritten pages with the misleading title of "Notes from the diary of Chief Justice Brearley."[11] But the whereabouts of the original diary — and whether Stryker's notes represented the full text of the diary or just a summary — remained a mystery. Recently, however, the almanac resurfaced at Valley Forge National Historic Park as part of the John Reed Collection. Curator Scott Houting describes the almanac as in "very poor condition and in urgent need of conservation." It is too fragile to be photocopied or photographed at the present time, but Houting confirmed the meticulous accuracy of Stryker's copy of the almanac's entries, and added that Brearley had underlined the names of important New York judges in one of the appendices.[12]

Brearley's entries for the winter and spring of 1776 are primarily a listing of court dates, with the principal exceptions being his attendance at an April 8 meeting of the "Committee of Safety at New Brunswick" and a May 10 "Field Day at Tom's River" for military exercises.[13]

As he wrote to his brother Joseph in Canada, the principal focus of the Monmouth County militia had been maintaining an adequate guard on the coast at Sandy Hook to prevent British raids. But the underlying and often-secretive nature of the conflict that pitted neighbor against neighbor in Monmouth County came to the fore in late May and early June of 1776. Thomas Fowler, a captured Loyalist described as a member of the Woodward gang, turned informant and testified before the Council of Safety that Loyalists had gathered to form their own militia at a special muster held in Upper Freehold at the mill complex of Richard Waln, a wealthy Quaker with Tory sympathies.[14]

The Provincial Congress responded quickly, issuing the following directive on June 3:

> Whereas authentick information has been received by this congress that a number of disaffected persons have assembled in the County of Monmouth, preparing by force of arms to oppose the cause of American freedom and to join the British troops for the destruction of this country; and it being highly necessary that immediate measures be taken to subdue these dangerous insurgents; it is therefore unanimously resolved that Colonel Charles Read, Lieutenant Colonel Samuel Forman, and Major Joseph Height [Haight] do take

> *two hundred of the Militia of Burlington County, and
> two hundred of the Militia of Monmouth, and proceed
> without delay, in order to quell the aforesaid insurrec-
> tion, and to disarm and take prisoners whomsoever they
> shall find assembled with the intent to oppose the friends
> of American freedom ...* [15]

Read, Forman, and Haight commanded the 2nd Regiment of
Burlington County Militia. Brearley, as colonel of the Monmouth
County Militia's 2nd Regiment, was in charge of the Monmouth
force, whose reliability was not entirely to his liking, as he
expressed in a letter "complaining of sundry disaffected persons
in his regiment" that was read aloud at the Provincial Congress
meeting on June 12.[16]

It was Brearley who reported to the Provincial Congress on
the state of the opposition in western Monmouth County, whose
meeting place at Waln's mills was just a few miles from his home.
On July 6, just two days after the Declaration of Independence
had been read publicly for the first time, Samuel Tucker,
president of the New Jersey Provincial Congress, reported to
John Hancock, president of the Continental Congress:

> *Colonel Brearley is just now arrived from
> Allentown, which is in the neighborhood of the
> Monmouth insurgents. He supposed that not more than
> one hundred have been over together. They had
> confederated under oath — at least part of them. About
> thirty are flying on board the enemy fleet, our militia in
> pursuit, and numbers of the lesser offenders coming
> back to their duty upon encouragement we thought
> proper to give such as shall appear to have been
> deluded. The leaders, if they can be apprehended, will be
> punished. If they escape, some of them have left estates.*

*The Colonel at Shrewsbury [Samuel Breese] had offered to resign, making great complaints of the backward will, "to say no worse" as he expressed himself, of the people, "so few of whom," he tells us, "are ready to turn out, (hiding themselves and deserting their homes), whenever he marched to defend the shores," that he is discouraged. As we hope the [7th Pennsylvania] rifle battalion will have little remaining to detain them in the upper end of the county, we have ventured to encourage him with the expectation of their assisting him on the lower end. The Freehold and Middletown people, who form a large battatlion, are, we believe, very hearty, and will assist as much as possible, both at Shrewsbury and the neighborhood of Sandy Hook.[17]*

Much had happened in the previous month.

On June 17, Colonel Nathaniel Heard of the Middlesex County Militia, operating under orders from the Provincial Congress, arrested Royal Governor William Franklin, who was adjudged an enemy of the people and then sent as a prisoner to Connecticut, marking the formal end of royal authority in New Jersey.[18]

The New Jersey Constitutional Convention adopted a new state Constitution under which a new Legislative Council and Assembly would be elected in August to replace the Legislature that had been dissolved by Franklin.

And in response to a call from the Continental Congress for the deployment of 13,800 militia, including 3,300 from New Jersey, to reinforce General Washington's army in New York,[19] the Provincial Congress on June 14 had authorized the creation of a force of five battalions, each with eight companies of seventy-eight men, to be enlisted through December 1 and to be "immediately got in readiness and marched to New York under the command of a brigadier-general."[20]

David Brearley was named lieutenant colonel of the First Battalion, which consisted of three companies from Bergen County, three from Essex and two from Burlington.[21] Brearley was second-in-command to Colonel Philip Van Cortland, and the overall command of what became known as "Heard's Brigade" was given to the militia commander who had arrested Franklin just three weeks before.[22]

On July 8, just two days after Tucker sent his report on the state of the Monmouth County uprising to Hancock, David Brearley's almanac records in typically laconic fashion: "Marched for New York."[23] One week later, Brearley took part in his first court-martial, as one of five officers directed to sit in judgment of the actions of Colonel Ritzema in a trial conducted at Mr. Motagnies Tavern.[24]

Brearley was going to war with a more sophisticated understanding of what could go wrong than most new officers, thanks to a carefully written, but sobering, letter from his brother. Joseph's letter of May 15 was not from Quebec, but from the "Camp at Sorell," and it was laced with frustration:

> Tho I arrived at this place but yesterday I am now just going upon command under Col Shreve over the River. Therefore have it not in my Power to acquaint you with Particulars only that soon after my arrival at Camp before Quebec I was sent upon command to Fort Levy, were I remained Till our retreat which I make no doubt you have ere this Heard of. If I had time would acquaint you of some Circumstances relative thereto but no doubt you will be acquainted. Our weakness were too conspicuous for our safety. Especially after the (British and Hessian) Reinforcements of the 6th Inst, I understand our people on the other side Retreated Immediately upon the Enemy sallying out tho I was

entirely kep Ignorant thereof. Indeed I was ordered by my Commanding Officer here Col Nicholson to prepare for a Storm the next evening, the pollicy of which cannot Determine unless Designed to Render me Incapable of saving my Baggage. I maintained my Post till nearly next Morning after our retreat on the other side when I was Informed of the Circumstances as they were. I found I must Follow which after Getting my men in Proper order to the amount of 2:00 in the morning of the 7th I began my Retreat which after a Toilsome March of 8 Days I accomplished to this place being near 140 miles (without Provisions only what we received of the Inhabitants & where I met with a number of our army with verry Considerable reinforcements of Artilery etc. Unlucky for us it was not sooner. The Main body of our Troops rested at Point D'Shambo but we expect they will join us every Day. Something very Important you may Depend will shortly appear of Great Consequence to this Department of America in General. God bless you My Dr Brother. I wish time would permit me to give you a more consequential Intelligence. Adieu

    Joseph Brearley

    Our retreat was so managed as to lose all our Baggage to a Trifle. Ammunition. Cannon. Provision &c[25]

General John Sullivan arrived at Camp Sorel on June 4 with fresh troops and promptly ordered an attack on Three Rivers. Joseph Brearley's company was part of the force of 2,000 men under General William Thompson that crossed the St. Lawrence River in bateux under cover of darkness, hiked through a swamp, and then attacked the city in the morning. They were quickly defeated by a larger British force. Thompson

DAVID BREARLEY AND THE MAKING OF THE UNITED STATES CONSTITUTION

was taken prisoner, and Joseph Brearley was wounded, but escaped. The American troops retreated in bateux to Isle au Noix, a swampy, malarial island in the Sorel River near Lake Champlain, where fifteen to twenty soldiers died each day from sickness. A week later, the army retreated to Crown Point, and news of the defeat was sent to Congress. "Our army at Crown Point is an object of Wretchedness," John Adams wrote to his wife Abigail on July 7, "enough to fill a humane Mind with Horror, Disgraced, defeated, decimated, dispirited, diseased, naked, undisciplined, eaten up with Vermin — no Clothes, Beds, Blankets, no Medicines, no Victuals, but Salt Pork and flour."[26] Soon thereafter, the army retreated all the way back to Fort Ticonderoga, where they would remain for months.[27]

The campaign to conquer Canada — and Joseph Brearley's first military experience — was effectively over, just as David Brearley's first — and equally unsatisfying — military campaign was about to begin.

It is unclear whether Brearley and his company took part in the disastrous Battle of Long Island, in which British General William Howe rolled up the lightly guarded flank of the Continental Army at Jamaica Pass in Brooklyn, killing about 970 Americans and taking another 1,079 captive at a cost of just sixty-three British and Hessian lives and 337 wounded or missing. Only a desperate counterattack led by New Jersey-born General William Alexander, Lord Stirling, who was surrounded and captured, managed to blunt the British onslaught long enough for the rest of the army to retreat to their Brooklyn Heights redoubts.

When General Washington arrived the following day, he immediately directed the construction of new fortifications, as a steady rainstorm made further British attacks that day unlikely. If Brearley's unit did not take part in the Battle of Long Island, then it was among the six regiments of reinforcements that Washington ordered ferried across from Manhattan on August 28, bringing his total strength on Long Island to 9,500 men — more than half of the Continental army.

With the impending arrival of British warships in Long Island Sound, however, Washington realized that his position was untenable and ordered his troops ferried across the East River to Manhattan. All night, John Glover's Marblehead regiment rowed and sailed the army across the river to safety, aided in the final hours by a dense fog that hung on after sunrise.[28]

Brearley's almanac entry for August 29 is typically brief: "Left Long Island tonight." On September 9, Brearley records, Heard's Brigade "Marched to Mt. Washington," whose fortifications would fall to the British two months later.

On October 18, Brearley and the New Jersey troops "Moved toward White Plains" and "Reached the Plains" two days later. Washington's troops had more than a week to dig in before Howe launched his assault on October 28. The Battle of White Plains was a standoff, with the Continental Army losing 175 men and the British and Hessians more than 200. Before Howe could renew his assault, Washington slipped away north to North Castle on the Croton River. Or, as Brearley chose to record it in his entry for October 31, "Advanced 6 miles above White Plains."[29]

When Howe moved his troops from White Plains to transport ships on the Hudson River, Washington and his generals rightly concluded that the British general was planning to attack Fort Washington and invade New Jersey. Washington decided to "throw over a body of our Troops" into the Jerseys. He would march one-third of his army — the 5,000 men whose homes were in New Jersey, Pennsylvania and farther south — to New Jersey to link up with the 3,600 troops defending Fort Washington and Fort Lee.[30]

Brearley's company "Marched to Peekskill" on November 8, "Crossed the North River" on November 10, "Marched to Sniders Landing" the following day, "Marched to Tappan" on November 14, "Marched to Hackensack" on November 15, and "Marched to English Neighborhood" (now Leonia) on November 16.[31] That day, Fort Washington fell to a British assault with the loss of all 2,700 men, including 2,200 who were captured.

Fort Lee was abandoned to the advancing British and Hessians on November 19, and the next day Brearley and the New Jersey brigade, whose December 1 enlistment expiration was rapidly approaching, continued to retreat over the Hackensack River at New Bridge Landing. On November 21, the troops "Marched to Aquackanouck bridge" (now Passaic City), and as soon as the last troops had cleared the rickety wooden bridge over the Passaic River, Washington had the bridge destroyed.[32]

Brearley and his company presumably were among the 5,410 troops with Washington in and around Newark on November 23, although Brearley makes no mention of Newark in his almanac. The next entry, dated November 28, reports "Marched to Scotch Plains," followed by "Marched to Brunswick" on November 29.[33]

It was in New Brunswick the following day that Washington and his top generals "paraded the troops whose enlistments were expiring and pleaded with them to stay. They were badly trained and equipped, but he needed every man."[34]

But on Sunday, December 1, almost all of General Heard's Brigade of 800 New Jerseyans and General Beall's 1,200-man Maryland brigade left camp, and others began deserting, leaving Washington with no more than 3,400 men.

For the New Jersey troops whose terms of enlistment were expiring, it was more than a question of enlistment dates. They knew that British and Hessian troops had plundered the farms in

Bergen County and other areas they had abandoned in their withdrawal across the Jerseys.

Their homes were now in the path of the advancing enemy force. The week before, Washington had dispatched the 250-strong New Jersey State Regiment under Colonel Samuel Forman to suppress yet another incipient uprising by Monmouth Tories emboldened by British successes.[35] Brearley's home and family were on the likely route of march.

Brearley's last almanac entry for 1776, dated December 1st, reports: "Marched to Allentown."[36] With his home state under direct attack, Brearley would return to his post as colonel of the Second Regiment of the Monmouth County Militia.

Brearley also may have known that the New Jersey Council and Assembly had already made recommendations in September for the establishment of a new brigade of four battalions that would give preference in the selection of officers to those who had been serving in Heard's Brigade. While Brearley was marching to Scotch Plains on November 28, committees representing New Jersey's regiments had already elected him to serve as lieutenant colonel of the Fourth Regiment, Second Establishment, under Colonel Ephraim Martin.[37]

Brearley's performance in the preceding months also had won the respect of Washington. In a letter from Morris Town to Colonel Forman asking him to raise a new regiment, Washington urged, "I wish it may be agreeable to you to appoint Henderson or Brailey your Lieutt. Colo. if they, or either of them Incline to serve again."[38] With Brearley already named a lieutenant colonel, Forman took Washington's advice and appointed Thomas Henderson on January 12, 1777.[39]

It is one of the great ironies of the Revolutionary War that very few New Jerseyans fought in the most famous battle in state history, the first Battle of Trenton. But David Brearley's brother, Joseph, may be one of those who did.

Captain Joseph Brearley and the rest of Maxwell's Brigade, whose terms of service were due to expire November 29, left Fort Ticonderoga two weeks earlier and arrived back in New Jersey in December. While every single private "went off to a man" as soon as they reached home, a few officers accompanied General Arthur St. Clair and joined Washington's army in time to take part in the historic crossing of the Delaware and surprise attack on the Hessian garrison in Trenton.[40]

Joseph's eighty-year-old widow, Rachel McClary Brearley, stated in a December 7, 1836, application for a pension that her husband had been wounded in the leg by a musket ball at the Battle of Trenton on December 26, 1776.[41] But the battle was such a success for the Americans that it was easy to count the wounded — two officers and two enlisted men — after the battle. Brearley was not one of them.[42] However, the widow's story about her husband's wound, related sixty years after the battle, may be a simple case of confusion; he did return home after the Trenton campaign with a war wound, even if it was suffered at Three Rivers.

He also returned home disillusioned with the Continental Army.

On November 29, the same day that his younger brother had been rewarded with election as lieutenant colonel of the new Fourth Battalion, Joseph Brearley's hopes for promotion were shattered when Captain Richard Howell, who had been junior to him in rank, was promoted to major in the reconstituted Second Battalion, Second Establishment.[43]

In a letter dated January 22, 1777, written from Maidenhead, a prideful Joseph Brearley turned down his commission as captain:

*It is with great reluctance that I address you on a subject I had hoped to never have had the occasion to mention, but by appointing my junior officer to Command me, I think myself bound in Honour to signifie the non-acceptance of the appointment given me.*

*I always admired the character of a Soldier and it has been my study and the height of my ambition to approve myself one.*

*I entered the Army with the purest intentions, being thoroughly convinced of the Righteousness of our cause, and determined, if I lived, to see the matter out. I should therefore want candour was I to deny that I feel the keenest disappointment. It has always been allowed by the best of Judges that Military Promotions should be Regular, unless some remarkable Acts of Merit or Baseness should appear, neither of which (to my knowledge) was the case in the Company I served in.*

*I entered the cause early, had the honor to lead the first company from this State into Canada, and during the campaign have had the satisfaction to meet the Approbation of the Officers under whom I served.*

*Were I therefore to accept the present Appointment, I should want that Spirit which is necessary to constitute a good officer, and the World might rightly conclude that I defend the indignity offered me.*

*You have put it out of my power to serve in a military capacity, yet it shall be my constant study to promote the independence, happiness and welfare of my country ...*[44]

The Legislative Council accepted Joseph Brearley's resignation on February 5, ending his career in the Continental

Army. But Brearley was as good as his word in his commitment to the cause of independence.

Just six weeks later, on March 15, Joseph Brearley was commissioned first major of the 1st Battalion of the Hunterdon County Militia by Governor Livingston. He and his regiment fought at the Battle of Springfield, the critical "forgotten victory" of June 23, 1780, and served as mustermaster to ensure that Hunterdon County met its quota for troops from 1780 until the end of the war.[45]

In the 1880s, Joseph's granddaughter, Louisa Brearley, recounted the family stories she heard in her childhood:

> He not only received no compensation as an officer during the Revolutionary War, but every pound of meat and every bushel of grain that could be spared from the farm was sent to supply the troops. I heard Grandma say that impatient of the rigid economy, she exclaimed, "Father, I believe you grudge every piece of meat I take from the casks." The old patriot replied, "Oh, Rachel, remember how hungry the boys must be in camp."[46]

After a single year, Joseph Brearley's days in camp were over. His brother David's were just beginning.

# CHAPTER FIVE

# The New Jersey Brigade

## Brandywine and Germantown, Valley Forge and Monmouth

*"The condition of the New Jersey troops is such that it would be criminal to keep silent longer … four months' pay for a private will not procure his wretched wife and children a single bushel of wheat… New Jersey soldiers are as brave as any. Why they should be neglected is a problem in politics hard to explain."*

— Lt. Col. David Brearley and Col. Israel Shreve, in a letter to Governor William Livingston,February 7, 1778[1]

The New Jersey Brigade in which Brearley was to serve for the next thirty months was placed under the command of newly promoted Brigadier-General William Maxwell, the colonel who had commanded Joseph Brearley's Second Battalion in the Quebec campaign. It took four months to organize "Maxwell's Brigade." Brearley's Fourth Battalion was ready to go in late February, but it was not until late April that the Third Battalion was fully organized and the Brigade ready to take the field.[2]

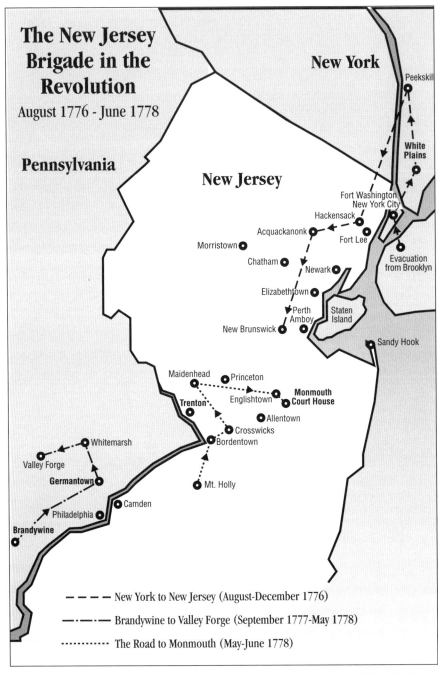

The New Jersey
Brigade in the
Revolution

New York

August 1776 - June 1778

Peekskil

Pennsylvania

White
Plains

New Jersey

Fort Washington
New York City

Hackensack

Acquackanonk

Fort Lee

Morristown

Chatham

Newark

Evacuation
from Brooklyn

Elizabethtown

Perth
Amboy

Staten
Island

New Brunswick

Sandy Hook

Maidenhead

Princeton

Monmouth
Court House

Trenton

Englishtown

Allentown

Crosswicks

Whitemarsh

Bordentown

Valley Forge

Germantown

Mt. Holly

Camden

Philadelphia

Brandywine

– – – – New York to New Jersey (August-December 1776)

–·–·– Brandywine to Valley Forge (September 1777-May 1778)

············ The Road to Monmouth (May-June 1778)

TriArt Graphics

By the time the regiment was ready to move, Brearley apparently had been transferred from the newly formed Fourth Battalion to serve as lieutenant colonel of the prestigious First Battalion. Stryker's voluminous 872-page *Official Register of the Officers and Men of New Jersey in the Revolutionary War*, compiled in 1872, records Brearley's appointment as "Lieutenant Colonel, First Regiment, to date January 1st, 1777." But it is more likely that Brearley was transferred after March 15, when the First Battalion's colonel, Silas Newcomb, was promoted to brigadier-general of the New Jersey Militia and Matthias Ogden moved up from lieutenant colonel to colonel to replace him.[3]

A fiery leader known for his "reckless gallantry" in battle, Ogden was just twenty-two years old when he suffered a serious shoulder wound in the December 31, 1775, dawn assault on Quebec in which General Montgomery had been killed. As Stryker tells the story, the young Ogden

> ... was taken prisoner and sent to British headquarters, and, being admired for his bravery, was invited to a seat at the officers' mess. At this table an officer, just arrived from England, asked the company to drink a toast, and Ogden, rising with the rest, heard the toast proposed, "Damnation to the Rebels!" Instantly, he flung his glass and its contents in the face of the British officer, exclaiming, "Damnation to the man who dares to propose such a toast in my presence!" Of course, a challenge was passed, but the British commanding officer would not allow Ogden, as his prisoner, to accept it.[4]

The four-month delay in the New Jersey Brigade taking the field was undoubtedly a welcome relief for Washington's quartermaster-general, who was having trouble feeding the troops who been encamped in Morristown since arriving in early January fresh from their victories in Trenton and Princeton. Washington's military chest was also exhausted, as he wrote in a February 13 letter seeking $4,000 for the bounty and subsistence of the new Fourth New Jersey Regiment that Brearley had raised.[5]

For Brearley, the delay was particularly welcome. The home front needed his attention. Elizabeth was pregnant with their fourth child, conceived during the month he had spent suppressing Tory activities near their Allen's Town home. Furthermore, Monmouth County once again was in a state of civil war.

Emboldened by British victories and Washington's retreat from New Jersey, Tory farmers and plantation owners around Waln's mills — the same group whose activities Brearley and the militia disrupted in June — had resumed their activities.

In December, prosperous Tory plantation owner Anthony Woodward Jr., his nephew, several cousins, and other Tories burst into Isaac Rogers' store in Allen's Town and demanded the surrender of all of the pork in Rogers' storehouse. "When one of Rogers' clerks suggested that he weigh the pork before surrendering it, the Tories would not allow it, saying that it was Continental pork."[6] The barrels of pork were "conveyed to the British fleet then lying off Sandy Hook."[7] Isaac had never recovered from the trauma.

On February 8, Brearley witnessed Isaac Rogers' will providing for the dispersal of his home, store and tavern in Allen's Town and several farms and estates he owned in nearby Upper Freehold and in Middlesex County.[8] Just over a month later, on March 14, Isaac died at the age of forty-nine. The cause of his death is not certain; it may have been lingering illness. "Vile Tories!" exclaimed the *Pennsylvania Evening Post*, in its death notice. "It cannot go unnoticed, that through your gross abuse and continual harassing, you brought on him a dejection of spirits and a broken heart, by which he fell a sacrifice to your villainous conduct."[9]

Nine days later, on the morning of March 23, Elizabeth Brearley gave birth to a third daughter, Esther. Esther joined a household that included her brother William, sisters Elizabeth, Mary, and her stepsister, Harriet Luttrell, now about sixteen years old. It had been a difficult pregnancy, and Elizabeth was not well. Brearley was able to spend another month at home before     leaving to rejoin the army.

On April 25, Brearley recorded in his almanac, his battalion "Marched to camp," and then "Marched to Bound Brook" on May 24.[10] The New Jersey Brigade was deployed at Elizabethtown, Bound Brook and Spanktown (now Rahway), where its familiarity with the terrain and local sources of information would be advantageous for monitoring both British and Tory activities.

Brearley's May 19, 1777, report to Governor Livingston on the capture of a local Tory, Giles Williams, is typical of the state of civil war that existed in the Jerseys throughout 1777 and 1778:

> SIR.-Your Excellency will have delivered herewith a certain Giles Williams, who left this state last summer with Elisha Lawrence and others, and joined the enemy on Staten Island; he has for some time past been lurking in the Pines with a set of villains, but was very luckily taken last night on the edge of the Pines, by Lieut [William] Barton, and sent up to this place.[11]

The Elisha Lawrence with whom Williams had escaped was the last royal sheriff of Monmouth County and was serving as colonel of the First Battalion of the New Jersey Royal Volunteers. Lawrence's property was sold at Waln's mill on April 5, 1779, and he was forced to emigrate to Great Britain.[12]

Brearley was with his command less than two months when he received news that his wife Elizabeth had become more seriously ill. He requested a furlough and left camp on June 21.[13]

For six weeks, Elizabeth battled to stay alive, but on August 3, Brearley recorded in his almanac, "Mrs. Brearley died 8 o'clk PM." Her obituary, which appeared in *The Pennsylvania Gazette*, reported:

> *On the 3rd instant died at Allentown in New Jersey, Elizabeth Brearley, wife of Colonel David Brearley, after a long and painful illness, which she bore with great fortitude, it may with truth be said of this Lady, that her external form (for she was eminently beautiful) was but a fair copy of her mind; and it would be doing injustice to her memory, not to say, that she possessed all the qualities that adorn human nature.*[14]

Elizabeth's death left Brearley a widower with a sixteen-year-old stepdaughter and four children under the age of ten, including the infant Esther, who would be known as Hettie. Over the next week, he buried his wife and made arrangements for the care of his children until his return from military duties. He did not have to look far for a solution.

Hannah Tallman Rogers, whose husband Isaac's death had left her a widow with seven children, would also care for Brearley's infant daughter Hettie. Brearley's papers include an October 30, 1777, payment of nine pounds to Mrs. Rogers for "keeping daughter." Presumably, Mrs. Rogers also helped Brearley's stepdaughter, Harriett Luttrell, watch over Brearley's children William, Elizabeth, and Mary.[15] Most likely, the adjoining houses functioned as a single family unit. For Brearley, money was never plentiful. An Allen's Town storekeeper's ledger shows Brearley's account for "cheese, butter, veal and 3 1/2 years rent @

£8,14,3," an amount totaling £88 for the years 1775 to 1777, his first three years of Revolutionary War activity, would not be paid off in full until 1783.[16]

Nine days after his wife's death, Brearley rejoined his regiment, arriving just in time to participate in the fall campaign for Philadelphia. On August 24, Brearley recorded, the "Army marched through Philadelphia" and by September 5 had reached White Clay Creek near Newport, Delaware, where Washington hoped to intercept General Howe's army. But Howe skirted Washington's flank, setting off a race by the two armies to the Brandywine River, the last natural barrier before the Schuylkill River and Philadelphia.

On September 9, Brearley reported, the New Jersey Brigade "Marched to Chadd's Ford."[17] While most of the army dug in on the other side of the river, the New Jersey Brigade and other units under Maxwell's command were dispatched forward as an advance skirmish line to intercept the British. Field command of the New Jersey Brigade passed to Ogden as the senior colonel, which put Brearley in command of the 169-man First Battalion.

Two days later, at about nine o'clock in the morning, the Battle of Brandywine began. Maxwell's troops were attacked by Ferguson's Riflemen and the Queen's Rangers, who served as the shock troops for Hessian General Knyphausen's Division.

Maxwell's orders were to delay the advance, and the New Jersey troops fought bravely, firing from cover as they fell back in an orderly fashion from line to line, then across Chadd's Ford to rejoin their comrades on the east side of the creek.

Several times, Washington sent Maxwell's Brigade and some of Nathanael Greene's troops in quick sallies across the river to disrupt British entrenching parties. Knyphausen's troops inexplicably failed to attack across the river. What Washington didn't know was that Knyphausen's attack was a feint, designed to occupy the Americans while 8,000 of General Howe's troops crossed the Brandywine upsteam unnoticed.[18]

When Washington realized he had been outflanked, he shifted most of his army north to meet Howe, while leaving Maxwell's Brigade and General Wayne's troops to hold off Knyphausen's division. The New Jerseyans and Pennsylvanians inflicted heavy casualties when the British troops finally crossed the river at five-thirty in the afternoon. The Continentals were holding their own in the fierce battle when the British and Hessian troops who had defeated Washington's main body suddenly emerged from the woods to the north. "The enemy outnumbering us four to one, turned our right flank and broke us off platoon after platoon," Lieutenant John Shreve wrote.[19]

Shreve's father, Colonel Israel Shreve, had two horses shot out from under him and was "severely wounded in the thigh....When we stopped to dress his wound, and unbuttoned his breeches at the knee, the bullet, which had been flattened on one side by striking the bone, rolled down on his boot," the lieutenant recalled.[20] Major Joseph Bloomfield also was seriously wounded, "having a Ball with the Wad shot through my left forearm & the fuse set my coat and shirt on fire."[21] The battle ended in darkness. The New Jersey Brigade lost seven killed, twelve wounded, nineteen captured and thirteen missing. The next day, the army "Marched to the Falls of Schuylkill," Brearley wrote.

The Americans lost 1,400 men, ten cannons, and a howitzer, while British casualties totaled 576, including ninety killed. The road to Philadelphia was now open, and on September 26, Howe occupied the city where the Continental Congress had met and where the Declaration of Independence had been signed just fourteen months before.[22]

While the Battle of Brandywine was a defeat, the Americans had fought well, and fresh troops were arriving from New Jersey and New York. When Washington learned three weeks later that

Howe had divided his army, he decided to attack the main British encampment at Germantown, hoping that a victory would enable him to recapture Philadelphia.

Maxwell's Brigade, which had fought for more than ten hours at Brandywine, was initially kept in reserve at Germantown, but was still involved in some of the most bitter fighting in the October 4 battle. Washington's morning attack sent most of the British troops reeling in retreat, but six companies of the British 40th Regiment barricaded themselves inside Cliveden, the palatial mansion of Pennsylvania's last Crown-appointed chief justice.

When American cannonballs bounced off the mansion's two-foot-thick walls, Maxwell's Brigade was ordered to attack the house. Repeated charges by companies and smaller groups primarily drawn from the First Regiment commanded by Ogden and Brearley and the Third Regiment under Colonel Elias Dayton failed to capture the impromptu fort. The New Jerseyans "attacked with great intrepidity, but were received with no less firmness,'" a British officer later wrote, "the fire was well directed and continued, the rebels nevertheless advanced and several were killed with bayonets getting in at the windows and upon steps attempting to force their way at the door."[23]

The toll among officers was particularly high, Dayton recalled:

> *At this place fell Capt. McMyer and Ensign Hurley of Col. Ogden's regiment; Capt. Conway, Capt. Morrison, Capt. Baldwin and Lt. Robinson wounded of the same regiment, together with about 20 men; of my regiment, Lt. Clark and Ensign Bloomfield were wounded, and 18 men killed and wounded; my horse was shot under me at the same place, within about three yards of the corner of the house.*

*(Then) came on perhaps the thickest fog known in
the memory of man, which, together with the smoke,
brought on almost midnight darkness, it was not
possible it one time (I believe for the space of nearly half
an hour) to distinguish friend from foe five yards
distance.*[24]

Maxwell then moved his troops back behind the cherry trees
at the entrance to the estate and kept up a steady fire on the house
from there. Washington arrived with his senior staff, and agreed
with General Henry Knox that the "castle" could not be
bypassed. The British shot and killed an American adjutant who
approached Cliveden with a white flag seeking their surrender. A
long cannonade, continuing musket fire from the New Jersey
Brigade, and a wave of charges by American officers trying to set
the house ablaze all failed to force the British to surrender.[25.] After
the battle, fifty-three American dead, mostly from the New
Jersey Brigade, would be buried by the British under the front
lawn where they fell.

Unable to take Cliveden by storm, the New Jerseyans
moved up to reinforce the main army. By this time, the American
troops were beginning to retreat. Some were out of ammunition,
some were lost, and in the darkness, two large American
detachments ended up firing upon one another — due partly to
confused orders from General Adam Stephen, who was
reportedly drunk.[26]

Howe would report 537 British killed, 300 American dead
on the battlefield, and 438 Americans captured. The New
Jersey Brigade listed twenty-two killed, forty-three wounded,
one captured, and twelve missing.[27] The dead included Major
James Witherspoon, Maxwell's brigade major and son of the
Reverend John Witherspoon, president of the College of New
Jersey and signer of the Declaration. Captain Joseph Morris

of the First Battalion would die of his wounds two months later.[28]

The defeats at Germantown and Brandywine, which had seemed winnable fights, aroused grumbling both within the army and from Congress. Maryland Congressman Charles Carrollton, who had complained to Washington in September that two unnamed top officers were "much addicted to liquor," sharply criticized Maxwell's leadership during the assault on the Chew House:

> It is evident that our men do not want resolution, but they want discipline, if they could have been rallied after the repulse from Chew's house & had renewed the attack when the fog cleared away, it is more than probable that the Enemy rather than risk another onset would have retreated to Chester.[29]

Carrollton's assertion is debatable, but it came in the wake of a formal charge by Lieutenant Colonel William Heth of the Third Virginia Regiment that Maxwell had missed the opportunity to do "Great things" on the battlefield at Brandywine the previous month because he was drunk. "We had opportunities – and any body but an old-woman, would have availd themselves of them – He is to be sure – a Damnd bitch of a General."[30] Earlier in the campaign, the Marquis de Lafayette had described Maxwell as "the most inept brigadier-general in the army."[31]

A court of inquiry headed by General Nathanael Greene concluded that Maxwell "was once ... disguised with liquor in such a manner, as to disqualify him in some measure, but not fully, from doing duty; and that once or twice besides his spirits were a little elevated by spiritous liquor."[32] The panel left it up to Washington to decide whether to seek a formal court-martial, but Maxwell demanded one. A court-martial headed by General

John Sullivan that included Captain William DeHart of the Second New Jersey Regiment acquitted Maxwell, but a scapegoat still had to be found. General Adam Stephen, the fifth and final general to face a court-martial, was found guilty of drunkenness at Germantown and was dismissed from the army.

Maxwell's acquittal was popular with the rank-and-file, who had always liked the rough Scot. Brearley and his fellow officers were unconvinced, but they decided to bide their time.

Generals were not the only ones who found themselves suddenly subject to stricter discipline. Washington ordered Brearley and other ranking officers on October 19 to "appoint Genl Courts Martial in their respective Brigades for the trial of all non Commiss'd Officers and Privates, now in the provost" for trial the following morning. Ensign Clement Wood of the Fourth New Jersey, who had disregarded Brearley's October 14 order to rejoin his regiment, was missing; he would be court-martialed and discharged the following month.[33]

Strategic maneuvering continued for more than a month. Brearley's diary records that his battalion "Crossed Schuylkill and recrossed" on October 21, "Crossed again" on October 22, and the following day "At the lower ferry and recrossed" for the fourth time in three days.[34]

Finally, on November 2, the army encamped at Whitemarsh for a month and Brearley and his fellow officers settled into the trivia of winter officering. On November 6, Brearley hosted a "Court of Enquirey" in his quarters to determine whether soldiers serving in the 7th Pennsylvania were entitled to be transferred to the 9th Pennsylvania, in which they said they had enlisted.[25] A week later, Brearley and other officers were directed to meet the following day "to compare the wants of their Brigades & agree on the manner which the clothes shall be distributed."[36] The "wants" were great, as Brearley and Shreve would later write to the New Jersey Legislature.

The troops marched to Swedesford on December 11 and the following day crossed the Schuylkill River on a wobbly, makeshift bridge in an area called the Gulph. They were forced to bivouac at the Gulph for several days after a snowstorm and icy rain made roads impassable. On December 18, the soaked and miserable troops observed a Day of Thanksgiving declared by Congress for the American victory over Burgoyne's army at Saratoga in October.

As Joseph Plumb Martin wryly recalled, "We had nothing to eat for two or three days previous except what the trees of the forests and fields afforded us, but we must now have what Congress said, a sumptuous Thanksgiving to close the year of high living ... it gave each man half a gill (about half a cup) of rice and a tablespoon of vinegar!"[37]

Brearley's troops "Marched to Valley Forge" on December 19, he recorded in his almanac. Two days later, he was at Lancaster, Pennsylvania, but he "Returned to camp" on Christmas Day, and bought State Lottery tickets in the amount of 1.856 for Polly Brearley, 1.857 for Betsey Brearley, and 7.625 for his stepdaughter Harriet Luttrell.[38]

Christmas Day offered no holiday feast. Soldiers' diaries already spoke bitterly of a diet of "fire cakes" — flour and water batter fried on a griddle. The next day, the soldiers awoke to find four more inches of snow on the ground.

Brearley's troops followed specifications laid out in orders in building sixteen-by-fourteen-foot log cabins with walls six and a half feet high, a wood board roof and stone fireplace. Most huts were dug into a pit about two feet below ground with a dirt floor and cloth hung over the doorway. Identical officers' huts were built behind the enlisted men's cabins. They were equally drafty, damp, and smoky, but probably less crowded than the enlisted men's huts, each of which housed twelve soldiers.[39]

Brearley's legal training was put to use again soon after his arrival at Valley Forge, as he was called upon to preside over courts-martial on January 3 and again on January 6. As described in Washington's General Orders for January 11:

> At a General Court Martial held 3rd. instant in Lord Stirling's division, whereof Lt. Colo. Brearly was President, John Rea, Quarter-Master in 6th. Pennsylvania Regiment charged with fraudulent Practices in said Regiment, ordering Lieut. Gibbons in the Provost, and behavior unbecoming the character of an Officer or a Gentleman, was tried and by the unanimous opinion of the Court was found guilty of a breach of 21st. Article of 14th. section of the articles of War and sentenced to be discharged from the service.[40]

The following year, Lt. James Gibbons, the officer who had been the target of the discharged officer's wrath, would be brevetted captain for his bravery in leading an advance wing in the July 15, 1779, assault on Stony Point.

The second case also involved charges against an officer with a Pennsylvania regiment:

> At the same Court held 6th. instant, was tried Lieutt. (John) Hays of 12th. Pennsylvania Regt. charged with breaking open officers Chests at Bethlehem and ungentlemanlike behavior. The Court unanimously acquit him of the first charge, but guilty of a breach of 5th. Article of 18th. Section of the articles of War and sentence him to be dismissed from the service.

"The Commander in Chief approves both these sentences and orders them to be carried into execution accordingly," the Washington's General Orders for January 11 noted.[41]

Brearley "Left camp" on January 10, he recorded in his

almanac. He had not seen his children in five months after leaving them abruptly following the death of their mother, and there would be no further fighting until the spring. He also used his time away to assess the military and political situation in New Jersey. He was at Morristown on January 29, at Brunswick three days later, and at Salem on February 9.[42]

It is also possible that he and Colonel Israel Shreve, commander of the Second New Jersey Battalion, went to New Jersey to personally deliver their petition to the Governor and Legislature on behalf of the officers of all four New Jersey battalions. Their petition stated:

> *The condition of the New Jersey troops is such that it would be criminal to keep silent longer…four months' pay for a private will not procure his wretched wife and children a single bushel of wheat…New Jersey soldiers are as brave as any. Why they should be neglected is a problem in politics hard to explain."* [43]

Governor Livingston specifically addressed the letter from Shreve and Brearley in his February 16 annual address to the Legislature. "As it is presented by authority and in behalf of the whole of the troops raised in this state, and I conceive the matters contained in it to be of great importance to the army, I cannot but recommend it as a matter worthy of your early attention to remedy the evils complained of," Livingston said.[44]

Brearley and Shreve returned to camp at Valley Forge together on February 24, the day after Baron Friedrich Wilhelm Augustus von Steuben arrived to train the troops. They almost did not make it. As Shreve wrote to his wife Polley the following week, "As Colo : Brearly and I Came from Jersey we were near being taken by the British Light horse. But happaly escaped."[45] How they managed to escape is unclear: Shreve weighed 320 pounds, and "no horse was able to carry him faster than a walk."[46]

Brearley remained in camp at Valley Forge for almost a month. He noted in his almanac on February 28 that he had "subscribed 3 dollars for Dunlops paper." On February 11, while in New Jersey he had "subscribed for Collins' paper."

Relations between Maxwell and his senior officers, which were never good, had continued to deteriorate over the winter, and with the new campaign season approaching, Brearley and the cream of New Jersey's officer corps decided to act. On March 2, they bypassed Washington and their division commander, Lord Stirling, by directing a "Memorial of Jersey Field Officers agt. Genl. Maxwell" to a Congressional committee that had been in residence near Valley Forge since January. The missive to Congress, which Brearley undoubtedly had a hand in drafting, states:

> Confident, that a partial inquiry only, is not intended; but that a thorough purgation should take place: we, in duty to our country, take upon ourselves the disagreeable task, of giving the character of our Brigadier-General. We are sensible of the impropriety of such a measure, did it proceed from any other motive, than that of the strictest justice, and greatest necessity. Could you be informed, through any other channel, we would wish to be silent. Our eminent and impartial Commander in chief cannot be supposed to be minutely acquainted, with the character of every officer. He must be informed from capital events, or accidental intelligence. Our Major-General [Stirling] cannot judge, from the essential principles. His Lordship never having seen him [Maxwell] in the field of action, the theatre, on which Genius is displayed, and the great criterion of an officer and soldier.

*Who then shall determine? Are there any more proper than we, who have served with him from the first entering the army, and have been witnesses to his conduct in every occasion.*[47]

Brearley and his colonel from the First Regiment, Matthias Ogden, both signed the petition, as did Colonel Israel Shreve and Major Richard Howell of the Second New Jersey, Lieutenant Colonel Francis Barber and Major Joseph Bloomfield of the Third, and Major John Conway of the Fourth New Jersey. The seven had "impeccable service records," and four of them had been wounded in the fall campaign.[48] Colonel Elias Dayton, who was in line to succeed Maxwell if the general was dismissed, did not sign the petition, but he made it clear that he agreed with its sentiments by proffering his resignation to Washington, citing ill health and personal problems. When Washington acceded to Dayton's request on March 8,[49] Shreve immediately wrote to Washington pointing out on "that Lieut: Colo: Brearley is the first Lieut: Colo: of the State and upon every principle intitled to the vacancy."[50]

No action was taken by the Congressional committee on the New Jersey officers' petition. Dayton ultimately reconsidered and decided to stay with his command; when the embattled Maxwell finally resigned on July 25, 1780, Dayton succeeded him as Brigadier-General of the New Jersey Brigade and served until the end of the war.[51]

Despite, or perhaps to avoid, the turmoil, Brearley returned home again on March 20 for what he probably thought would be his last trip to New Jersey for a while. He "Returned to Camp" on March 28.[52]

May Day, a traditional holiday adopted by the Continental Army, was celebrated with special fervor at Valley Forge, because the day before, news of the French alliance had reached

Washington's headquarters. Brearley and the New Jersey Brigade's officers celebrated with a barbecue, and the rank-and-file marched around the maypole and held a dance.[53] Five days later, Washington, his wife, Martha, and his generals joined the New Jersey Brigade on the parade ground for a more formal celebration of the alliance, including cannon and musket salutes and huzzas for Washington and the King of France.[54]

In May, the Continental Congress decided to require loyalty oaths from all senior officers and political leaders, which met with some resistance, although not within the New Jersey Brigade. "[Lt.] Colos. Brealey and [Francis] Barber informs me that the Officer of their Regiments are now ready to take the Oaths," Washington wrote to Lord Stirling on May 11, "and as their is some little boggle in the matter in other Corps I must beg your Lordship to administer them without delay as it will be a good example to others."[55]

On May 25, Ogden, Brearley and the rest of Maxwell's Brigade began moving from Valley Forge to more familiar ground. Henry Clinton, who had replaced Howe, was reportedly preparing to evacuate Philadelphia, and he was going to go through New Jersey. Brearley knew that his hometown of Allen's Town, strategically located on the Lower York Road, the highway connecting New Jersey's two provincial capitals, Burlington and Perth Amboy, lay directly on the British route of march.

On June 2, Brearley reports, he "Joined the reg't at Mount Holly." When Clinton evacuated Philadelphia and began his march across New Jersey to meet a fleet assigned to transport his troops from Sandy Hook, the New Jersey Brigade, knowing its home state's terrain, was detached from the main army and joined with General Philemon Dickinson's New Jersey militia in harassing the British troops.[56]

Brearley and his fellow officers were "feasting on Turtle &

Punch" with the leading citizens of Mount Holly on June 21 when word came that the British Army was on the march north.[57] The New Jersey troops fought "a smart skirmish" with advance elements of the British at Crosswicks, near Bordentown, on June 23.[58] During the skirmish, Colonel Elias Dayton "was in front of the enemy & again had a horse wounded."[59]

Ironically, on the following night, while Brearley and the New Jersey Brigade camped in Maidenhead, where Brearley's father and brother still lived, the British occupied Brearley's hometown of Allen's Town. The following morning, British Generals Clinton and Lord Cornwallis arranged their order of march and headed toward Sandy Hook by way of Monmouth Courthouse (present-day Freehold).

Washington placed all of his advanced forces, including Maxwell's Brigade, Morgan's Riflemen and General Wayne's Pennsylvanians, under the command of the Marquis de Lafayette with orders to "take the first fair opportunity to attack the rear of the enemy."[60] Command, however, passed the following day to General Charles Lee.

Two days later, the largest pitched battle of the war began less than ten miles east of Brearley's home with several small skirmishes. When the British rear guard turned to fight, the American troops began to retreat under what they believed to be orders from Lee. When Washington sent two aides forward to find out why his troops were retreating, they ran into an infuriated New Jersey Brigade. David Rhea, Brearley's neighbor in Allen's Town and his replacement as lieutenant colonel of the Fourth Battalion, expressed strong disapproval. Colonel Matthias Ogden in great anger called out to one of Washington's aides, Lieutenant Colonel Harrison, "By God! They are flying from a shadow."

Ogden persuaded Maxwell to allow him and Brearley to form up their First Battalion in an orchard to cover the retreat, and Major Aaron Ogden, who had replaced the slain Witherspoon as brigade major after Germantown, offered to help. Maxwell then sent Major Ogden to find Lee for further orders. When the impetuous future New Jersey governor found Lee and told him that his brother's battalion "would give the enemy a warm reception," Lee sent back a messenger ordering Colonel Ogden "to hold his position to the last extremity and cover, if possible, the movement of Lee's division over the narrow bridge" leading away from the battlefield. Then, thinking this was a particularly good idea, Lee sent Major Ogden back with orders to have the Second, Third, and Fourth New Jersey Battalions cover the retreat too. Maxwell promptly commandeered two retreating cannon and turned to face the enemy.

When Lee's troops were safely over the bridge, the New Jersey Brigade withdrew and linked up with Lord Stirling's command on the left wing of the American army. Stirling's arrival was the first evidence the New Jerseyans had that Washington had confronted Lee, ordered the retreat halted, and sent Lee back with orders to "check the enemy" until Washington could bring up the main army.

The battle raged back and forth, and Ogden's and Brearley's First Battalion continued to distinguish itself. At one point, when two American brigades stationed behind a hedgerow gave way under a furious assault by British infantry and cavalry, Ogden's troops again covered the withdrawal and were the last to leave the field, reforming in an orderly fashion on a nearby slope.

Recognizing that "the men, who had been on the march and in the battle since the early morning, were worn out with hunger, thirst and fatigue," Washington ordered the New Jerseyans to the rear and continued the battle with fresh troops. The battle concluded with General Wayne's rout of the British grenadiers and General Clinton's withdrawal from the field late that night. While Clinton's goal was to march his army to Sandy Hook for embarkation, the Battle of Monmouth marked the first major engagement between the two armies since Saratoga in which the Americans possessed the battlefield the following morning. Each army lost about 350 killed.[61]

Brearley presumably rode to Allen's Town after the battle to see his family and inspect his home, but if he did so, he did not record the trip in his almanac. The "Brigade marched into Elizabeth Town" on July 12.[62]

Brearley's competence continued to attract Washington's notice. On August 8, Washington wrote to General Maxwell stating that:

> I am uncertain whether you may not already have a party somewhere in Monmouth County, but however this may be, it is my wish you should without delay have one of 50 men stationed under a very vigilant and intelligent Officer at some place in that County most convenient for commanding a view of the Hook and its environs; in order to watch the motions of the Enemy's Fleet and to advise me from time to time of every thing that passes, of all Vessels that arrive to them, or go out from them. Lieut. Colo. Brearly, [Lt. Col. David] Rhea or Major [Richard] Howel[l] would either of them be very proper for this business.[63]

There was no need for Maxwell to select an officer. Maxwell had already written to Washington the day before informing him that Lord Howe's fleet had sailed from Sandy Hook the previous day, presumably bound for Rhode Island.[64]

For Washington's army, it was a relatively uneventful summer and fall, as Brearley's almanac records. Brearley made weeklong trips to Philadelphia from July 20 to July 28 and from September 20 to September 28. On October 5, the Brigade

"Marched to Second River" and "Returned to Elizabeth Town" nine days later. Brearley "Went to Trenton" on November 2, "Returned to Elizabeth Town" on November 15, attended a court "Vendue in Trenton" on December 9.[65] By this time, Washington's Army was being stationed throughout the Watchung Mountains for its second winter in New Jersey, which would be known as the Middlebrook Encampment.

On February 11, 1779, he noted "Fourth regiment reduced," a reference to the reorganization of the Continental Army under which New Jersey's four regiments were merged into three larger regiments, with Ogden and Brearley remaining as colonel and lieutenant colonel of the First Regiment.

Four days later, Brearley left camp for personal reasons — for a wedding that would further unite the Brearley and Rogers families. "Harriet married," Brearley records in an almanac entry for February 16.[66] The wedding was held in the Brearley home.

Three generations later, a Brearley relative would describe Harriet as "a wilful, wayward and troublesome girl." Harriet "did not inherit her mother's beauty, but she must have been an attractive woman," she added,[67] although a Rogers relative described her as "like her mother very beautiful."[68]

Harriet, not quite nineteen, was marrying James Rogers, the second-oldest son of Hannah Tallman Rogers, who had been raising the Brearley children along with her own. Mrs. Rogers had been remarried the year before to Joseph Haight, the Burlington County militia major with whom Brearley had chased Tories in June 1776.[69] Haight owned the Allentown Mills, and his wife would continue to look after Brearley's four children.

James Rogers, who had just turned sixteen and needed his mother's consent to marry, had inherited the family home, store and tanyard in Allen's Town. Whether Harriet Luttrell was pregnant is uncertain, but likely, considering James' extreme youth at the time of the ceremony. The first of their seven children, Benjamin, was born in 1780, but no month of birth is given.[70]

Brearley spent almost two weeks at home before returning to camp on February 28 for a relatively uneventful two months of waiting for winter and the spring rains to end, making the roads passable again for armies.

On May 11, he records, "First regiment marched from Elizabeth Town."[71] With the war drawing down in the north, Maxwell's three New Jersey regiments had been assigned to join Major-General John Sullivan in a 3,500-man expeditionary force against the Iroquois, who had been waging an effective campaign against settlers in the Wyoming Valley.[72] The New Jersey regiments arrived in Easton, Pennsylvania, in late May. "First regiment marched from Easton" on June 1 and "Arrived at Wyoming," the predetermined rendezvous for the campaign, on June 4, Brearley reported.[73]

Brearley's career in the Continental Army had less than a month to go.

Robert Morris, who had been serving as New Jersey's first Supreme Court chief justice since February 5, 1777, wrote to Governor Livingston in early June informing him of his desire to resign:

> I accepted my present office to manifest my resolution to serve my country. I mean to do the duty of it while I hold it according to my best judgment. Whenever the Legislature think they can fill it more advantageously, the tenor of my commission shall not disappoint them.[74]

On June 10, the two houses of the New Jersey Legislature met in joint session to select Morris' replacement. The *Pennsylvania Gazette* printed its announcement on June 16:

> At a Joint-Meeting of the Legislative Council and
> Assembly of this State, on Thursday last, Lieut. Col.
> David Brearley was elected Chief Justice, in the room of
> the Hon. Robert Morris, Esq. Who hath resigned.[75]

Brearley was notified of his appointment by messenger, but
when he did not respond, Livingston wrote to Brearley on June
30 from Chatham:

> I took it for granted that you would be notified of
> your appointment to the office of Chief Justice of this
> State, by the Chairman of the joint meeting [Caleb
> Camp], whose Business I take it to be. But having
> reason to think by what Colonel [Elias] Dayton said that
> it has been neglected, I hereby inform you of your said
> appointment, & congratulate you upon it. If you accept
> of the office, as I believe every friend to his Country
> heartily wishes You to do, it is to be hoped that you will
> enter upon the execution of it, as soon as your present
> military connections will permit, there being four Courts
> of Oyer & Terminer appointed, at which your atten-
> dance will be of importance.[76]

On July 2, when Colonel Charles Armand's Independent
Corps was reassigned and ordered to report to Washington's
headquarters in New Windsor, New York, Brearley accompanied
them to make his separation from the army.[77] "The appointment
was in a measure forced upon him, as he preferred to remain in
the army," *The Judicial and Civil History of New Jersey*
acknowledged, "but gave way to the solicitations of the
Legislature that he would accept the position."[78]

Brearley's pride in his Continental Army service and his
reluctance to leave was evident from his letter to Congress, which

was read in public session on July 22. In it, Congress was told, Brearley stated:

> ... that the State of New Jersey, to which he belongs, has lately appointed him chief justice of that State, an office important and honourable, but not lucrative, and have requested him in the strongest manner to retire from the army and enter upon the duties of that office; but is very desirous of holding his rank in the army without pay.

Congress voted, on the motion of Elbridge Gerry, with whom Brearley would serve as a delegate to the Constitutional Convention eight summers later, "That the desire of Lieutenant Colonel David Brearley, Jun. to hold his rank in the army, after he shall have accepted the office of chief justice of the State of New Jersey, cannot be complied with."[79]

Washington chose John Conway, a major in the Third New Jersey Regiment who had been wounded at the Battle of Germantown,[80] to replace Brearley as lieutenant colonel of the First Regiment on July 17[81] and the New Jersey Legislature officially certified the appointment the following March 29 in Chief Justice Brearley's courtroom.[82]

But confusion would linger for more than a year over when Brearley actually resigned from the Army to take over as chief justice. In the summer of 1780, Robert Hanson Harrison, one of Washington's aides-de-camp, wrote to Brearley over Washington's signature from the headquarters near Passaick Falls (now Paterson):

> Dr Sir: I have to request that You will be so obliging as to inform me by the earliest opportunity, at what time you accepted the appointment of Chief

*Justice of this State. My reason for this request is, a Board of General Officers have determined on a late occasion, that Several Officers in the Jersey line ought to take rank from that time, and that reference should had to You to fix it. I have the Honor etc.*[83]

Whatever the effective date of Brearley's resignation, it is clear that the reluctant chief justice knew he was scheduled to open the Court of Oyer and Terminer on July 27 at the Monmouth County Courthouse in Freehold, just west of the battleground where he and Ogden had helped to cover Lee's withdrawal a year before. Ogden would be on his way to further military glory, and Brearley was envious.

# CHAPTER SIX

# Chief Justice

## *Holmes v. Walton* and the
## Precedent of Judicial Review

*"Whatever may be the case in other countries, yet, in this, there can be no doubt, that every act of the legislature, repugnant to the Constitution, is absolutely void."*

— William Paterson, Associate Justice of the
U.S. Supreme Court, ruling in the 1795
case of Van Horne's Lessee v. Dorrance [1]

The New Jersey Constitution that was adopted by the Provincial Congress on July 2, 1776 — the same day that the Continental Congress was voting its approval of independence in Philadelphia — vested most of its power in the two houses of the new Legislature. The governor would be elected annually at a joint session of the Council and Assembly, and the same two houses would select the Supreme Court justices. The terms of all judges were limited, and the Legislature had the power to reduce the judges' salaries at any time.

Consequently, the New Jersey Legislature did not find it easy to fill the post of chief justice, especially in the middle of a revolution. Many of the most prominent lawyers had sided with the Crown and others were serving in the military or in the more powerful legislative branch of government.

Two months after adoption of the New Jersey State Constitution, the Council and Assembly met in joint session and elected Richard Stockton to be the new state's first chief justice. As New Jersey's most respected lawyer, Stockton was the logical choice. In July, the Princeton lawyer had been one of five New Jerseyans to sign the Declaration of Independence, but his revolutionary credentials went back much earlier. In 1765, he had been the first to publicly urge the New Jersey legislature to send delegates to the Stamp Act Congress. But Stockton declined the appointment to the Supreme Court without publicly giving any reason.

A few days later, on September 4, 1776, the two houses elected John De Hart, a Hopewell farmer, to be chief justice, but he too declined. Later that same day the two houses voted again and this time they voted to offer the job to two candidates in the hope that one would accept. Francis Hopkinson, a former member of the Council, became the third candidate in four days to turn down the post of chief justice, but Samuel Tucker accepted. Tucker had served as president of the Provincial Congress until August 21, when it was dissolved so that the new state Legislature — created under the new state Constitution adopted July 2 — could take over. However, Tucker held the position for only three months before he resigned.[2]

On February 5, 1777, the two houses of the Legislature met again in joint session and chose Robert Morris to serve as chief justice. Perhaps the legislators were counting on heredity: After all, Morris' father, Robert Hunter Morris, had served as a long tenure as chief justice under the Crown. They were hopeful his son would stay in the post for more than a few months.

Ten days later, the two houses met again and selected Isaac Smith and John Cleves Symmes as associate justices, both of whom were still serving when David Brearley was chosen as chief justice two-and-a-half years later.[3]

Brearley knew of the difficulties that the Legislature had filling positions on the Supreme Court. Supreme Court justices not only heard appeals, but also had to travel the circuit, presiding over the Courts of Oyer and Terminer that functioned as trial courts in the Revolutionary War era. Brearley opened Monmouth's Court of Oyer and Terminer on July 27, 1780, and closed it on August 13. Five days later, he opened the Middlesex Court of Oyer and Terminer in Cranbury. That session did not end until August 28.[4]

On September 7, in Hillsborough, Brearley presided over the Supreme Court for the first time. The most important decision he made during the five-day session was to postpone ruling on what would prove to be the most important case he would ever handle — one that would establish the principle of judicial review almost a quarter-century before *Marbury v. Madison*. His predecessor, Chief Justice Morris, had agreed to hear the appeal of the controversial case, *Holmes v. Walton*, in which two Monmouth County men were charged with trading with the enemy.

Brearley, who spent the first year of the Revolution as a colonel in the Monmouth County Militia chasing Loyalists and suppressing similar trade with the enemy, wanted time to study the case and ordered oral arguments delayed until the next Supreme Court session, to be held in Burlington in November.

The law in question was passed by the Legislature on October 8, 1778, in an effort to eliminate trading with the enemy, who had been largely driven to Staten Island in the wake of the British withdrawal that followed the Battle of Monmouth. To encourage private citizens to aid the army and the militia in cracking down on illegal smuggling, the Legislature made it "lawful for any person or persons whomsoever to seize and secure provisions, goods, wares and merchandize attempted to be carried or conveyed into or brought from within the lines of encampments or any place in the possession of the subjects or troops of the King of Great Britain."

The 1778 law required the alleged smuggler and his goods to be brought before a justice of the peace, who was required to grant a trial by jury under the provisions of a February 11, 1775, law stating "that in every case where a jury of six men give a verdict as aforesaid there shall be no appeal allowed."[5] If the defendant was found guilty, the smuggled goods were to be sold and the proceeds divided among those who had seized them.

Brearley undoubtedly knew the plaintiff. Elisha Walton had enlisted as an ensign at the beginning of the war and served as captain of the First Regiment of the Monmouth County Militia while Brearley was colonel of the Second Militia Regiment.[6]

Walton had since been promoted to first major of the First Regiment of the Monmouth County Militia, and it was in that capacity that he detained John Holmes and Solomon Ketcham, charging them with illegal trading with the enemy. The goods seized included 700 to 800 yards of silk, 400 to 500 yards of silk gauze, and many other items of "such a quantity and such a quality as could not be purchased in all the stores of New Jersey." The value of the seized goods was later estimated to be "twenty nine thousand, four hundred and twenty-eight pounds, thirteen shillings and fourpence half penny," or about $70,000 in the depreciated Continental currency of the day — enough to make Walton a very wealthy man.[7]

Walton brought Holmes and Ketcham before John Anderson, a Monmouth County justice of the peace, and on May 24, 1779, a duly constituted jury of six ruled in Walton's favor. Holmes and Ketcham, however, had already applied to the

Supreme Court to consider their case, and outgoing Chief Justice Morris, in one of his last official acts, issued a writ of *certiorari* that bequeathed the case to Brearley.

In a four-page written appeal to the New Jersey Supreme Court filed in November 1779, attorney William Willcox offered a series of arguments for overturning the verdict. The seventh reason cited was: "Because the jury sworn to try the above cause and on whose verdict judgment was entered, consisted of six men only, when by the Laws of the Land it should have consisted of twelve men."[8]

As he was developing his appeal, in which some clauses were crudely crossed out, Willcox evidently began to feel that the constitutionality of the jury trial was his strongest point because he also filed a single page entitled "Additional reasons why the Judgment of the Justice given in this Cause or Plaint should be reversed." Three of the four reasons cited were:

> For that the Jury who tried the said plaint before the said Justice consisted of six men only contrary to law.
> For that the Jury who tried the said plaint before the said Justice consisted of six men only contrary to the constitution of New Jersey.
> For that the proceedings and trial in the said plaint in the Court below, and the Judgment thereon given were had and given contrary to the Constitution, practices, and Laws of the Land.[9]

No records were kept of the oral arguments made in the case by Willcox or the questions posed by Brearley and his fellow justices at the hearing on Thursday, November 11, in Trenton. It was clear that the case raised fundamental constitutional issues.

Brearley and his associate justices heard all the arguments

as to why they should overrule the previous verdict; they knew the case would be controversial. When the court session ended on Monday, November 15, the minutes of the Supreme Court stated simply that "the court will further advise on the arguments had on this cause until the next term." With the Supreme Court not scheduled to meet again until April 4, that meant Brearley and his fellow justices would have five months to think about his ruling.[10]

Brearley's almanac contains a single cryptic entry for the following month: December 13 is marked "Came to Mr. Higbee's." Joseph Higbee was a leading citizen of Trenton, a member of St. Michael's Episcopal Church, and the father of a beautiful, twenty-eight-year-old unmarried daughter named Elizabeth, who quickly attracted the attention of the thirty-four-year-old widower chief justice.

Brearley found time to visit his former comrades-in-arms "At Camp" on January 13, presumably in the Morristown area where Washington's army was marking its second consecutive winter behind the safety of New Jersey's Watchung Mountain range. On February 16, he attended a session of the New Jersey General Assembly, and on March 27, he presided over the Court of Oyer and Terminer in Somerset County.[11]

When the Supreme Court reconvened on April 4, 1780, Brearley still was not ready to decide the case of *Holmes v. Walton*. "The court not being ready to give judgment on the reasons filed and argued in this cause — Ordered, that a *curia advisare vult* until next term be entered; on motion of Mr. Elias Boudinot," the Supreme Court minutes reported.[12] "*Curia advisare vult*" meant that the court wanted to consider the case in all of its aspects. Boudinot, a top New Jersey attorney who had read law under Richard Stockton and would be elected     president of the Continental Congress just two years later, was now the lead attorney on the appeal.

Brearley presided over the Court of Oyer and Terminer in Sussex County on April 18, but when the Supreme Court reconvened on May 8, the case of *Holmes v. Walton* went unmentioned. This meant that no verdict would be given in the case until at least September — sixteen months after the initial trial and verdict in Monmouth County and ten months after oral arguments before the Supreme Court.

Brearley spent the summer on the judicial circuit, his almanac shows. He presided over the Court of Oyer and Terminer at Somerset on May 22, the Court of Oyer and Terminer for Bergen County on June 6, Middlesex Court on June 20, Burlington Court a week later, and the Court of Oyer and Terminer in Salem on August 22.[13] Undoubtedly, the *Holmes v. Walton* case was never far from his mind.

As a ranking officer in both the Monmouth County Militia and the New Jersey Line of the Continental Army, Brearley would have had clear disdain for Holmes and Ketcham, whose trade with the enemy had been on such a scale that it would have made them very wealthy if they had been able to slip past Major Walton's militia and sell their goods. Affirming their guilty verdict would be popular with the soldiers and with the citizenry.

But *Holmes v. Walton* also raised complex constitutional issues and offered an opportunity to affirm the rule of law and the primacy of constitutional rights. Section XXII of the New Jersey Constitution of 1776  specifically stated:

> That the common law of England, as well as so much of the statute law as have been heretofore practiced in this colony shall still remain in force, until they shall be altered by a future law of the legislature; such parts only are excerpted as are repugnant to the rights and privileges contained in this Charter; and that the inestimable right of trial by jury shall remain

confirmed as a part of the law of this colony, without repeal forever.[14]

If the words "without repeal forever" were not sufficiently clear, the importance of this right to the framers of the New Jersey Constitution was underscored by their decision to require members of the Legislature to take an oath not to assent to any law repealing or annulling "that part of the twenty-second section respecting the trial by jury."

In both East Jersey, where the Proprietors had ruled, and in West Jersey, where Brearley's father found himself in prison for leading the land riots against the West Jersey Society, "trial by jury" meant trial by a jury of twelve:

> In addition to immemorial custom, the "common law" of England, which may have been held to have had validity in this case, two documents may have been appealed to as fundamentally relevant and as constituting in New Jersey a part of the "law of the land:" the first, Chapter XXII. of the West Jersey "Concessions and Agreements" of 1676, "Not to be altered by the legislative authority," which begins thus, "That the trial of all causes, civil and criminal, shall be heard and decided by the verdict or judgment of twelve honest men of the neighborhood." The second was a formal declaration of the "Rights and Privileges" passed by the House of Representatives in East Jersey on March 13, 1699, and accepted by the governor and council, which asserted that "all trials shall be by the verdict of twelve men."[15]

Laws passed by the Assembly in West Jersey in November 1681 and the Assembly in East Jersey in March 1683 also specified the right to trial by a jury of twelve men.[16]

Brearley opened the Supreme Court in Trenton on September 3, 1790, but it was not until September 7, five days into the session, that he was ready to issue his verdict in *Holmes v. Walton.* In what was probably an oral opinion delivered from the bench, Brearley declared:

> *This cause having been argued several terms past and the court having taken time to consider the same, and being now ready to deliver their opinion ... on motion of Mr. Boudinot for the plaintiffs, judgment is ordered for the plaintiffs, and that the judgment of the justice in the court below be reversed and the said plaintiffs be restored to all things.*[17]

The dry, understated language from the Supreme Court minutes quoted above belies not only the importance of the decision, but the furor it aroused. For the first time in American history, a court had asserted the concept of judicial review, including the right to declare laws passed by a legislature unconstitutional.

Patriotic citizens reacted angrily to the ruling, and petitions of protest poured into the Legislature. On December 8, in the state Assembly, "a petition from sixty inhabitants of the county of Monmouth was presented and read, complaining that the justices of the Supreme Court have set aside some of the laws as unconstitutional, and made void the proceedings of the magistrates, although strictly agreeable to the said laws, to the encouragement of the disaffected and great loss to the loyal citizens of the state and praying redress."

Similar petitions came in from Middlesex and Essex counties, which, like Monmouth, bordered the British and Loyalist stronghold of Staten Island. One petition read in the Assembly on November 21, 1780, requested that the Legislature make jury verdicts in seizure cases final and not subject to review by the Supreme Court.[18] In their view, Holmes and Ketcham were traitors and deserved to be treated as such.

Angry citizens in the counties bordering the British lines did not know that Brearley and his fellow justices had written to the Legislature on May 13 — four months before the *Holmes v. Walton* verdict — suggesting that a new law be passed giving the court the option of sending cases reversed on technicalities back to the lower court for a new trial. In response, the Legislature on June 17 enacted a law stating:

> *That in all such causes where the judgment of the justice shall be reversed in the supreme court on certiorari for informality of proceedings, or any other cause not essential to the merits of the suits, such judgment of reversal shall only affect the parties with respect to the costs of the suit; and it shall and may be lawful for the supreme court on such reversal to award a new trial on the merits in the court below where the cause was originally determined ...[19]*

Perhaps it was those back-channel relationships that made it easy for the Legislature to disregard the protest petitions pouring in from the border counties. Brearley's almanac notation that the "Assembly met" on September 13 may well indicate a visit by the Chief Justice to the Legislature six days after the ruling, most likely to explain and build support for his decision.

Certainly, Brearley remained in high esteem in the Legislature. It was in the midst of the public furor over the *Holmes v. Walton* decision that Brearley found himself nominated as a candidate for governor. Brearley, who was in the process of building a strong relationship with the popular Livingston, certainly harbored few illusions about his chance of being elected and may not have campaigned at all for the position. In any case, Livingston won reelection at an October 30, 1780, meeting of the Joint Council with twenty-eight votes. Brearley finished second with six votes, followed by Philemon Dickinson with two.[20]

Two months later, Brearley won a more important vote when the Legislature on December 22, 1780, passed a law ratifying Brearley's decision by requiring judges, on the demand of either party in such cases as *Holmes vs. Walton*, to grant a jury of twelve men.[21]

The decision by Brearley and his associate justices was doubly important. It was the first state court ruling affirming the constitutional right of trial by jury, coming six years before the 1786 Rhode Island decision in *Trevett v. Weeden* and seven years before the North Carolina ruling on *Bayard v. Singleton*.[22]

But more important was the precedent set by the New Jersey Supreme Court for the right of the judiciary to rule on the constitutionality of state laws.

More than two decades would pass before another New Jersey chief justice, Andrew Kirkpatrick, would explicitly cite the New Jersey Legislature's acquiescence to Brearley's decision in *Holmes v. Walton* as establishing a precedent for legislative recognition of judicial authority to rule on the constitutionality of state laws.[23]

But Governor Livingston, in a June 7, 1782 message to the Assembly urging passage of a stronger seizure statute, already implicitly recognized the right of the Supreme Court to rule on the constitutionality of laws when he stated:

> *...if an act of legislation can constitutionally be made, declaring that no person in whose possession any goods, wares or merchandise shall be seized and captured as effects illegally imported from the enemy,*

*shall be entitled to such a writ (of replevin) ... it would probably encourage such seizures and give additional check to that most pernicious and detestable trade...*[24]

Gouverneur Morris, in a 1785 speech to the Pennsylvania Legislature opposing legislation introduced to repeal the charter of the National Bank, specifically cited the *Holmes v. Walton* precedent:

*A law was once passed in New Jersey which the judges pronounced unconstitutional, and therefore void. Surely no good citizen can wish to see this point decided in the tribunals of Pennsylvania. Such power in judges is dangerous, but, unless it somewhere exists, the time employed in framing a bill of rights and form of government was merely thrown away.*[25]

Two years later, Morris and Brearley would grapple with the issue of constitutional review by an independent judiciary on the federal level as fellow delegates to the Constitutional Convention, and Brearley and his fellow New Jersey delegates would keep that principle in mind while developing the "New Jersey Plan," which strengthened the power of the judiciary.

William Paterson, Brearley's ally in those constitutional debates, was serving as New Jersey's attorney general at the time of the *Holmes v. Walton* ruling and he issued a similar opinion while serving as associate justice of the United States Supreme Court in 1795. In his opinion on a circuit case, *Van Horne's Lessee v. Dorrance*, Paterson would contrast the supremacy of Parliament under the British system with the supremacy of the Constitution in the new nation:

*Whatever may be the case in other countries, yet, in*

*this, there can be no doubt, that every act of the legislature, repugnant to the Constitution, is absolutely void.*[26]

Brearley's and Paterson's position would become enshrined as the judicial bedrock of the federal system in 1803, when Chief Justice John Marshall issued his landmark ruling in *Marbury v. Madison* that it "is emphatically the province and duty of the judicial department to say what the law is." Marshall did not cite precedents in his opinions, but he undoubtedly knew of *Holmes v. Walton* from Paterson, who was still serving as associate justice.[27]

The decision in *Holmes v. Walton,* issued at the end of his first year as chief justice, would be Brearley's major intellectual contribution to New Jersey and American jurisprudence, but his day-to-day conduct of his office did much to shape the evolving state judicial system and to cement a close working relationship with Governor Livingston that would have important ramifications not only for New Jersey, but for the creation of the federal system of government.

Like most governors and their chief justices, Livingston and Brearley kept up a constant correspondence on pardons and other legal issues. For example, Brearley wrote to Livingston on February 6, 1781, to report:

At the Courts of Oyer and Terminar and General Gaol-Delivery lately held in the County of Monmouth, the following persons were Capitally convicted, and are sentenced to be executed on Friday next, to wit, Robert James for High Treason whose case I have before stated to your Excellency: Humphrey Wade and John Parker for Horse-Stealing, their cases are very clear –

*they were in company in stealing the Horses, and taken together on them, at a place called Squancum in Shrewsberry, they acknowledged to the Party who took them, that they Stole the Horses out of the pasture of John Coward of Upper-Freehold — Wade is an elderly man, Parker is a youth of about seventeen years of age ...*[28]

None of the three were hanged that Friday. Unknown to Brearley, Wade and Parker had escaped two days before. Robert James would be pardoned by the Privy Council the following month on Brearley's recommendation.

Brearley and Livingston frequently conferred on how to resolve difficult cases in a way that would be suspect once the new federal Constitution established a strict separation of powers. Typical was the case of Lt. Col. William Klein of the German Volunteers, who came to the colonies from Hamburg in 1778 to fight the British. Congress put Klein in charge of luring his fellow Germans to desert from the British, but he appears to have been inept, and the German Volunteers requested that he be removed from command. On January 29, 1781, Livingston wrote to Brearley asking his advice on the Klein matter, and Brearley wrote back the following day:

*I am really at a loss with respect to Lieutenant Colonel Klein, as Congress dont incline to have anything to do with him. I think it would be very hard to punish him by the laws of this State, for attempting to go within the Enemies Lines, and to set him at liberty will be an encouragement for him to attempt it again. If, therefore, he can give, almost any sort of, security, that he will not return into this State again, I believe it would be best for your Excellency to permit him to pass over into Pennsylvania, and from Philadelphia he may probably find his way to Europe.*[29]

Livingston took Brearley's advice. Nine days later, Klein signed a written letter of parole promising not to return to New Jersey and went to Philadelphia, where Congress voted him a year's pay to underwrite his return home "as there is no further use of him here."[30]

As New Jersey's chief justice, Brearley sometimes found himself in the unusual position of representing civil authority against the military, and state officials knowing Brearley's good standing with General Washington took advantage of the access afforded by that relationship. On August 11, 1780, Brearley wrote to Washington:

> Complaint has been made to me by a member of the Legislature of Somerset County, together with other reputable inhabitants, that a detachment of Major Lees light dragoons have quartered themselves upon the Inhabitants of that County near Rocky Hill, without any Order of Law, are impressing forage by their own authority, and committing other great outrages on the inhabitants — The persons particularly complained against, are, Captain Rudolph, Doctor Irvin and one Stephen Lewis (supposed to be a commissioned officer) — I have forborn giving any warrant for them, well knowing that every fresh wanton infraction of the Law, would meet your Excellencys utmost disapprobation, and that your desire to support order, and the rights of Citizens, would induce you to deliver them, to be dealt with agreeably to the just laws of the State.[31]

As a wartime chief justice, however, Brearley was more often concerned with making sure that the county sheriffs he supervised kept a close eye on Tory activities. On January 11, 1782, he reported to General Alexander, Lord Stirling, who had been placed in charge of the Army's Northern Department, which included New Jersey, that:

> I despatched the Sheriff of Burlington down to Egg-harbour, who returned yesterday, and informs me that the enemy have not made any fortifications on Osbourne's Island, as was supposed; but that there are a considerable body of armed boats which ply constantly between Egg-harbour and New-York, — some of which are always at Egg-harbour, in order to carry off deserters and others who choose to go to New-York. Colonel Lawrence of Monmouth was down at the same time, with a party of Militia; and on his approach, the enemy, who were in the village, at the Meeting-house, fled over the beach, where, by means of their boats, they were in a state of perfect security.
>
> Unless these fellows are routed, all the sea-coast for many miles must be given up to the enemy; yet I know of no possible means of accomplishing it, but by sending a superior force by water, so as to cut off their retreat to New-York. If this could be effected, they might then very easily be demolished.[32]

He signed the letter "Colonel David Brearley," reflecting the rank he had reassumed in the Monmouth County Militia upon his return from Washington's Continental Army.

Trading with the enemy, the *Holmes v. Walton* issue, continued to be a major focus of Brearley and New Jersey's court system throughout the war. On May 13, 1782, Brearley wrote to Livingston about actions he had taken to crack down on abuses involving flags of truce:

> ... at the time we were holding of a special Court in

*Essex last winter, information was made to me that very improper uses were made of Flags of Truce passing between Elizabeth Town & Staten Island. That they had become the Vehicle of clandestine trade & commerce, with the Enemy. That this business was carried on by people of the worst characters, who had fled from us. That we had no Post kept at Elizabeth Town at that time and that no military officer was stationed there. It then became me to make the necessary inquiry in this business. I therefore issued my warrant to the Sherif directing him to go to Elizabeth Town, apprehend & bring before me those who were there under colour of Flags of truce.... When the Sheriff got to Elizabeth Town, there were at that point, no less than three Boats from Staten Island, carrying General [Cortland] Skinners flag Orders, some of which had been there for a week; and so bold were they in this business, that the ostensible reason for one of them, as mentioned in the Orders, was for two or three of those Miscreants, to visit their Friends at Elizabeth Town.*

*Perhaps it may be unnecessary further to observe to Your Excellency, that all those who were apprehended by the Sheriff were taken two Miles from their Boats, without any leave given by an officer of ours. Indeed some of them had been riding about the Country in sleighs. ...*

Brearley reported to Livingston that he had discharged some of the men apprehended, but that he had charged John Smith Hetfield and Abner Badgley with "High Treason" and put them in prison. They "had joined with the Enemy long since the passing of the treason Act" and "by the Laws of Nations are not protected by Flags of Truce," Brearley explained. He added that he had discharged Job Hetfield because he had previously been taken prisoner and exchanged by the military.[33]

As chief justice, Brearley handled at least fifteen cases in which slaves or former slaves sought freedom for themselves or their children. Invariably, the Brearley Court ruled for manumission, according to a report certified by Joseph Bloomfield, New Jersey's Attorney General from 1783 to 1792 and later President of the New Jersey Society for Promoting the Abolition of Slavery.[34]

In one of his first manumission cases, during the September 1782 term, Brearley ruled against Edmund Bainbridge, the son of the anti-Proprietary leader of the same name who led the riders who freed his father from the Trenton jail in 1747. The elder Bainbridge had given a slave named Nelly to his daughter Abigail as a New Year's Day gift when she was a child. Abigail, who had married a relative of Brearley's half-brothers, set Nelly free in her will, and the Brearley Court ruled that her brother had no right to challenge Nelly's manumission and keep her as a slave.[35]

In a 1783 case, *Mercy Hill v. William Leddell*, the Brearley Court ruled that Mercy Hill, born to a slave woman in Massachusetts and put into indentured servitude as an infant, should not have been "by some Means sold as a Slave," and was entitled to her freedom.

Leddell, a lawyer, was the defendant in an even more complicated case two years later involving a slave named Quamini, whose Morris County owner, Captain Augustine Bayles, promised Quamini "that if he would be honest, faithful, and industrious, he never should serve any other Master, but should be free at the said Captain Bayles's decease." However, Bayles "on his Death-Bed, considering that his Wife would be left very destitute of Help, directed that the said Negro Quamini should continue in her Service during her Widowhood, and that then he should be free." When his widow, Keziah, remarried,

Quamini ended up in Leddell's hands, still a slave. The Brearley Court ordered Quamini freed.[36]

In a 1787 case, *The State against John B. Oliver and his Wife*, the Court ordered Oliver to post bond of £500 over the alleged ill treatment of a slave named Kate; the dispute was later settled out of court.[37] Finally, in an April 1789 case, *The State against David Lyon*, the Court ruled that two children born to a slave, Flora, after her marriage to a freedman, Joseph Reap, could not be pressed into slavery. As in the case of Quamini, the Court cited the intentions of Flora's former master, Dr. Joseph Eaton, who had declared himself "principled against slavery," and the payment of wages to Flora by Dr. Eaton's widow and son as evidence of her free status.[38]

Brearley did not own any slaves, although he did purchase the contract of an indentured servant on April 8, 1780. The contract called for the "Negro boy named Lewis, seventeen years of age, to serve him for Term of thirteen years from the date hereof, at the expiration of which term said Negro is become free."[39] When Brearley died, Lewis' services were "not wanted by the family." As one of Brearley's executors, James Mott gave Lewis "Liberty to travel for a few days (not leaving thirty miles from this Place) to find a master of his Own Choice" for the remaining two years and seven months on his contract.[40]

Brearley's courtship of Elizabeth Higbee from 1780 to 1783 not only added some stability to his personal life, but shifted the focus of his life from Allen's Town, where he had raised his first family, to Trenton, where both his wife-to-be and his Supreme Court office were located.

Little is known of Brearley's home life in the period between the death of his first wife Elizabeth in August 1777 and his subsequent marriage to Elizabeth Higbee on April 17, 1783, but it could not have been easy for his children. For the first two years after their mother's death, he served virtually full-time in the Continental Army, and over the next four years, his job as chief justice kept him on a monthly circuit from courthouse to courthouse to preside over Courts of Oyer and Terminer.

While his stepdaughter, Harriet, had been married in January 1779, William, Elizabeth, and Mary, were able to live again with their father once he returned home from the army. However, his younger daughter, Hettie, who had been just four months old when her mother died, evidently remained in the care of the widow Hannah Rogers in Allen's Town for three more years until she was five years old.[41] It is not until August 1, 1782, that Brearley records in his almanac, "Brought Hetty home."[42]

Brearley's son, William, resented his relationship with Elizabeth Higbee. William was still "quite young" when he "left home and went to sea, in consequence of an act for which he incurred his father's displeasure," W. H. Brearley reported in his family genealogy. According to other family sources, he had quarrelled with his new stepmother, and his father sided with her against his son.[43]

David Brearley immersed himself in Trenton civic life. On February 10, 1781, he joined with his future father-in-law, Joseph Higbee, and eighteen other leading citizens of Trenton in subscribing seven pounds, ten shillings each "for the purpose of erecting a School House in the said Town, and keeping up a Regular School for the Education of Youth, to be conducted under the Firm of the Trenton School Company."[44]

Brearley's fellow investors included Associate Justice Isaac Smith, Postmaster Abram Hunt, innkeeper Francis Witt, and William Churchill Houston, a professor of mathematics and natural philosophy at the College of New Jersey (later Princeton University). Houston was about to begin a law practice and would soon be appointed by Brearley as clerk to the Supreme

Court, where their work on legal issues would grow to encompass the politics of the nation.

Brearley's subscription enabled him to send a child to the school at no charge, but despite his growing prominence, money in the Brearley household was never abundant.

While Brearley's title of chief justice was a prestigious one, he, like so many other public officials and soldiers, had difficulty living on deflated Continental currency. On November 22, 1781, he wrote angrily to John Mehelm, Esq.:

> It is with great reluctance that I am induced to address you on a subject which principally concerns myself, but when the circumstances are fully understood, I trust I shall be justified in doing it. It is with respect to the Salary which I have received as Chief Justice of this State. — It is very certain that the Legislature intended that what they gave should be a decent and moderate support, but unfortunately for me, the good intentions of Legislature have hitherto been defeated, by the depreciation of paper money. As it is totally incompatable with the Honor and Dignity of the Legislature of a Free and virtuous People to permit their Servants to suffer by confiding in and faithful serving them; so I have not a doubt but that they will do complete and ample justice when accounts are fairly exhibited to them, for which purpose I have inclosed a state of all the monies that I have received, with the fair value therof, as nearly as I can ascertain it, whence it will be apparent that I have not been supported. And herefore permit me to observe that from the frequency, the duties and nature of the office, I am entirely precluded from following any other business; it is therefore obvious that the support of myself and Family

*rests upon the Salary of Office. — And, Sir, permit me*
*further to observe, that, I have never asked or sought for*
*Place or Office, neither have I ever refused my services*
*where my country have called for them, and so long as I*
*am enabled to live with decency, I shall serve cheerfully,*
*but when that is withheld, it will be sufficient notice*
*from me, that I am no longer useful, and I will then retire*
*without reluctance.*[45]

Brearley's rise to increasing public prominence was underscored in June 1781, when the College of New Jersey
bestowed upon him an honorary master of arts degree. Brearley
was part of a distinguished class of honorary degree recipients.[46]
Also receiving honorary masters of arts degrees were Major
General Nathanael Greene and Pierre-Eugene du Simitiere, "a
gentleman of literary merit, a native of Geneva, and residing in
the city of Philadelphia." Thomas McKean, president of
Congress, received a doctor of laws degree. Ironically, long after
Brearley's death, then-Governor McKean would serve as a
trustee for the funds bestowed on Brearley's stepdaughter,
Harriet Luttrell, by her nobleman Irish father.

Brearley and Elizabeth Higbee were married on April 17,
1783, at St. Michael's Episcopal Church in Trenton,[47] two days
after peace was proclaimed in Trenton following news of the
signing of the Treaty of Paris. The Higbee family had been
longtime members of St. Michael's, and the couple delayed their
wedding to await the reopening of the Anglican church. The
church had been closed from July 1, 1776, until January 1, 1783,
because its congregation included so many Loyalists. It was used
during the war as a hospital for soldiers of the Continental Army.
When it reopened for normal church services and activities in
January, the building needed much repair. Brearley took the time

to organize the repair efforts, and by April, the church was sufficiently refurbished to host their wedding.[48]

Brearley went on to serve as Warden of St. Michael's Church, and also took on a principal leadership role in two major fraternal organizations that would cement old relationships and provide important connections in the years ahead.

On May 13, 1783, just a month after news of the peace treaty reached the United States, Major General Henry Knox, the Baron von Steuben and other officers of Washington's Army met in cantonment on the Hudson River and created the Society of the Cincinnati, named for the Roman general who had saved the city from invaders and then returned to his plow. A hereditary society that would be open for membership to any officer who had served at least three years in the Continental Army, the Society of the Cincinnati vowed "an incessant attention to preserve inviolate those exalted rights and liberties of human nature for which they have fought and bled, and without which the high rank of a rational being is a curse instead of a blessing."[49]

When New Jersey's state chapter was formed, Brigadier General Elias Dayton was elected as president and Lieutenant Colonel Jonathan Forman as vice president. But Forman apparently resigned or stepped aside during those first months, and Brearley replaced him as vice president, a position he would hold until his death.[50]

Brearley also continued his involvement in the Fraternal Order of the Masons, which he apparently joined through Military Lodge No. 19 of Pennsylvania while serving with the Continental Army, presumably during the Brandywine-Germantown campaign or the winter that followed at Valley Forge. Records of early Masonic lodge activity in New Jersey are sparse, although a Monmouth County lodge was warranted by the Grand Lodge of Pennsylvania in 1779 and a military lodge for the New Jersey Line of the Continental Army in 1782.[51]

Where Brearley attended Masonic meetings in the early to mid-1780s is not known, but he was sufficiently prominent and involved to be elected as Grand Mason when New Jersey's Masonic lodges held their first state convention on December 18, 1786, at the White Hall Tavern in New Brunswick to establish a Grand Lodge of New Jersey.

The prominent positions held by Masons in New Jersey can be judged simply from a roster of the officers elected along with Brearley: Robert L. Hooper, vice president of New Jersey's Legislative Council; Assemblyman Daniel Marsh; Maskell Ewing, the clerk of the state Assembly, an Army colonel, and the sheriffs of Morris and Hunterdon counties filled the remaining five elected positions for the new Grand Lodge.[52]

The year before, the Brearleys had moved from Allen's Town to a house on Pennington Road in Trenton, near his duties as Supreme Court justice and his wife's family as well. By this time, the family included daughters Elizabeth, Mary and Hetty from his first marriage, and Elizabeth Higbee had given birth to their first child. As Brearley recorded in his almanac under February 10, 1785: "Joseph born 7 o'clock morning." He was presumably named for Brearley's brother, Joseph.[53]

Eight months later, David Brearley Sr., the patriarch and first in the family to rebel against Royal authority and privilege, died almost four decades after his arrest for treason and four years after the "world turned upside down" at Yorktown. Under October 4, 1785, his son recorded simply, "My father died."[54]

Just over a year later, on November 3, 1786, Brearley recorded the birth of his second son: "David born half after 11 at night." His almanac would end that year with a mix of typical entries: November 14: "Supreme Court." November 28: "Winter set in, the Delaware closed without snow." November 30: "Bergen Court." December 4: "Dreadful snow storm." December 5: "Essex Circuit." December 19: "Middlesex Court."[55]

One entry for September 27, 1786, records his attendance at "Convention in Burlington." Brearley served as a delegate from St. Michael's Episcopal Church to the New Jersey Diocesan Convention, during which rules and regulations were adopted that set the guidelines for the future Constitution of the Episcopal Church for the Diocese of New Jersey. One of the convention tasks that Brearley undoubtedly relished was the rewriting of the Episcopal church service to take out all references to the King.[56]

Two months later, Brearley would be assigned to serve as a delegate to another constitutional convention, with much greater ramifications for the nation. Left out of Brearley's almanac entries for November 1786 was the following letter:

> November 23, 1786
> The State of New Jersey
> To the Honorable David Brearley, William Churchill Houston, William Patterson, and John Neilson Esquires. Greeting.
>
> The Council and Assembly reposing especial trust and confidence in your integrity, prudence, and ability, have at a joint meeting appointed you the said David Brearley, William Churchill Houston, William Paterson, and John Neilson Esquires, or any three of you, Commissioners to meet such Commissioners, as have been or may be appointed by the other States in the Union, at the City of Philadelphia in the Commonwealth of Pennsylvania, on the second Monday in May next, for the purpose of taking into Consideration the State of the Union as to trade and other important objects, and of devising such other Provisions as shall appear necessary to render the Constitution of the federal Government adequate to the exigencies thereof.
>
> In Testimony whereof...the Great Seal of the State

is hereunto affixed. Witness William Livingston Esquire, Governor, Captain General and Commander in Chief in and over the State of New Jersey and Territories thereunto belonging Chancellor and Ordinary in the same at Trenton the Twenty third day of November in the Year of our Lord one thousand seven hundred and Eighty six and of our Sovereignty and Independence the Eleventh.

Wil. Livingston

Bowes Reed[57]

# CHAPTER SEVEN

# The New Jersey Idea

## Taxation, Trade, and the Challenge to the Confederation Government

*"... the Idea of extending the powers of their deputies to other objects than those of Commerce, which has been adopted by the State of New Jersey, was an improvement on the original plan, and will deserve to be incorporated into that of a future Convention ... (to) render the constitution of the Federal Government adequate to the exigencies of the Union.."*

— Resolution of the Annapolis Convention,
September 11, 1786 [1]

The groundwork for the Constitutional Convention of 1787 was actually laid in 1786, when the Virginia Legislature, at the suggestion of James Madison, passed a resolution urging each state to send delegates to a convention to be held in Annapolis to discuss Congress' exercise of power over trade.[2]

No state in the nation had a greater stake in this issue than New Jersey.

Virginia Governor Edmund Randolph's letter to Livingston arrived as New Jersey was in the middle of a major dispute with Congress over its failure to make interest payments on the national debt, of which ten percent was owed to New Jerseyans — twice the amount that the state's population would suggest. The dispute was tied inextricably to larger issues, including the weakness of Continental and state currency, the taxation of imports, and the inability of the Confederation government to solve these and other complex problems under Articles of Confederation that required unanimity for every decision.

As far back as June 1778, in its objections to the Articles of Confederation then under consideration, New Jersey recommended that Congress, not the individual states, be given the power to tax imports as a means of supporting the national government.[3] New Jersey ratified the Articles in November — even though the government created was not in the state's best interest.

Brearley fully understood the impact of the currency crisis. Brearley, as chief justice; Philemon Dickinson, commanding general of the New Jersey militia, and six other prominent New Jerseyans had painstakingly signed their names to tens of thousands of dollars issued by the State of New Jersey in 1780 and 1781. Just above the "D. Brearley" signature, the State of New Jersey promised payment of "One Spanish milled Dollar," plus five percent interest per year, by December 31, 1786. The New Jersey Assembly authorized the first state currency issue of $600,000 (the equivalent of £250,000) on June 9, 1780, in response to a March 18, 1780, resolution by Congress, which had promised to back the bills. The front of each dollar explicitly promised that "The United States ensure the Payment of the within BILL, and will draw Bills of Exchange for the Interest annually, if demanded." The following year, on January 9, 1781, the New Jersey Assembly authorized a second currency issue of

£30,000 in the more familiar, and presumably trustworthy, English denominations of shillings and pence. Brearley once again was one of the designated signers of the notes.[4] But Congress did not have the money to cover the interest on these notes or other debts.

As the national currency depreciated in value until it was "not worth a Continental," Congress in February 1781 finally decided to seek approval by the states for a five percent tax on certain imports and prizes of war. New Jersey and eleven other states approved the measure. But Rhode Island refused, and under the Articles of Confederation, unanimity was required.[5]

The tax proposal was revived in 1783, but three years later, only New Jersey and seven states had agreed. New York, not surprisingly, and Georgia rejected the plan. New York and Pennsylvania were levying high tariffs on imported goods coming in through New York City and Philadelphia; without a major port of their own, residents of New Jersey — a "barrel tapped at both ends," in the famous phrase attributed to Benjamin Franklin — were paying a sizable percentage of the import duties that supported its larger neighboring state governments.[6] Paying import taxes to the national government would ensure that at least some of the money was spent in New Jersey's interest.

Meanwhile, the Confederation Congress, which like the Continental Congress during the war lacked the necessary clout to raise enough money to meet the nation's needs, had stopped paying even the interest on its debt. Of the estimated $2.5 million owed to New Jerseyans, "half of this sum was represented by Continental Loan Office Certificates (similar to War Bonds) and the remainder by certificates issued by Army quartermasters and commissaries in payment for supplies and by notes given to soldiers for their pay."[7]

New Jersey's Legislature, therefore, decided informally in December 1783 – and formally in December 1784 — to refuse to pay any further requisitions made by the Confederation government and instead to levy an $83,358 annual tax on its own citizens to pay for the interest on the national debt. A further tax of $33,333 was added to cover the interest due on the state government's $750,000 debt for payments for militia, supplies, and soldier's pay.

New Jersey's taxes were now the highest in the nation, but it was the only state that had figured out how to pay its creditors.

"We stand like Tantalus to our Chin in water, and are notwithstanding perishing with thirst," William Churchill Houston, clerk to Brearley's Supreme Court, complained in a letter to Livingston. "But perhaps, as it often happens, these Difficulties will bring us sooner into the proper Systems and Forms of political Administration."[8]

The direct challenge to the Confederation government posed by New Jersey's action did not become apparent until September 1785, when Congress issued a new requisition of $3 million from the states, of which New Jersey's quota was $166,716.

Abraham Clark, one of New Jersey's five signers of the Declaration of Independence and a legislator whose influence was second only to Livingston's in New Jersey during the Confederation years, asserted in a letter to two of New Jersey's congressional representatives, "This is a burden too unequal and grievous for this State to submit to." New York and Pennsylvania, he noted, once again would raise their quotas of taxes through import duties paid partly by New Jersey residents, while New Jersey's citizens would be asked to pay the new Confederation levy entirely from their own resources. Furthermore, Congress had decided that New Jersey would be given no credit after January 1, 1786, for any interest payments it made to its own creditors. New Jersey also lacked the ability that other states such as Virginia possessed to sell western lands to finance its quota.[9]

William Paterson was one of the few prominent New Jerseyans who favored the requisition, arguing that the overall effect of the Confederation plan would be to spread the national debt more evenly among the various states. In a May 1786 petition that anticipated the strong Federalist position he would take as a delegate to the Constitutional Convention and later as Governor and U.S. Supreme Court justice, Paterson argued:

> *The more the Interests of the States are intertwined, the more close and perfect will be their Union; the more sure and permanent will be the Basis on national Credit & Honor. It is generally supposed, that New Jersey has a surplus of Certificates; and therefore it is emphatically the Interest of New Jersey to adopt the Resolution.*[10]

However, Clark's view, which resonated with legislators angered by eight years of perceived injustices in the Confederation governmental system and similar slights and inequities perpetrated by neighboring states, easily carried the day. On February 20, 1786, by a 32-3 vote, the Legislature resolved that it would not pay its requisition to Congress until every state agreed to the revived 1783 plan to allow Congress to tax imports "or at least until the several States, having the Advantage of Commerce which they now enjoy solely from the joint Exertions of the United States, shall forbear exacting Duties or Imposts upon Goods and merchandise for the particular Benefit of their respective States, thereby drawing Revenues from other States whose local Situations and Circumstances will not admit their enjoying similar advantages from Commerce."[11] Subsequent legislation drafted by Clark directed New Jersey's congressional delegation to oppose any revenue measure until these conditions were met.

New Jersey Congressman John Beatty was one of those

who feared that his state's defiance could destroy the fragile Union, but Virginia's Henry Lee wrote to Washington that he thought New Jersey was justified: "Perhaps this intemperance in Jersey may bring this state [New York] to acquiese in a system of finance long ago approved by ten states and whose operation might have saved the difficultys which impend over the union."

Congress' response was to appoint a three-member delegation headed by Charles Pinckney of South Carolina to travel to New Jersey to meet with the rebellious Legislature. In a speech to the Assembly, Pinckney asserted that small states like New Jersey would have more to fear from the dissolution of the Confederation than larger states, and added that if New Jersey wanted to strengthen the powers of the central government, it should direct its congressional delegation "to urge the calling of a general convention of the states, for the purpose of amending and revising the federal system."[12] William Grayson, a second member of the delegation, added in his address that a new government was unlikely to give small states the same position of equality in votes that they held under the Articles of Confederation.

Clark was unmoved, but Thomas Griffith of Gloucester County moved and won passage for a half-hearted, face-saving resolution four days later that rescinded the Legislature's defiant refusal to pay the requisition, while making no effort to actually raise the $166,716 requested.

While New Jersey proved "willing to remove as far as in their power every Embarassment from the Councils of the Union," the lesson of the confrontation in Trenton was not lost on Congress.

Grayson noticed a new willingness among some members of Congress to recommend a new convention to amend the Articles of Confederation. Pinckney's recommendation that Congress take a hard look at the state of the national government resulted in the appointment that summer of a committee to recommend amendments to the Articles to "render the federal government adequate to the ends for which it was instituted."

The New Jersey Legislature was not going to wait for Pinckney or Congress. Virginia Governor Randolph's letter to Livingston and a follow-up letter from Patrick Henry inviting New Jersey's participation in a convention to be held in Annapolis to discuss whether to expand Congress' power to regulate trade awaited an answer, and the New Jersey Legislature was quick to respond.[13]

On March 20, three days after passing the Griffith resolution, the Legislature appointed Clark, Houston, and James Schureman, a thirty-year-old merchant who had been a prisoner of war, as delegates to the Annapolis Convention:

> ... to take into Consideration the Trade of the United States; to examine the relative Situation and Trade of the said States; to consider how far a uniform System in their commercial Regulations _and other important matters_ may be necessary to their common Interest and permanent Harmony; and to report to the several States Such an Act relative to this grand Object, as when unanimously ratified by them will enable the United States in Congress assembled effectually to provide for the Exigencies of the Union ...[14]

New Jersey's charge to its delegates to consider not only trade, but "other important matters" necessary to the common interest was a clear expansion of the mission envisioned for the Annapolis Convention by Madison and Randolph.

Only five states — Virginia, New York, Pennsylvania, Delaware, and New Jersey — were represented when the Annapolis Convention convened on September 11, 1786. The twelve delegates included seven who would participate in the

Constitutional Convention in Philadelphia, including Randolph, James Madison, John Dickinson, and Alexander Hamilton.[15]

While the delegates decided that the attendance was too small to proceed with substantive deliberations, the delegates voted, at the suggestion of Clark, to call for another convention in Philadelphia the following May.[16] Furthermore, they added in their report to the various state legislatures "that the Idea of extending the powers of their deputies to other objects than those of Commerce, which has been adopted by the State of New Jersey, was an improvement on the original plan, and will deserve to be incorporated into that of a future Convention ... [to] render the constitution of the Federal Government adequate to the exigencies of the Union."[17]

On February 21, 1787, Congress voted to authorize the Philadelphia convention with the "sole and express purpose of revising the Articles of Confederation" – a broader mandate than the Annapolis Convention enjoyed.

"The 'New Jersey Idea,' emerging from the words, 'other important matters,'" historian Richard McCormick wrote, "had become the bridge between Annapolis and Philadelphia."[18]

For David Brearley, the bridge between Annapolis and Philadelphia was the man whose legal career he had encouraged and whom he had appointed as clerk to the Supreme Court. William Churchill Houston, who was appointed with Brearley as one of the four New Jersey delegates to the Philadelphia Convention, had the advantage of participating in the Annapolis Convention deliberations and meeting both Randolph and Madison. Houston and Madison also shared a bond as fellow graduates of the College of New Jersey at Princeton.

New Jersey was the first state to appoint delegates to the Constitutional Convention, and Brearley and Houston would have months to plot strategy for the upcoming convention in their Supreme Court offices in Trenton. Their relationship was somewhat complicated. Houston, who is often described as brilliant, had the classical education that Brearley lacked and had served as a delegate to the Continental Congress in 1779. But while Houston was two years older, it had been Brearley who had encouraged Houston to study law, and it was Houston who had worked for Brearley for the past six years.[19]

Brearley and Houston also had served together as two of the seven commissioners from five states who met in Trenton in 1782 and decided the dispute between Connecticut and Pennsylvania over ownership of the Wyoming Valley in favor of Pennsylvania.[20] That experience underscored the need for a federal court system.

Brearley also knew a second New Jersey delegate, William Paterson, very well. Paterson served as attorney general during Brearley's first four years as Supreme Court chief justice, then retired from government service after the war to set up a private law practice. Paterson's biggest caseload was before Brearley: Paterson handled 482 separate cases before the New Jersey Supreme Court, usually representing the rich and powerful.[21] Paterson had the added advantage of having served as a delegate to the New Jersey Constitutional Convention of 1776, where he grappled with many of the issues concerning constitutional powers that New Jersey's delegation would now address on a larger scale.

John Neilson, a wealthy Middlesex County resident, would soon withdraw, leaving Brearley, Houston and Paterson as the New Jersey delegation when the convention opened.

New Jersey's delegation would be the youngest at the convention. Brearley, Houston and Paterson were all in their early to mid-forties — old enough to have served in significant positions during the Revolutionary War, but young enough to be part of the generation that would govern the new nation under the new Constitution they were sent to Philadelphia to create. Only Paterson, however, would live long enough to fulfill that promise.

# CHAPTER EIGHT

# Virginia vs. New Jersey

## Forging a Large-State/Small-State Compromise

*"If we must have a national government, what is the remedy? Lay the map of the confederation on the table, and extinguish the present boundary lines of the respective state jurisdictions, and make a new division so that each state is equal — then a government on the present system will be just."*

— David Brearley critiquing the Virginia Plan June 9, 1787 (from the notes of Robert Yates) [1]

The Constitutional Convention was scheduled to open on Monday, May 14, but it would be eleven days before seven states could muster the voting quorums needed to formally open the convention. David Brearley made the ferry and stagecoach trip from Trenton in the middle of that first week. Knowing Paterson was not scheduled to arrive until May 20 and Houston until May 25, Brearley wanted to make sure New Jersey's interests were represented from the beginning.

Brearley quickly discovered that, as in most constitutional conventions, the most important work was being done in committee, only this time the committee was self-selected: The blue-ribbon Virginia delegation had taken it upon itself to produce a draft constitution for consideration by the full convention in a series of daily private meetings that were not open to participation by other convention delegates.[2]

The Virginia committee meetings were James Madison's idea. There was a certain logic in Virginia assuming the leading role in writing the initial document that would set the parameters for the upcoming convention debate. After all, Virginia had proposed and convened the Annapolis Convention the year before. But there was a certain hubris as well, fostered by the First Colony's awareness that it was not only by far the wealthiest and most populous state, but also had sent the most prestigious and most capable delegation to the convention.

George Washington came out of a four-year retirement from public life to join the Virginia delegation, and most delegates assumed that he would not only be elected president of the Constitutional Convention, but also the first chief executive of the new government that the convention would create.

George Mason, author of Virginia's "Declaration of Rights," and Judge George Wythe, a signer of the Declaration of Independence, were famous throughout the nation. Governor Randolph would be the lead orator and floor leader for the Virginia resolutions, but it was the young Madison, who had spent months studying the history of federations and republics, who provided the impetus and the intellectual underpinnings for the Virginia Plan.[3]

Like Brearley, the scholarly Madison did his best work in small committees; historian Clinton Rossiter contends that "this 'consultation among the deputies' of Virginia, which he (Madison) brought together and then pushed delicately toward the end he had in mind, was the most consequential" contribution made by Madison to the Constitution — more important than any work he did during the ensuing three months of debate or in his coauthorship of the Federalist Papers to ensure the Constitution's passage.[4]

Delegates from the smaller states understood what Virginia's decision to unilaterally frame the debate would mean for their interests. It was tacitly understood that no new national government could succeed without the support and participation of the four large states — Virginia, Pennsylvania, Massachusetts, and New York. By Monday, May 21, it was clear to small-state delegates like George Read of Delaware that the Virginia Plan was likely to propose replacing the equality of states in the current Confederation Congress with at least one legislative house based on population. As Read wrote to John Dickinson:

> By this plan, our state may have a representation in the House of Delegates of one member in eighty. I suspect it is to be of importance to the small states that their deputies should keep a strict watch upon the movements and propositions from the larger states, who will probably combine to swallow up the smaller ones by addition, division or impoverishment; and if you have any wish to assist in guarding against such attempts, you will be speedy in your attendance.[5]

Brearley and Paterson, who had arrived the Philadelphia the day before, would have had the same concern. Perhaps the New Jersey Legislature — meeting in Burlington less than twenty-five miles upriver from Philadelphia — had picked up similar signals. With Neilson's resignation and Houston's ill health, the Legislature voted on Friday, May 18, to add to the delegation the state's two leading politicians, Governor Livingston and

Congressman Abraham Clark, a signer of the Declaration and one of the driving forces behind New Jersey's 1786 refusal to pay the tax levy imposed by the Confederation Congress. Livingston wrote to Brearley the following day not only to inform him of the appointments, but to underscore his willingness to drop any other business, if necessary, to join the delegation immediately, if needed:

> *The State has added to our Delegates in Convention, Mr. Clark & myself. I expect that by the middle of next week at farthest we shall have a full representation by the attendance of Mr. Clark and Mr. Paterson. Mr. Houston's ill state of health which I sincerely regret will I fear prevent his going tho' he told me that he intended it. It will be more agreeable to me, & what is of more consequence more useful to the State in my opinion that I should remain here during the sitting of the Legislature which I imagine will not be protracted beyond three weeks. After the rising of the Assembly, I will upon sufficient notice to prepare for the Journey cheerfully take the place of any one of you that shall choose to return home & your Delegation should during the Sitting be unavoidably reduced to two I will leave the legislature & go to the Convention rather than that the State should for a single day be unrepresented in it but in that case I should wish to have notice sufficient to enable me first to go to Elizabeth Town where I should want two or three days to arrange my own affairs & prepare for the Journey.[6]*

Brearley and Paterson knew that the addition of Livingston and Clark would add stature to the New Jersey delegation — stature that would be needed for the anticipated large-state/small-

142

state struggle ahead. When they took their seats on Friday, May 25, for the long-awaited official convening of the Constitutional Convention, they were also gratified to discover that the ailing Houston had made it to Philadelphia after all. Houston's attendance gave New Jersey the quorum of three members required for the officially designated delegation of five to cast votes at the convention.[7]

Four of the seven smallest states were not yet represented — Connecticut and Maryland, whose delegates would arrive the following week; New Hampshire, whose delegates would not show up for two months; and Rhode Island, which boycotted the proceedings entirely.

Of the other three large-state delegations, New York sent Alexander Hamilton, but saddled him with John Lansing Jr. and Robert Yates, two political allies of Governor George Clinton, who opposed the convention. Massachusetts, recently torn by Shays Rebellion, sent Elbridge Gerry and an otherwise relatively weak delegation for a state whose "favorite sons" could have included Governor John Hancock, Samuel Adams, and John Adams, whose diplomatic duties kept him in London. Only Pennsylvania, with a delegation that included Benjamin Franklin, financier Robert Morris, and a pair of brilliant lawyers, James Wilson and Gouverneur Morris, sent a delegation that could compete in any way with Virginia's star-studded assemblage.[8]

Pennsylvania's alliance with Virginia was obvious. Robert Morris nominated Washington to serve as the convention's president, and the two Morrises had argued before the convention that the small states should not have equal votes to the large states during the convention. It was a stand that the Virginia delegation dissuaded them from pursuing on the grounds that it would be easier to persuade the small states to back off their insistence on equal votes in Congress if they felt they had an equal role at the convention. Nevertheless, it took two days for the Convention to agree on rules requiring a quorum of seven of the thirteen state delegations, with all decisions to be made by the majority of states fully represented, which now numbered eleven. The other important rule they unanimously approved was to keep all discussions and debates private and out of the press to enable delegates to deliberate without outside pressure.[9]

With the rules approved, Virginia wasted no time in putting the Virginia Plan before the Convention the following day. With Washington in the president's chair, Governor Randolph on May 29 unveiled a vision for a new government that was both exciting in its scope and threatening to the smaller states in its details.

Randolph detailed the defects of the Articles of Confederation, including the inability of the government it established to cope with the paper money crisis, the debt and the need to pass a federal trade duty to supersede the various state tariffs — all objectives of the New Jersey delegation to both the Annapolis Convention and the current Convention in Philadelphia. The Confederation Congress, he argued, was unable even to meet the first duty of government, to secure the common defense against foreign enemies and sedition from within, referring specifically to Massachusetts, where Shays Rebellion had recently been suppressed by the state government.[10]

Paterson began taking notes on each point for later review as Randolph read the fifteen resolutions of the Virginia Plan that he and Brearley had been waiting so eagerly to hear.[11]

The first resolution — "that the Articles of Confederation needed to be corrected and enlarged in order to accomplish the objectives proposed, namely common defense, the security of liberty, and the general welfare" — were fully in keeping with the "New Jersey idea," embodied in the New Jersey Legislature's instructions to its Annapolis and Philadelphia delegations.

Lieut. Colonel David Brearley, Jr.
circa 1776-1779

*TRADITION OF REVOLT: David Brearley's patriotic fervor, demonstrated by his service in both the Monmouth County Militia and the Continental Army (above), was in keeping with a family tradition of resistance. His father, David Brearley Sr., was charged with treason and jailed for his leadership of the 1745-47 anti-Proprietary land riots during the governorship of Jonathan Belcher (right).*

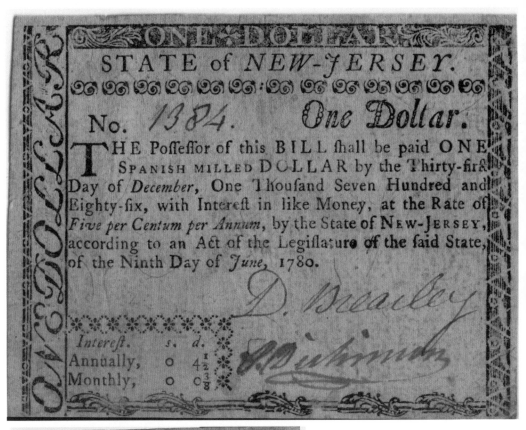

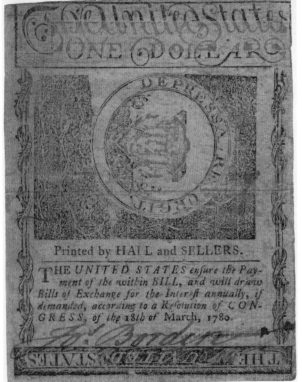

*CURRENCY AS SOUND AS ITS SIGNER: During the Revolution, respected patriots such as New Jersey Supreme Court Chief Justice David Brearley signed sheets of Continental currency (right) to instill faith in its value. The $1 bill on this page is signed on the reverse (above) by Brearley and by Major-General Philemon Dickinson, commanding officer of the New Jersey Militia. The default by the Confederation Congress on its promise on the front (left) to "ensure the Payment of the within Bill, and withdraw Bills of Exchange for the Interest annually" led the state government to assume responsibility for the interest owed to its citizens and to refuse to pay taxes levied by Congress – an act of defiance that helped lead to the Constitutional Convention.*

Collection of Donald Scarinci

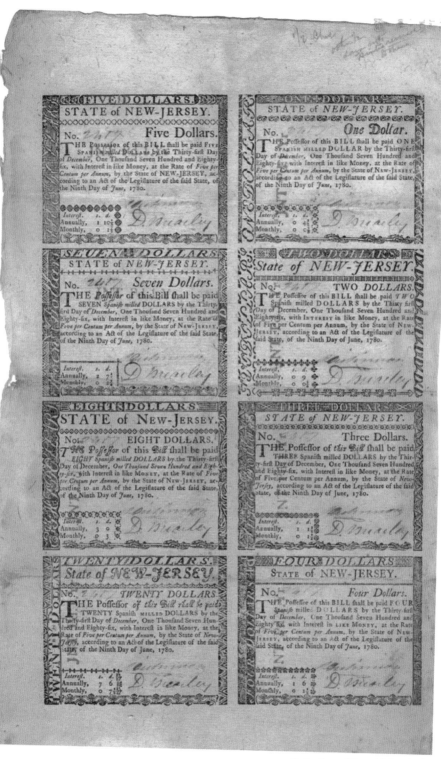

147

*THE NEW JERSEY DELEGATION: New Jersey's delegates to the Constitutional Convention included Governor William Livingston (above left), William Paterson (above right), and David Brearley (facing page).*

*SIGNING THE CONSTITUTION: Howard Chandler Christy's painting "The Scene at the Signing*

*of the Constitution" hangs in the U.S. Capitol in Washington, D.C.*

*BREARLEY MEMORIALIZED: A life-size statue of David Brearley stands in the Hall of Signers at the National Constitution Center in Philadelphia. The key New Jersey delegates are togeth-er in a group. Brearley (left) is shown listening to Pierce Butler of South Carolina. William Paterson is depicted importuning another Southern delegate, while William Livingston stands off to the side alone.*

Photo by Mark J. Magyar

The second resolution, as Read and Brearley had feared, asserted "that the rights of suffrage in the National Legislature ought to be proportioned to the quotas of contribution or to the number of free inhabitants, as the one or the other rule may seem best in different cases." This proposal to base votes in Congress on population or wealth was clearly in Virginia's self-interest, as not only the most populous state in both free and in slave population, but also the wealthiest due to its 300,000 slaves.

The next four resolutions called for a two-house national legislature, with members of the first house elected directly by the people of each state for a specific term, as was the case in the election of county representatives to state legislatures at the time, and with members of the second house elected indirectly by the various state legislatures. Members of the first house would be ineligible for reelection to ensure that its members would remain close to the people. This proposal represented a compromise between democrats seeking direct election and elitists who continued to favor indirect election. Each branch would be equal and would have broad legislative powers, including the authority "to veto laws passed by individual states" and to compel obedience by individual state governments.

Randolph proposed, but did not provide details for the election of, "a National Executive" to serve a single, specified term, the creation of a "council of revision" consisting of the executive and members of the judiciary to review the constitutionality of laws prior to their imposition, and the creation of a two-level "National Judiciary" to be chosen by the national legislature.

His plan also called for provisions to be made to admit new states to the union, to preserve the current boundaries of each state, and to provide a process for amendment of the new Constitution directly by the states without the approval of the national legislature.[12]

The Convention reconstituted itself as a Committee of the Whole to consider the Virginia resolutions. Brearley, Paterson, and Houston first signaled their displeasure two days later, when they voted against the resolution for direct election of the first house of the national legislature. It is not clear whether they did so out of opposition to direct popular election or, as is just as likely, out of opposition to the concept of representation on the basis of population called for under the Virginia Plan. New Jersey was on the losing side of a 6-2 vote with two state delegations split. Significantly, the other no vote came from South Carolina, and the divided delegations belonged to Delaware and Connecticut, all small states like New Jersey.[13]

Brearley and Paterson were already bracing for a long battle. In a June 1 petition they sent to the New Jersey legislature the following day requesting a requisition of five shillings a day to cover New Jersey's share of the convention costs, they predicted that the convention would last "two or three months."[14] They also knew that Houston was deathly ill with tuberculosis. The June 1 session was Houston's last, as he was forced to leave the convention he had helped to create in Annapolis the year before. Brearley immediately notified Livingston and Clark that New Jersey would be without a vote until one of them arrived to take Houston's seat. Livingston was as good as his word, arriving in the middle of deliberations on June 5 in time for New Jersey to vote on the last four resolutions decided that day.[15]

Days later, Brearley, Livingston, and Paterson learned not only that Houston would not be returning, as they had feared, but that the impressive Congressman Clark would not join their delegation at all. The June 7 letter came from a surprising source, Jonathan Dayton, who wrote:

> Mr. Houston formally resigned in consequence of his ill state of health. Mr. Clark has also resigned, but in

*his usual way that is very <u>informally,</u> because he thinks there is a kind of incompatibility in the two appointments [as a delegate to the constitutional convention and as a member of Congress]. I am therefore unfortunately the only one on the list of Supernumeraries.*[16]

Other members of the Confederation Congress had reached the same conclusion as Clark. Not a single member of Congress served as a Convention delegate. Dayton was young, just twenty-six years old,[17] and would add little to the ability of the New Jersey delegation to fight over the representation issue. Even so, Dayton would arrive June 21, bringing the New Jersey delegation back to its original strength of four.

New Jersey's delegates took no part in the debate that first week in June, although the votes by the delegation – made up of a governor, a Supreme Court chief justice, and a former state attorney general — began to reflect what would prove to be a pattern of limiting the power of the national legislature, favoring the executive and judicial branches, and protecting the rights of small states. New Jersey voted with the majority on June 8 to reject a push by Virginia, Pennsylvania, and Massachusetts to give the national legislature the right to overturn any laws passed by an individual state that it deemed improper. Such a provision would not only give the largest states virtual veto power over smaller states like New Jersey, but also would infringe upon what Brearley and the New Jersey delegation saw more properly as a judicial prerogative.

As New Jersey's Supreme Court chief justice, Brearley personally had exercised that power seven years earlier in his landmark decision in *Holmes v. Walton*. Brearley's ruling was the first time in the young nation's history that a judge declared a law unconstitutional, and legislators and judges in other states took notice. Two years earlier, in 1785, Gouverneur Morris of Pennsylvania, who would prove to be one of the most influential delegates at the convention, specifically cited Brearley's precedent to the Pennsylvania legislature in warning against passage of a law he considered to be unconstitutional.

By the summer of 1787, judges in Rhode Island and North Carolina also had declared laws unconstitutional, and the concept of judicial review was so well-established in the minds of the delegates that they did not explicitly write it into the Constitution. In arguing against the Virginia Plan's proposal to include judges on the proposed Council on Revision, Elbridge Gerry of Massachusetts pointed out that judges

> have a sufficient check against encroachment on their own department by their exposition of the laws, which involves a power of deciding on their constitutionality. In some states, the judges have actually set aside laws as being against the constitution. This was done, too, with general approbation.

The strongest statement on judicial review came from Madison himself during a debate on July 23. "A law violating a constitution established by the people themselves," he declared, "would be considered by the judges as null and void."[18]

While the issue of judicial review was implicitly decided, the battle over how to determine representation in the national legislature overshadowed every other question. As Delaware's Gunning Bedford noted in debate on June 8, Virginia and Pennsylvania would have one third of the votes in a legislature in which representation is based on population, while Delaware would have just one vote in ninety. "On this computation, where is the weight of the small states when the interest of one is in competition with the other on trade, manufactures and agriculture?" he demanded.[19]

Brearley and Paterson clearly were putting considerable

effort that week into a critique of the Virginia Plan's case for proportional representation based on population or wealth. Among the Brearley papers published by Secretary of State John Quincy Adams in the official *Journals, Acts and Proceedings of the Convention* in 1819 were the estimates Brearley developed of the number of votes to which each state would be entitled in the national legislature under Randolph's resolution to award representation based on tax effort or population.[20]

Brearley also made a careful copy of the Randolph resolutions. It was Brearley's copy of the Randolph resolutions that were published in Adams' compilation. The records that William Jackson, the convention's somewhat indifferent secretary, forwarded to Washington, the convention president, did not include a copy.

John Quincy Adams noted in his memoirs:

> It happened that General [Joseph] Bloomfield, a member of Congress from New Jersey, as executor of the will of David Brearley, one of the members of the Convention, had come to the possession of his papers, among which were several important ones relating to the proceedings of the Convention. He sent them all to me.[21]

The long preparation that Brearley and Paterson put into planning for the debate over representation can be seen in the five drafts of speech preparations made by Paterson. Scholar Max Farrand notes that "A is a long and elaborate draft; B is the same in shorter form with some additional notes; C includes some notes for reference; D seems to consist of catch-words; and E is an elaboration of one or two points."[22]

On Saturday, June 9, Brearley and Paterson were ready and asked that debate be reopened on Randolph's proposal "that the rights of suffrage in the national legislature ought to be apportioned to the quotas of contribution, or to the number of inhabitants, as the one or other rule may seem best in different cases."[23]

The choice of the scholarly Brearley, rather than the more charismatic Paterson, to open the debate underscores the critical, and most likely equal, role that Brearley played in the development of the New Jersey Plan and other strategies to protect small-state interests. While none of Brearley's notes remain from his opening speech, much of it can be reconstructed from the extensive notes taken by Madison, Robert Yates of New York, and Rufus King of Massachusetts; Paterson, who knew what Brearley was going to say, jotted down just a few lines in his notes.

Brearley opened by saying he was sorry that the Virginia Plan had introduced the question of equality among the states.[24] "The present question is an important one," Brearley said. "On the principle that each state in the union was sovereign, congress, in the articles of confederation, determined that each state in the public councils had <u>one</u> vote. If the states remain  sovereign," he argued, the Virginia Plan's proposal to base representation on population or tax assessment "is founded on principles of injustice."[25]

Representation on such a basis "carried fairness on the face of it; but on a deeper examination was unfair and unjust." Based on his population estimates, Brearley said, in a Congress made up of ninety members, Virginia would have sixteen votes and Georgia but one. Brearley argued that in such a Congress,

> There will be 3. large states and 10 small ones. The large States by which he meant Massts. Pena. & Virga. will carry every thing before them. It had been admitted, and was known to him from facts within N. Jersey that where large and small counties were united into a district for electing representatives for their district, the

*large counties always carried their point, and Consequently that the large States would do so. Virga. with her sixteen votes will be a solid column indeed, a formidable phalanx. While Georgia with her Solitary vote, and the other little States will be obliged to throw themselves constantly into the scale of some larger one, in order to have any weight at all.*[26]

Brearley noted that he "had come to the convention with a view of being as useful as he could in giving energy and stability to the Federal Government."[27] New Jersey's state legislature, as the delegates knew, sent its delegates to the Annapolis Convention committed to strengthening the national government and was the first state to vote to send a delegation to Philadelphia. But this issue of representation was critical. "This vote must defeat itself, or end in despotism," he warned,[28] adding that he was "astonished" and "alarmed" when "the proposition for destroying the equality of votes came forward."[29]

Brearley acknowledged that on its face, "the Rule of confedn." that gives each state an equal vote "is unequal."[30] "Is it fair then it will be asked that Georgia should have an equal vote with Virga.?" Brearley asked, then answered his own question by acknowledging it would not be fair.[31] He then went on to propose a novel solution:

*If we must have a national government, what is the remedy? Lay the map of the confederation on the table, and extinguish the present boundary lines of the respective state jurisdictions, and make a new division so that each state is equal — then a government on the present system will be just.*[32]

The proposal to eradicate existing state lines and redraw a

nation of thirteen equal districts was arguably the most radical proposal put before the Convention. Whether Brearley believed he could win enough support to implement such a plan is unclear. It certainly was an excellent debating point to throw out in challenge to the large-state delegates who were so willing to strip the small states of their political power, and the Pennsylvania delegation, in particular, treated Brearley's argument seriously.

Clearly, Brearley's proposal, if implemented, would have benefited New Jersey and similar small states. The issues of national vs. state control over tariffs and the taxation of trade — the issues that had inspired the Annapolis Convention and sparked New Jersey's 1786 refusal to pay taxes levied by the Confederation Congress — had yet to be raised in the first three weeks of debate. Any redrawing of state lines would double New Jersey's tax base and perhaps secure for the state a port on which it could impose tariffs, as New York State and Pennsylvania did.[33]

Brearley was followed immediately by Paterson, who reiterated Brearley's arguments, but went further in questioning the very legitimacy of the Virginia Plan. Paterson noted that the Convention was convened by Congress, the various state legislatures, and the people they represented in order to amend the Articles of Confederation that brought the states together, not to form a national government:

> The idea of a national Govt. as contradistinguished from a federal one, never entered into the mind of any of them, and to the public mind we must accommodate ourselves. We have no power to go beyond the federal scheme, and if we had the people are not ripe for any other. We must follow the people; the people will not follow us.

Paterson noted that "a confederacy supposes sovereignty in

the members composing it & sovereignty supposes equality."[34] If such equality does not exist, the recommendations of the Convention must create it, he asserted, underscoring Brearley's argument:

> If we are to be considered as a nation, all State distinctions must be abolished, the whole must be thrown into hotchpot, and when an equal division is made, then there may be fairly an equality of representation.[35]

Paterson noted that the Virginia Plan contemplated proportional representation based on population or tax contribution, and he challenged the fairness of a system based on wealth. "There was no more reason that a great individual State contributing much, should have more votes than a small one contributing little, than that a rich individual citizen should have more votes than an indigent one," Paterson contended.[36]

He noted that "in every state the individual Citizens have equal votes though their property is unequal,"[37] then asked "Is a man, for example, possessing a property of £4000 to have 40 votes to one possessing only £100?"[38]

> Such a principle would never be admitted, and if it were admitted would put B (the man with £1000) entirely at the mercy of A (the man with £4000). As A. has more to be protected than B, so he ought to contribute more for the common protection. The same may be said of a large State wch. has more to be protected than a small one. Give the large States an influence in proportion to their magnitude, and what will be the consequence? Their ambition will be proportionally increased, and the small States will have everything to fear.[39]

Mere representation is not sufficient to guarantee the rights of smaller states, he said, noting that Congressman Joseph Galloway had proposed before the war that the colonies be given representation in Parliament.

> *Suppose, as it was in agitation before the war, that America had been represented in the British parliament, and had sent 200 members; what would this number avail against 600? We would have been as much enslaved in that case as when unrepresented; and what is worse, without the prospect of redress.*[40]

Alluding to Pennsylvania delegate James Wilson's threat that "the large States might be reduced of confederating among themselves, by a refusal of the others to concur," Paterson stated:

> *Let them unite if they please, but let them remember that they have no authority to compel the others to unite. N. Jersey will never confederate on the plan before the Committee. She would be swallowed up.*[41]

"I therefore declare, that I will never consent to the present system, and I shall make all the interest against it in the state which I represent that I can. Myself or my state will never submit to tyranny or despotism," Paterson stated. He laid down the gauntlet to Madison, Wilson, and other proponents of proportional representation: If no accommodation were made to the smaller states, New Jersey would not join the new nation.[42]

Brearley's and Paterson's speeches marked the first important challenge to the presumption that the Virginia Plan, which had won votes on every important point to date, would be the basis for a new national government. James Wilson of

Pennsylvania quickly responded to the challenge that Brearley and Paterson had posed.

Wilson said he hoped that a majority, or at least a minority, of the states would enter into a new confederation if the present Articles of Confederation were dissolved, and he contended that it would be equally defensible to allocate proportional representation on the basis of population or wealth:

> ... in districts as large as the States, the number of people was the best measure of their comparative wealth. Whether therefore wealth or numbers were to form the ratio it would be the same. Mr. P. admitted persons, not property to be the measure of suffrage. Are not the citizens of Pena. equal to those of N. Jersey? does it require 150 of the former to balance 50 of the latter. Representatives of different districts ought clearly to hold the same proportion to each other, as their respective constituents hold to each other.

"If the small States will not confederate on this plan, Pena. & he presumed some other States, would not confederate on the any other," he warned. "... If N.J. will not part with her Sovereignty it is in vain to talk of Govt."

Wilson concluded by agreeing with Brearley that "A new partition of the States is desireable, but evidently & totally impracticable."[43] Viewed through the prism of Pennsylvania's self-interest, it would have indeed been "impracticable" for Wilson's state to cede one third of its territory and wealth to Brearley and Paterson's Greater Jersey.

Hugh Williamson of North Carolina chimed in to point out that if state governments believed it just to allocate representation in their legislatures on the basis of population, then the national government should do the same.[44]

Paterson, realizing that he and Brearley did not have the votes to win the question that day, pushed successfully to postpone a vote on the Virginia Plan's proposal to base representation on tax contribution or population until the next session, which would be Monday.[45] That would give the New Jerseyans all day Sunday to lobby the various state delegations for votes. They would need help. Pennsylvania's eight-member and Virginia's seven-member delegations gave the large states an added advantage in both lobbying and presence.

That day, presumably following the debate, Brearley dashed off a short, but firm letter, to Jonathan Dayton:

> We have been in a Committee of the Whole for some time, and have under consideration a number of very <u>important</u> propositions, some of which, however, have as yet been reported. My colleagues, as well as myself, are very desirous that you should join us immediately. The importance of the business really demands it.[46]

Although Dayton was young, another voice to assist in planning, lobbying, cajoling and debating would help — particularly since Livingston was shy about public speaking and reluctant to take an active part in the public debate.

By Monday, June 11, the day that a stifling heat wave struck Philadelphia, Paterson and Brearley had begun to win important allies. Roger Sherman of Connecticut opened the debate by proposing that one house of the new national legislature be selected on the basis of population, and that each state have one equal vote in the second house:

> As the States would remain possessed of certain individual rights, each State ought to be able to protect itself; otherwise a few large States will rule the rest. The

*House of Lords in England ... had certain particular rights under the Constitution, and hence they have an equal vote with the House of Commons that they may be able to defend their rights.*[47]

Sherman's speech was a clear indication that Connecticut, the second-largest state in New England in population, nevertheless saw itself as a small state not only in relation to its Massachusetts and New York neighbors, but also to giant Virginia and Pennsylvania, and to the growing slave populations of the Southern states whose value in determining representation based on wealth or population had yet to be determined.

The latter point was immediately underscored when John Rutledge of South Carolina proposed to make "quota of contribution" the basis of representation in the first branch of the legislature, which would give greater weight to the human wealth possessed by the slave states of Virginia, North and South Carolina, and Georgia.

Alarmed by the growing number of representation proposals, Rufus King of Massachusetts and Pennsylvania's Wilson promptly moved for a vote on the principle of allocating representation by "some equitable ratio" in the first house, hoping to win a quick victory.

The precariousness of New Jersey's situation under such a scenario was highlighted when King pointed out that if representation was based on national revenue, "it was probable that imports would be one source of it. If the actual contributions were to be the rule the non-importing States, as Cont. & N. Jerse, wd. be in a bad situation indeed. It might so happen they wd. have no representation." Again, King noted, this was "a powerful argument" for the imposition of a five percent national tariff to replace state tariffs.[48]

The tariff issue was one of the New Jersey delegation's

priorities, but it appeared nowhere in the Virginia Plan read by Randolph three weeks before. Now, the delegations were being asked to vote on a resolution that could base representation on tax contribution without knowing how that would be determined.

Washington's presidency of the Convention and his personal desire to remain aloof from the debate kept the First Virginian out of the fray, but Benjamin Franklin, second only to Washington in influence and respect, chose this moment to throw his weight into the debate on the side of the large-state delegations. Franklin was too ill to make lengthy speeches, but his mind was still sharp, and he gave Wilson a lengthy speech to read on his behalf.

Franklin's speech implicitly chided the New Jersey delegation, particularly Paterson:

> It has given me a great deal of pleasure to observe that till this point, the proportion of representation, came before us, our debates were carried on with great coolness & temper. If any thing of a contrary kind, has on this occasion appeared, I hope it will not be repeated; for we are sent here to consult not to contend, with each other; and declarations of a fixed opinion, and of determined resolution, never to change it, neither enlighten nor convince us.

Franklin said he had hoped that representatives of the new Congress would represent the interests of the nation as a whole, rather than the interests of particular states — a not-so-subtle barb aimed at Brearley and Paterson. If members of Congress were to represent narrow state interests, that made the case for representation by population all the more compelling.

Franklin dismissed Paterson's argument that colonial representation in Parliament would have been meaningless because the colonies' two hundred representatives would have been outvoted by Britain's six hundred. He pointed out that Scotland's interests were not forsaken, even though Scotland was outnumbered forty to sixteen by England in the House of Lords.

However, he took seriously the suggestion of Brearley, whom he characterized as "an honorable gentleman," to throw out state boundaries and redraw thirteen equal states:

> I should, for my own part, not be against such a measure, if it were found practicable. Formerly, indeed, when almost every province had a different Constitution, some with greater[,] others with fewer privileges, it was of importance to thc borderers when their boundaries were considered, whether by running the division lines, they were placed on one side or the other. At present when such differences are done away it is less important. The Interest of a State is made up of the interests of its individual members. If they are not injured, the State is not injured. Small States are more easily well & happily governed than large ones. If therefore in such an equal division, it should be found necessary to diminish Pennsylvania, I should not be averse to the giving part of it to N. Jersey, and another to Delaware. But ... there would be considerable difficulties in adjusting such a division; and however equally made at first, it would be continually varying by the augmentation of inhabitants in some States, and their (more) fixed proportion in others; and thence frequent occasion for new divisions ...

This, of course, is the method under which congressional district lines are redrawn after every census. But instead, Franklin challenged the smaller states to pay for equality, if they valued it so. "Let the weakest State say what proportion of money or force it is able and willing to furnish for the general purposes of the Union," Franklin said, then let each state match that amount. If New Jersey's 138,000 residents wished to be equal in Congress with Pennsylvania's 341,000, then let them tax themselves at more than twice the rate to pay for that equality.[49]

Whether Franklin's words, delivered by Wilson, had any effect on the debate is uncertain, but the principle of representation according to some equitable ratio passed easily, by a 7-3 vote. Massachusetts, Connecticut, and Pennsylvania joined Virginia and the other three Southern states in voting yes. New Jersey and Delaware voted no, and the delegation from Maryland, a mid-sized state with a sizable slave population, split on the issue. New York went against its own large-state interests in voting no, but the three-man delegation's two anti-Federalist representatives were more interested in obstructing a new Constitution than in the particulars of any individual vote. A mild surprise was the yes vote cast by Georgia, the smallest state in the union, although one that expected to grow rapidly.[50]

The reason for the Southern solidarity immediately became apparent as Wilson and Charles Pinckney of South Carolina quickly called for a motion to base representation in the first house of Congress "in proportion to the whole number of white & other free Citizens & inhabitants of every age sex & condition including those bound to servitude for a term of years and three fifths of all other persons not comprehended in the foregoing description, except Indians not paying taxes, in each State."[51]

This was the standard the Confederation Congress used in September 1785 in apportioning the level of tax contribution required from each state — the levy New Jersey had refused to pay.

Elbridge Gerry of Massachusetts objected that "the idea of property ought not to be rule of representation. Blacks are property, and are used to the southward as horses and cattle to the northward; and why should their representation be increased to the southward on account of the number of slaves, than horses or oxen to the north?"[52]

Madison, however, said such questions could be taken up by a subcommittee, and the states then voted 9-2 for what would become the infamous "three-fifths clause," with only New Jersey and Delaware — small states both in population and in number of slaves — voting no.[53]

Sherman then insisted on a vote on his measure providing for equality of representation in the second house of Congress. "Every thing he said depended on this," Madison recorded in his notes. "The smaller States would never agree to the plan on any other principle" than voting equality in the second house.[54]

This time, Connecticut, Maryland, and anti-Federalist New York joined New Jersey and Delaware in voting for small-state interests, but Massachusetts, Pennsylvania, Virginia, the Carolinas, and Georgia held firm and defeated the motion 6-5.

Wilson and Alexander Hamilton, the lone New York Federalist delegate, then moved immediately for representation in the second house based on the same population plus "three-fifths rule" as in the first house, and won by the same 6-5 vote.[55]

The issue was decided. The large states and the slave states had won. Brearley and Paterson were fuming, knowing that the absence of the New Hampshire and Rhode Island delegations had cost them the majority in a convention that now appeared to be the last meaningful political forum in the nascent nation in which voting would be based on the equality of states.

The next resolution called for guaranteeing the boundaries of all current states, which would effectively end discussion of Brearley's proposal to redraw thirteen equal states, a concept that had drawn at least lip-service consideration from the most influential Pennsylvanians, Wilson and Franklin.

Speaking for the small states, George Read of Delaware argued that "the idea of guarantying territory ... abetted the idea of distinct States wch. would be a perpetual source of discord. There can be (no) cure for this evil but in doing away States altogether and uniting them all into (one) great Society."

Read's vision of one "great Society" lost by a 7-4 margin, with New Jersey, Delaware, Connecticut, and Maryland again finding common cause in defeat.[56]

The day dragged to a close with indifferent debate over whether the newly constituted Congress would have the right to consent to constitutional amendments and whether loyalty oaths to the new national Constitution should be required from state officeholders.

On Tuesday, June 12, and Wednesday, June 13, the delegates quickly ran through the remaining resolutions, approving three-year terms for one house of Congress and seven-year terms for the other, agreeing that judges should be appointed by the Senate, and resolving other issues of judicial and legislative jurisdiction with relatively little debate.[57]

Brearley, Paterson, and Livingston sat in silence, biding their time. If Madison and the Virginians could take it upon themselves to write the principles for a new federal Constitution, so could they.


On Thursday, June 14, as the Constitutional Convention prepared to vote on the nineteen resolutions adopted from the Virginia Plan over the preceding three weeks preparatory to the formal writing of the new Constitution, Paterson rose and asked for a one-day postponement. As Madison dutifully recorded,

*It was the wish of several deputations, particularly that of New Jersey, that further time might be allowed*

*them to contemplate the plan reported from the Committee of the Whole, and to digest one purely federal, and contradistinguished from the reported plan.*[58]

It is unclear how long Paterson, Brearley, and other unhappy delegates had been working on their own plan, but Paterson said he "intended to give in principles to form a federal system of government materially different from the system now under consideration" and that he expected to be ready by the following day.[59]

In putting together what came to be known as the New Jersey Plan, Brearley, Paterson, and Livingston took allies wherever they could find them. Unlike the self-selected group that developed the Virginia Plan, the group that developed the New Jersey Plan was open to all. It was "a composite production" in which Paterson and Brearley, the Delaware delegation, Connecticut's Sherman, Luther Martin of Maryland, and the anti-Federalist John Lansing Jr. of New York "all had a hand," historian Clinton Rossiter noted.[60]

Connecticut and New York were opposed to replacing the Confederation concept with a strong national government, while New Jersey and Delaware actually favored a strong national government, but not if it was constituted on the basis of proportional representation. As John Dickinson, the respected senior statesman from Delaware, explained to an impatient Madison in an aside:

> *You see the consequences of pushing things too far. Some of the members from the small States wish for two branches in the General Legislature, and are friends to a good National Government, but we would sooner submit to a foreign power, than submit to be deprived of an equality of suffrage, in both branches of the*

*legislature, and thereby be thrown under the domination
of the large States.*

The New Jersey Plan that Paterson read to the assembled
Convention on Friday morning, June 15, was indeed an
amalgamation, but constitutional scholars are too quick to
dismiss it as "A Backward Step" — the title that historian William
Peters chose for his chapter on the New Jersey Plan in *A More
Perfect Union,* his bicentennial history of the Constitutional
Convention.[61]

Madison, Wilson, and other advocates of the Virginia Plan
undoubtedly fumed uncomfortably as Paterson presented the
small states' alternative vision. But while it was couched in the
conservative context of revising the Articles of Confederation,
the New Jersey Plan actually proposed an expanded vision of the
scope of national government. It dealt specifically with lingering
issues of the regulation and taxation of trade, and strengthened
the powers of the executive and judicial branches of government
in counterbalance to the strong national legislature envisioned in
the Virginia Plan.

As Governor Randolph of Virginia had done just seventeen
days before, Paterson opened the June 15 session by reading the
resolutions of the New Jersey Plan.[62]

The first resolution — "that the Articles of Confederation be
revised, corrected, and enlarged, as to render the Federal
Constitution adequate to the exigencies of government and the
preservation of the Union" — was a clear nod to the interests of
his New York and Connecticut allies.

The second resolution directly addressed New Jersey's
longstanding concern with the inability of the Confederation
Congress to raise funds to pay the national debt — of which New
Jersey citizens held a disproportionate share — and to make the
regulation of trade an issue of national jurisdiction that would

undercut New York's ability to finance its budget by levying tariffs on imports headed for New Jersey. The resolution specifically authorized Congress

> ... to pass acts for raising a revenue, by levying a duty or duties on all goods or merchandise of foreign growth or manufacture, imported into any part of the U. States ... to pass Acts for the regulation of trade & commerce as well with foreign nations as with each other ....

The third resolution authorized taxes to be raised based on population and the "three-fifths rule" included in the Virginia Plan.

The fourth resolution followed the Virginia Plan in calling for the federal executive to be elected by Congress, but provided greater independence for the executive branch by barring Congress from initiating impeachment proceedings except upon application by a majority of the nation's governors. Ironically, the New Jersey Plan envisioned the appointment of several executives, even though New Jersey and New York were the only two states with single chief executives at the time.[63]

The fifth resolution strengthened the independence of the judiciary from Congress by requiring judges to be appointed by the federal executive, not by the Senate, as the Virginia Plan had recommended and the delegates had voted to do just a few days before.

This emphasis on the independence of the executive and judicial branches, which would become a hallmark of the new Constitution's separation of powers, was clearly a major goal of the New Jersey delegation that included a governor, a Supreme Court chief justice, and a former attorney general who had chafed under pressure from the New Jersey Legislature.

But it was the sixth resolution clearly establishing national authority over the states that should have most gratified — and astonished — Madison:

> Resolved that all Acts of the United States in Congress ... and all Treaties made & ratified under the authority of the U. States shall be the supreme law of the respective states... and that the Judiciary of the several States shall be bound thereby in their decisions, any thing in the respective laws of the Individual States to the contrary notwithstanding; and that if any State, or any body of men in any State, shall oppose or prevent ye. carrying into execution such acts or treaties, the federal Executive shall be authorized to call forth ye power of the Confederated states to enforce and compel an obedience to such Acts or an Observance of such treaties.

That clause clearly was intended to signal to the large-state advocates of a strong national government that states like New Jersey and Delaware were committed to just as strong a national government, if their objections on the representation issue could be met.

Finally, the New Jersey Plan called for the enactment of provisions to add new states to the union, to make naturalization laws apply uniformly in every state, and to make state laws apply equally to offenses committed by residents and non-residents.

These nine resolutions are listed in virtually every history of the Constitutional Convention as making up the full New Jersey Plan because they are the resolutions listed in Madison's notes for the day.[64] Rufus King, a Madison ally who also who took notes, listed just seven of the resolutions, skipping the seventh and eighth.[65]

Three other texts of the New Jersey Plan are in existence, and they were left by three of its principal authors. Brearley's manuscript and Paterson's papers both contain eleven resolutions and are identical in wording. Luther Martin's notes on the New Jersey Plan (printed in *Dunlap's Maryland Gazette and Baltimore Advertiser* on February 15, 1788), which is evidently an earlier version, lists sixteen resolutions in a different order, but significantly, the Martin text agrees with the Brearley and Paterson texts on the wording for the two missing resolutions.[66]

The first of the missing resolutions called for every state governor, legislator, and judge to be bound by oath to support the new "Articles of Union."

The second declared that "provision ought to be made for hearing and deciding upon all disputes arising between the United States and an individual state respecting territory."[67] This resolution was aimed squarely at what the New Jersey delegation regarded as Virginia's boundless ambition. While seven states laid claim to western lands during the Confederation period, with most claims running roughly parallel to their state's existing northern and southern borders, Virginia's appetite for expansion was ravenous. Virginia at one point claimed all of the present-day states of Ohio, Kentucky, Indiana, Illinois, Michigan, Wisconsin, and Minnesota. New Jersey, which had no territorial claims, wanted the western lands used as a source of revenue for the national government, which would benefit all the states. In the early 1780s, New Jersey failed in its efforts to bring a suit against Virginia challenging its western land claims. The new resolution was designed to establish a constitutional basis for such suits.[68] Advocates for the New Jersey Plan decided at the last minute to drop the proposal; if it had been introduced, Madison would certainly have noted such an attack.

The New Jersey Plan, like the Virginia Plan, envisioned a stronger federal government to replace the Confederation model.

"No government could be energetic on paper only, which was no more than a straw," Paterson noted, referring to both plans.[69]

New Yorkers Lansing and Hamilton, usually on opposite sides, found common ground in recommending that both the Virginia resolutions and the New Jersey Plan be considered together by the full Convention meeting as a Committee of the Whole.[70] The following morning, Saturday, June 16, Nathaniel Gorham of Massachusetts once again replaced Washington in the chair as debate resumed over the proper form of the new government — over issues that had seemingly been decided two days before.

Lansing opened the debate by expressing his preference for the New Jersey Plan over the Virginia Plan. New York "would never have concurred in sending deputies to the convention, if she had supposed the deliberations were to turn on a consolidation of the States, and a National Government." He warned that the states would "never feel a sufficient confidence in a general Government to give it a negative on their laws."[71]

But once again, it was Paterson who made the central case for the New Jersey Plan.

He reminded his fellow delegates that "the large States acceded readily to the confederacy. It was the small ones that came in reluctantly and slowly. N. Jersey & Maryland were the two last," with New Jersey objecting to the Confederation Congress' lack of power over trade, and both New Jersey and Maryland objecting to Congress' inability to appropriate vacant lands for the benefit of all, he noted.[72]

"When independent societies confederate for mutual defense, they do so in their collective capacity; and then each state for those purposes must be considered as one of the contracting parties," Paterson said. "Destroy this balance of equality, and you endanger the rights of the lesser societies by the danger of usurpation in the greater."[73]

Once again, Paterson repeated his call to redraw state lines in order to create thirteen equal political entities, "and we shall see whether the Citizens of Massts. Pena. & Va. accede to it."[74]

Wilson once again took the lead role in criticizing the New Jersey Plan, arguing that power should be vested in citizens, not states, and adding that the Constitution should be submitted to the citizens, not to the state legislatures, for ratification. He noted that it was not the larger states who had blocked the national impost tax, but a small state, and asserted that a single Federal Executive was preferable to several sharing power, as envisioned in the New Jersey Plan.[75]

But it was Charles Pinckney of South Carolina who understood the politics driving the New Jersey Plan most clearly. "The whole comes to this," Pinckney said. "Give N. Jersey an equal vote, and she will dismiss her scruples, and concur in the Natil. system."[76]

The next session day, Monday, June 18, was taken up entirely by an Alexander Hamilton monologue. Hamilton critiqued both the Virginia and the New Jersey Plans as inadequate, and laid out eleven resolutions that would have created a much more powerful national government than Madison or the New Jerseyans had envisioned. Under Hamilton's plan, the chief executive and Senate were to hold office for life, and the governors of the states were to be appointed by the chief executive.[77]

Not surprisingly, Hamilton's plan drew no support, and on the following day, Madison himself took to the floor as the lead proponent for the Virginia Plan he had designed, but previously been content to let Randolph and Wilson advocate.

Madison noted that the current Confederation was weak, and that violations by individual states "had been numerous & notorious. Among the most notorious was an Act of N. Jersey herself; by which she <u>expressly refused</u> to comply with a constitutional requisition of Congs. — and yielded no farther to the expostulations of their deputies, than barely to rescind her vote of refusal without passing any positive act of compliance."

He warned that dissolution of the union would threaten the smaller states more than participation in a national government on a less-than-equal status, then focused on the central political issue:

> The great difficulty lies in the affair of Representation, and if this could be adjusted, all others would be surmountable," Madison said. "It was admitted by both the gentlemen from N. Jersey [Brearley and Paterson] that it would not be just to allow Virga., which was 16 times as large as Delaware an equal vote only. Their language was that it would not be safe for Delaware to allow Virga. 16 times as many votes.
>
> The expedient proposed by them was that all the States should be thrown into one mass and a new partition made into 13 equal parts. Would such a scheme be practicable?
>
> But admitting a general amalgamation and repartition of the States, to be practicable, and the danger apprehended by the smaller States from a proportional representation to be real; would not a particular and voluntary coalition of these with their neighbors, be less inconvenient to the whole community, and equally effectual for their safety. If N. Jersey or Delaware conceive that an advantage would accrue to them from an equalization of the States, in which case they would necessaryly form a junction with their neighbors, why might not this end be attained by leaving them at liberty by the Constitution to form a junction whenever they pleased?[78]

The Madison forces won a procedural vote to postpone consideration of the New Jersey Plan by a 9-2 margin, then moved a resolution calling for the Committee of the Whole "not to agree to the Jersey propositions, but to report those offered by Mr. Randolph." The Virginia Plan was reaffirmed by a 7-3 vote, with New Jersey, Delaware, and New York voting no, and the Maryland delegation split. Connecticut, under Sherman's leadership, voted with the majority, but still hoped for a compromise.[79]

Brearley and Paterson knew that the dynamics of the convention and the state-by-state ratification fight that would follow demanded greater consensus. The large states would eventually have to compromise.

When Jonathan Dayton finally arrived on June 21, Brearley, as previously arranged, went home for a quick visit.[80] He was back at his seat in the convention six days later. Based on Brearley's notes on the debate of the day, a three-hour rambling oration by Maryland's attorney general, Luther Martin, it was clear that little had changed while he was away:

> Have those who upon the present plan hold 1/12 part of the Votes, a 13th part of the weight, – certainly not – upon this plan they sink to nothing.
>
> The Individual right of Citizens is given up in the State Govts. they cannot exercise it again in the Genl. Government.
>
> It has never been complained of in Congress — the complaint there is the want of general powers.[81]

Paterson, meanwhile, had also left the Convention, apparently to try a case in the Burlington Court. The case "did not continue as long as I expected," Paterson wrote to his wife.

He got back to Philadelphia about ten o'clock on Friday night, June 29.[82]

The following morning, backed by the full New Jersey delegation of Paterson, Livingston, and Dayton, Brearley requested that Washington, as president of the Convention, "write to the Executive of N. Hamshire, informing it that the business depending before the Convention was of such a nature as to require the immediate attendance of the deputies of that State. In support of his motion he observed that the difficulties of the subject and the diversity of opinions called for all the assistance we could possibly obtain."[83]

Paterson immediately seconded Brearley's motion

The motive of the New Jersey delegates was transparent. Madison added parenthetically in his notes that "it was well understood that the object was to add N. Hamshire to the no. of States opposed to the doctrine of proportional representation, which it was presumed from her relative size she must be adverse to."

Rutledge immediately objected, arguing that the New Hampshire delegation "can attend if they choose. Rho. Island might as well be urged to appoint & send deputies. Are we to suspend the business until the deputies arrive?"

King reported that he had written to the New Hampshire delegation, and that they were delayed for personal reasons — which turned out to be a lack of money for travel — while Wilson worried that such a message would break the Convention's rule of secrecy and cause "a great alarm."[84]

Brearley's motion died by a 5-2 vote, with Massachusetts, Connecticut, Virginia, and North and South Carolina in opposition, Maryland divided, and Pennsylvania and Delaware not yet on the floor. Only New York, whose majority opposed a strong central government, joined New Jersey in favor of the proposal.[85]

Two days later, however, on July 2, New Jersey and the small-state forces won a significant victory when the full Convention deadlocked 5-5 on Connecticut delegate Oliver Ellsworth's motion calling for equal representation – one senator from each state – in the upper house. As they had several weeks before, New Jersey, Delaware, Connecticut, New York, and Maryland supported equal representation, but this time Georgia's delegation was split, leaving the large states without the 6-5 majority they had previously enjoyed.[86]

Hopelessly deadlocked, the convention decided for the first time to create a committee of eleven members — one from each state — to try to work out a compromise.[87] Paterson wrote to his wife that day, "It is impossible to say when the Convention will rise — Much remains to be done, and the Work is full of Labour and Difficulty."[88] Paterson passed up the opportunity to return home for a short visit, and suggested that Livingston go instead, reasoning that since Livingston was New Jersey's chief of state, he would have more urgent affairs to address. Livingston left Philadelphia on July 3, as did many other delegates, for the anniversary of independence holiday. He promised to return by mid-month and requested to be kept continually informed on the Convention happenings during his absence.

On July 9, the committee chairman, Gouverneur Morris of Pennsylvania, presented the report of the committee set up to determine representation in the first Congress. Out of a Congress of fifty-six members, Virginia would have nine representatives; Pennsylvania, eight; Massachusetts, seven; New York, North Carolina, and South Carolina, five; Connecticut and Maryland, four; New Jersey, three; New Hampshire and Georgia, two; and Delaware and Rhode Island, one. Morris acknowledged that the numbers were "little more than a guess," that both population and wealth were considered as factors in apportioning seats, and that Georgia, with a smaller population than Delaware, had been given two representatives to Delaware's one in anticipation that its population would grow rapidly before the new Constitution would take effect.[89]

With Morris' numbers showing conclusively how the "three-fifths rule" would swell representation for the Southern states, Paterson chose that day to deliver a speech opposing the inclusion of slaves in determining representation in Congress:

*Paterson considered the proposed estimate for the future according to the Combined rule of numbers and wealth, as too vague. For this reason N. Jersey was agst. it. He could regard negroes slaves in no light but as property. They are no free agents, have no personal liberty, no faculty of acquiring property, but on the contrary are themselves property, & like other property entirely at the will of the Master. Has a man in Virga. a number of votes in proportion to the number of his slaves? and if Negroes are not represented in the States to which they belong, why should they be represented in the Genl. Govt. What is the true principle of representation? It is an expedient by which an assembly of certain indivdls. chosen by the people is substituted in place of the inconvenient meeting of the people themselves. If such a meeting of the people was actually to take place, would the slaves vote? they would not. Why then shd. they be represented. He was also agst. such an indirect encouragemt. of the slave trade; observing that Congs. in their act relating to the change of the 8 art: of Confedn. had been ashamed to use the term "Slave" & had substituted a description.*[90]

In response, Madison (according to his own notes) "reminded Mr. Patterson that his doctrine of Representation which was in its principle the genuine one, must for ever silence the pretensions of the small States to an equality of votes with the large ones. They ought to vote in the same proportion in which their citizens would do, if the people of all the States were collectively met."

Speaking for Virginia's interest, Madison went on to suggest that states should be represented in one house based on population and in the second, "which had for one of its primary objects the guardianship of property, according to the whole number, including slaves."[91]

That Madison's view was shared across sectional lines was underscored by Massachusetts delegate Rufus King, who noted that he "had always expected that as the Southern States are the richest, they would not league thesmelves with the Northn. unless some respect were paid to their superior wealth ... Eleven out of 13 of the States had agreed to consider Slaves in the apportionment of taxation; and taxation and Representation ought to go together."[92]

The session ended with a 9-2 vote to name yet another committee with one representative from each state to determine proper representation in the House; Brearley was chosen to represent New Jersey.[93]

Paterson's speech on July 9 was apparently the first and last from the New Jersey delegation on the subject of slavery. New Jersey already had voted to bar the importation of slaves, and Brearley and Paterson both knew that what New Jersey might gain vis a vis such large states as Massachusetts and Pennsylvania if equal representation was ultimately won in the Senate would be offset somewhat by a relative loss of clout in the House of Representatives to Southern states if slaves were counted.

Paterson's notes in preparation for his July 9 speech

included a detailed breakdown of the number of inhabitants in each state:

*New Hampshire in 1774.......................................100,000*
*Massachusetts in 1774 .........................................400,000*
*Rhode-Island in 1783..............................48,538 Whites)*
*by a Return to the Legislature in Feby        3,331 Blacks)*
*Connecticut in 1774..............192,000 - 198,000 Whites)*
*(nearly) 6,000) Blacks*
*New York in 1756 ................................................95,775*
*in 1771................................................168,000*
*in 1786 .................219,996 - 238,885 Whites)*
*18,889 Blacks)*
*New Jersey in 1783 .............................................139,000*
*about 10,000 Blacks included*
*Pennsylvania —*
*Delaware —*
*Maryland in 1774 estimated at.............................350,000*
*Blacks 3/7 ..........................150,000*
*Virginia in 1774...................................................650,000*
*Blacks as 10 to 11 ..............300,000*
*In the lower States the accts. are not to be depended on —*

*The Proportion of Blacks*
*In Connecticut as 1 to 33.*
*The same ratio will answer for Massachusetts —*
*In Rhode-Island as 1 to 15 1/2.*
*In New York as 1 to 12 nearly.*
*In New Jersey as 1 to 13 nearly.*[94]

On July 10, the day after the Paterson speech, Brearley managed to work up more complete numbers, most likely in consultation with delegates from other states with whom he was serving on the new committee of eleven. Brearley's estimates showed:

| States | N. of Whites | N. of Blacks |
|---|---|---|
| New-Hampshire | 82,000 | 102,000 |
| Massachusetts Bay | 352,000 | |
| Rhode Island | 58,000 | |
| Connecticut | 202,000 | |
| New-York | 238,000 | |
| New-Jersey | 138,000 | 145,000 |
| Pennsylvania | 341,000 | |
| Delaware | 37,000 | |
| Maryland | 174,000 | 80,000 |
| Virginia suppd | 300,000 | 300,000 |
| North Carolina | 181,000 | |
| South Carolina | 93,000 | |
| Georgia | 27,000 [95] | |

Brearley's numbers apparently were used by the full convention. Months later, in a January 1788 speech to the South Carolina House of Representatives, Charles C. Pinckney reported that "the numbers in the states, according to the most accurate accounts we could obtain," were those cited by Brearley for New Hampshire, Rhode Island, Connecticut, New Jersey, and Delaware, and very close for Massachusetts (Pinckney estimated 360,000), New York (which Pinckney put at 233,000) and Pennsylvania (again 360,000 in Pinckney's estimate). With slaves included, Pinckney's figures for the five major slaveholding states were:

Maryland ............................................................218,000
(including three fifths of 80,000 negroes)
Virginia ............................................................420,000
(including three-fifths of 280,000 negroes)
N. Carolina ........................................................200,000
(including three-fifths of 60,000 negroes)
S. Carolina.........................................................150,000

*(including three-fifths of 80,000 negroes)*
*Georgia* ...............................................................*90,000*
*(including three-fifths of 20,000 negroes)*

"As we have found it necessary to give very extensive powers to the federal government both over the persons and estates of its citizens, we thought it right to draw one branch of the legislature immediately from the people, and that both wealth and numbers should be considered in the representation," Pinckney explained, then continued:

> *We were at a loss, for some time, for a rule to ascertain the proportionate wealth of the states. At last we thought that the productive labor of the inhabitants was the best rule for ascertaining their wealth. In conformity to this rule, joined to a spirit of concession, we determined that representatives should be apportioned among the several states, by adding to the whole number of free persons three fifths of the slaves. We thus obtained a representation for our property; and I confess I did not expect that we had conceded too much to the Eastern States, when they allowed us a representation for a species of property which they have not among them.*[96]

The committee on representation on which Brearley served reported on June 11 with a new proposal for a House of Representatives with sixty-five members, with Maryland gaining two seats, and New Hampshire, Massachusetts, Connecticut, New York, New Jersey, Virginia, and Georgia one each. Debate quickly sharpened on sectional grounds, with votes on successive motions to cut the size of New Hampshire's delegation and increase the representation of North Carolina, South Carolina,

186

and Georgia failing on sectional lines.[97]

Rufus King of Massachusetts remarked insightfully that "he was fully convinced that the question concerning a difference of interests did not lie where it had hitherto been discussed, between the great & small States, but between the Southern & Eastern." He questioned how four Eastern states with a population of 800,000 could have one-third fewer representatives than four Southern states whose population of 700,000 included three-fifths representatives for its slaves.[98]

After a long debate, the issue once again was sent back for further discussion by the committee of eleven on which Brearley was serving.

The continuing impasse worried Washington, who wrote in despair on July 10 to Alexander Hamilton, imploring him to return from New York:

> When I refer you to the state of the Councils which prevailed at the period you left this City — and add, that they are now, if possible, in a worse train than ever; you will find little ground on which the hope of a good establishment can be formed. — In a word, I <u>almost</u> despair of seeing a favourable issue to the proceedings of the Convention, and do therefore repent having had any agency in the business.
>
> The Men who oppose a strong & energetic government are, in my opinion, narrow minded politicians, or are under the influence of local views ...[99]

While Washington fretted, Randolph recognized that concessions would have to be made to "local views" if the nation was to achieve the "strong & energetic government" that most delegates, including Paterson and Brearley, desired.

The same day that Washington wrote to Hamilton, Randolph

sent an "accommodating proposition" to the small-state delegates. Randolph's "Suggestion for Conciliating the Small States" would have kept equitable representation in both houses of the National Legislature based on population or taxes paid, but it offered equal votes in the second branch for each state on thirteen of the most critical issues:

1. in granting exclusive rights to Ports.

2. in subjecting vessels or seamen of the U. States to tonnage, duties of other impositions

3. in regulating the navigation of Rivers

4. in regulating the rights to be enjoyed by citizens of one State in the other states.

5. in questions arising on the guarantee of territory.

6. in declaring war or taking measures for subduing a Rebellion.

7. in regulating Coin.

8. in establishing and regulating the post office

9. in the admission of new States into the Union

10. in establishing rules for the government of the Militia

11. in raising a regular army

12. in the appointment of the Executive

13. in fixing the seat of government

Randolph also was willing to consider requiring "a greater number of votes than a mere majority" for other key issues.[100]

Randolph's willingness to consider such a compromise undoubtedly emboldened Paterson, Brearley, and the other small-state delegates as they continued working on their alternative proposal. Randolph's "accommodation" was the floor – the compromise the small states could get today. Now the question was, how high was the ceiling?

The bitterness of the debates over representation worried the New Jersey delegation. Paterson could have been talking about more than the weather when he wrote his wife that "The heat here is and has been intense."[101]

On July 13, Dayton wrote to Livingston:

> *I have the mortification to inform your Excellency that altho we have been daily in Convention, we have not made the least progress in the business since you left us. It is unnecessary & would perhaps be improper, to relate here the causes of this delay, they will very readily occur to your Excellency from your knowledge of them heretofore.*
>
> *I must request that your excellency will be pleased agreably to the arrangement made at parting, to return to this place on Tuesday or Wednesday next at the latest.*
>
> *Mr. Paterson must leave this town the first day of August, & I must consequently be here to relieve (him) the last day of the month, let my stay at home (...) been ever so short. I shall therefore at best have (had) ten days...*[102]

But by the time Livingston received Dayton's letter on July 18 and prepared "to set out for that cool City & excellent fish market," as he wrote to John Jay from Elizabeth Town,[103] the Great Compromise had been reached.

On Monday, July 16, after more than five weeks of heated debate, the convention voted 5-4 in favor of a representation plan for Congress that called for a lower house of sixty-five members apportioned by population, with slaves counting as three-fifths for that purpose, and for equal representation among states in the Senate. New Jersey, Delaware, Connecticut, and Maryland were joined in voting for the compromise by North Carolina, which cast the deciding vote in an apparent effort to keep the convention together. Pennsylvania, Virginia, South Carolina, and Georgia voted no, with the Massachusetts delegation split.[104]

Randolph angrily took the floor and declared, "It will probably be in vain to come to any final decision with a bare majority on either side. For these reasons, I wish the Convention might adjourn, that the large states might consider the steps proper to be taken in the present solemn crisis of the business, and that the small states might also deliberate on the means of conciliation."[105]

Paterson called Randolph's bluff:

> I think with Mr. Randolph that it is high time for the Convention to adjourn, that the rule of secrecy ought to be rescinded, and that our constituents should be consulted. No conciliation can be possible on the part of the smaller states on any other ground than that of an equality of votes in the second branch. If Mr. Randolph will reduce to form his motion for an adjournment sine die, I will second it with all my heart.[106]

Rutledge recognized that the small states had won, even if Randolph did not. "The little states are fixed," Rutledge said. "They have repeatedly and solemnly declared themselves to be so. All that the large states then have to do is to decide whether they will yield or not. For my part, I conceive that although we cannot do what we think is best in itself, we ought to do something."[107]

The following day, a meeting of a number of large-state delegates failed to find a new proposal that could satisfy the small states. When the convention reconvened, Gouverneur Morris' motion to consider the vote of the previous day did not even receive a second.[108]

The Great Compromise would stand.

The United States would have a federal government, in which the people would be represented in the House and states would have an equal voice in the Senate.

It was a clear victory for Brearley, Paterson, and their Delaware, Maryland, and Connecticut allies over Madison, Wilson, and the powerful Virginia and Pennsylvania delegations.

Livingston returned to Philadelphia in time to participate in the July 23 vote giving each state two senators.[109] Brearley, Paterson, Dayton, and Livingston were pleased. And just as Pinckney had previously predicted, the New Jersey men raised no formidable objections during the remainder of the Convention.

Paterson left the Convention on August 1 to tend to his personal affairs. He received word from his wife that his legal practice was in dire need of his presence, and the paper money in which the New Jersey Legislature paid its delegates was of little value. As Paterson wrote to his wife, Euphemia White, on July 17:

> I shall be in want of some hard money in order to clear me of this town and therefor request you to send me by the first good opportunity about twelve pounds. It is to no end to draw upon the New Jersey treasury, as it contains nothing but paper money, which few people will take; which tested by gold must pay from 20 to 25 per cent and the Pa. paper is at present as bad, if not worse.[110]

Paterson made no mention as to when — or if — he would return to Philadelphia. In fact, he would be gone for six weeks and would not return until the Constitution was ready to be signed. This left Brearley, Livingston, and Dayton to tend to Convention details. All three men worked on various committees, dealing with such vital issues as state debts, navigation acts, and the slave trade.

On August 21, 1781, Brearley wrote to Paterson at (New) Brunswick, where he had spent the week on legal business:

> *Dear Sir:*
>
> *I was in hopes after the Committee had reported, that we should have been able to have published by the first of September. At present I have no prospect of our getting through before the latter end of that month. Every article is again argued over, with as much earnestness and obstinacy as before it was committed. We have lately made a rule to meet at ten and sit 'til four, which is punctually complied with. – Cannot you come down and alight with us, – we have many reasons for desiring this, our duty, in the manner in which we now sit, is quite too hard for three, but a much stronger reason is, that we actually stand in need of your abilities.*
>
> > *I am, most respectfully, dear sir,*
> > *your obedient humble servant*
> > *David Brearley* [111]

The following day, on August 22, no doubt to Brearley's chagrin, the Convention took time off to watch a demonstration of John Fitch's steamboat.[112] The delegates needed to blow off steam. Some of the most difficult moments of the convention still lay ahead.

# CHAPTER NINE

# Breaking the Constitutional Deadlock

## The Committee on Postponed Matters, the Electoral College, and the Vice-Presidency

*"Chaired by the faithful Judge Brearly ... this admirable committee moved in as a rescue party to make up the Convention's mind."*

— Clinton Rossiter, 1787: The Grand Convention [1]

For David Brearley and other proponents of a strong Constitution, Friday, August 31, was quite possibly the darkest day of the entire Constitutional Convention. From gavel to gavel, the debate that day was marked by despair and doubt, as one delegate after another questioned whether the Constitution as written could win ratification — and indeed, whether it should.

Madison, who felt that the Constitution on which were they were working was far superior to the existing Articles of

Confederation, proposed that approval by a bare majority of states and population — "Any seven or more states entitled to thirty three representatives at least in the House of Representatives" — should be sufficient for ratification.

But Roger Sherman of Connecticut said it would be "a breach of faith" to require ratification by any fewer than all thirteen states, given the unanimity required under the current Articles of Confederation. "Perhaps all the States may concur," he said hopefully, conveniently ignoring Rhode Island's boycott of the convention and New York's walkout.[2]

Luther Martin punctuated a lengthy debate over whether ratification should be required by state conventions or left up to state legislatures with the observation that in his state of Maryland, it didn't matter "whether the Legislature or the   people should be appealed to. Both of them would be generally against the Constitution."

Elbridge Gerry of Massachusetts denounced the system being established under the new Constitution as "full of vices" and said it would be improper to destroy "the existing Confederation, without the unanimous consent of the parties to it."

Gerry urged postponement of the whole question of ratification, and his motion was seconded by the influential George Mason of Virginia, "declaring that he would sooner chop off his right hand than put it to the Constitution as it now stands." Mason wanted the outstanding issues resolved, and if he did not agree with the solution, he wanted another convention.

Gouverneur Morris of Pennsylvania said he was ready for postponement to another convention "that will have the firmness to provide a vigorous Government, which we are afraid to do."

Finally, Virginia's Edmund Randolph, who had worked with Madison to create the Constitutional Convention, said that if "the final form of the Constitution should not permit him to accede to it, that the State Conventions should be at liberty to propose amendments to be submitted to another General Convention which may reject or incorporate them" – a proposal that raised the possibility that a new convention could undo all the work of the current convention, even if the states somehow ratified the Constitution.[3]

At the end of the day, after voting to allow ratification by conventions of nine states, the exhausted delegates agreed to a suggestion by Roger Sherman to refer all remaining unresolved issues, including how to elect a president, to a new Committee on Postponed Matters, made up like all other committees of one delegate from each state.[4]

The day's debate had underscored the fragility of the compromises worked out so far and the importance of the compromises to come, and that was reflected in the choice the various state delegations made. This new committee of eleven would be a particularly strong committee, and it would be made up of proponents of a strong Constitution.

The committee included such leading lights as Gouverneur Morris of Pennsylvania, Roger Sherman of Connecticut, and John Dickinson of Delaware. But just as important were those left off.

Virginia would be represented by Madison, not by the angry Randolph or the hostile Mason.

Maryland's committee member would be Daniel Carroll, not the irascible and verbose Luther Martin.

Massachusetts would be represented by Rufus King, not the uncompromising Elbridge Gerry.

South Carolina's choice was Pierce Butler, not the strong-willed John Rutledge.

Consciously or not, the state delegations were putting together a committee not only capable of, but committed to reaching the difficult compromises needed to avert another convention.

New Hampshire chose Nicholas Gilman, another advocate of strong government. North Carolina's Hugh Williamson was convinced of the need for strong government by the frustration he developed serving in the Continental Congress. Georgia chose its ablest delegate, Abraham Baldwin, whose critical switch of position in June had intentionally deadlocked the convention on the issue of representation in the Senate and opened the way for the Great Compromise.[5]

New Jersey's choice was easy: It was David Brearley, who not only had been there from the beginning, but had proved his ability to work with delegates from other states to forge new coalitions in developing the New Jersey Plan and ultimately incorporating its main principles into the Constitution that now had to be saved.

The choice of a chairman was left up to the committee members, and their choice was Brearley. Considering the importance of the committee, Brearley's selection as chairman was a mark of considerable confidence in his abilities.

The selection of Brearley reflected the emergence of a new bloc of seven states committed to a strong national government, but only within a federal context that recognized the rights of individual states. New Jersey, Connecticut, Maryland, and Delaware, who had fought together for the New Jersey Plan, now made up the core of a coalition that also included Massachusetts, Georgia, and recently arrived New Hampshire. Madison's Virginia, Pennsylvania, and the Carolinas were the new minority.[6]

Brearley wasted no time in getting his committee to work that evening. "Chaired by the faithful Judge Brearly," historian Clinton Rossiter wrote, "this admirable committee moved in as a rescue party to make up the Convention's mind."

The following morning, Brearley reported to the convention that his committee had already reached agreement on one issue.

He read the proposed language: "That in lieu of the 9th section of article 6, the words following be inserted viz. 'The members of each House shall be ineligible to any civil office under the authority of the U.S. during the time for which they shall respectively be elected, and no person holding an office under the U.S. shall be a member of either House during his continuance in office.'"[7]

Checks and balances required clear delineation among the executive, legislative and judicial branches, and this proposal would see to it by "ruling out any possibility of a parliamentary cabinet like those in Britain."[8]

Rutledge then made a similarly brief report from his committee on a proposed change to establish uniform bankruptcy laws, and the convention adjourned without debating either committee report.

As James McHenry reported taciturnly in his only note on the day's proceedings, "Adjourned to let the committee sit."[9] Brearley's committee had work to do.

While Madison, the convention's unofficial historian, and Rufus King of Massachusetts, who also kept periodic notes of convention debates, both sat on Brearley's committee, neither kept notes of the critical discussion, debate, deliberation, and compromise that shaped the committee's wide-ranging and often imaginative recommendations.

For Constitutional scholars, Madison's failure to do so, coupled with the absence of Brearley's papers on the subject, is frustrating, although it is often possible to reconstruct the likely committee battle lines based on both prior and subject debates on the convention floor and on the votes of individual states on proposed amendments to the committee's recommendations.

Brearley's committee made no further report when the Convention reconvened Monday, September 1, at ten o'clock in the morning, but most of the day's debate focused on the recommendation his committee had made Saturday to ban members of Congress from serving in any other federal office — which had been a highly controversial proposal to put before a convention in which forty-two of the fifty-five delegates had served in Congress and might plan to serve again.[10] No state government put such a prohibition on its state legislators.

King, Gouverneur Morris of Pennsylvania, and Hugh Williamson of North Carolina, all members of Brearley's committee, made it clear that they favored allowing members of Congress to fill positions that opened up in the executive branch.

But Roger Sherman of Connecticut worried that making members of Congress eligible to fill appointed positions "would give too much influence to the Executive" who controlled those jobs. Ultimately, though, it was Sherman who proposed the eventual compromise, under which members of Congress must give up their seats to fill executive or judicial branch vacancies, and would be barred from appointment to any new position or any position whose salary had been increased while they had served in office.[11]

As the chairman charged with bringing resolution to some of the convention's thorniest issues, Brearley did not participate in the convention debates on his committee proposals. He had a role model to follow in George Washington, who chaired the full convention with an even hand by steering clear of divisive debate.

It is clear, however, that Brearley favored the stronger language his committee originally proposed that would have barred members of Congress from filling any other federal position during the term to which they had been elected. New Jersey's delegation voted with Connecticut, Maryland and South Carolina against all three motions to water down the ban.[12]

The committee meeting that followed Monday's session was

one of the most productive and important committee meetings of the entire convention.

This quickly became clear shortly after ten o'clock in the morning on Tuesday, September 4, when Brearley stood at his seat and began to read from his own handwriting:

> The Committee of Eleven to whom sundry resolutions &c. were referred on the 31st. of August, report that in their opinion the following additions and alterations should be made to the Report before the Convention, viz.
>
> (1) The first clause of sect: 1. art. 7 to read as follow — "The Legislature shall have power to lay and collect taxes duties imposts & excises, to pay the debts and provide for the common defence & general welfare of the U.S."...[13]

For Brearley and the New Jersey delegation, announcement of this clause represented a matter of both personal and state triumph. New Jersey had sharply criticized the Articles of Confederation for failing to give Congress the power to tax and regulate trade. Rhode Island's refusal to grant the thirteenth vote needed to give Congress that power in 1783, and the subsequent refusal of New York and Georgia to approve a similar proposal in the years that followed, led directly to the Annapolis Convention of 1786. Randolph and Madison convened the Annapolis meeting in an effort to break the deadlock that denied Congress the power to tax and regulate trade. The "New Jersey Idea" to broaden the scope of the Annapolis Convention to include "other important matters" flowed directly out of the state's frustration with Congress' inability to pay interest on a war debt that was held disproportionately by New Jersey's citizens.

The New Jersey state government had struggled to raise the

taxes necessary to take on those interest payments when New York, in particular, was forcing New Jersey citizens to pay New York State duties on imports that came through its port. Giving Congress the power to tax trade had been a centerpiece of the New Jersey Plan developed by Paterson and Brearley in June. And now, with the anti-Federalist two-thirds of New York's delegation long departed for home, New York did not even have the necessary quorum to cast a vote against it.

Madison's unbound papers included his own copy of the "Reptt. of Come. of 11" on which Madison indicated that the power to tax trade to pay off the debt and provide for the "Common defence & Genl. welfare passed nem: con: and, as appears, without debate." As to the direct authorship of the proposal, Madison wrote in a note to himself — "Quer. if this report be not in the handwriting of Mr. Sherman?" — then answered his own question: "more probably in that of Mr. Brearley."[14]

A month or two earlier, this clause would doubtless have engendered a long and bitter debate. But on Tuesday, September 5, its importance paled in comparison to what was to come. Brearley offered a short clause giving Congress the power to regulate commerce "with the Indian tribes," in addition to foreign governments and the state governments, as previously agreed.

Then, in rapid succession, Brearley laid out a series of recommendations to select the president through an electoral college (the latest small-state/large-state compromise), to create a vice-president, to give the president the power to make treaties and to appoint Supreme Court justices, ambassadors, and the entire executive branch of government, to allow the president and vice-president to serve successive four-year terms, and to provide a process for their impeachment and removal from office.

Brearley began innocuously, reading undoubtedly in the same judicial tone he used to deliver judgments from the New

Jersey Supreme Court bench. He mentioned the vice-presidency for the first time almost in passing as he unveiled what would prove to be a controversial, yet "ingenious mechanism" for the election of the president. The President, Brearley read:

> 'Shall hold his office during the term of four years, and together with the vice-President, chosen for the same term, be elected in the following manner, viz. Each State shall appoint in such manner as its Legislature may direct, a number of electors equal to the whole number of Senators and members of the House of Representatives, to which the State may be entitled in the Legislature. The Electors shall meet in their respective States, and vote by ballot for two persons, of whom one at least shall not be an inhabitant of the same State with themselves; and they shall make a list of all the persons voted for, and of the number of votes for each, which list they shall sign and certify and transmit sealed to the Seat of the Genl. Government.... The President of the Senate shall in that House open all of the certificates; and the votes shall then & there be counted. The Person having the greatest number of votes shall be the President, if such number be a majority of that of the electors, and if there be more than one that have such a majority, and have an equal number of votes, then the Senate shall choose by ballot one of them for President: but if no person have a majority, then from the five highest on the list, the Senate shall choose by ballot the President. And in every case after the choice of the President, the person having the greatest number of votes shall be vice-president ...

Brearley provided no rationale for the electoral college or the vice-presidency, but continued reading. The Brearley committee's next major recommendation required the President to be at least thirty-five years of age, a natural born citizen of the United States or a citizen at the time of the adoption of the Constitution – a concession to the eight convention delegates born abroad, including Hamilton, Randolph, and Gouverneur Morris, who might have presidential ambitions.

As to the duties of the vice-presidency, which had not existed before that morning, Brearley read:

> The vice-president shall be ex-officio President of the Senate, except when they sit to try the impeachment of the President, in which case the Chief Justice shall preside, and excepting also when he shall exercise the powers and duties of President, in which case & in case of his absence, the Senate shall chuse a President pro tempore. – The vice President when acting as President of the Senate shall not have a vote unless the House be equally divided.

The Brearley committee, which had been stacked with some of the staunchest nationalists at the convention, clearly intended to strengthen the office of the president at the expense of the Congress, as Brearley's next clause showed:

> The President by and with the advice and Consent of the Senate, shall have power to make Treaties; and he shall nominate and by and with the advice and consent of the Senate shall appoint ambassadors, and all other public Ministers & consuls [Brearley interlined the words "& consuls" above "Ministers" on his copy], Judges of the Supreme Court, and all other Officers of the U–S –, whose appointments are not otherwise

*herein provided for. But no Treaty except treaties of peace [Again, "except treaties of peace" is interlined by Brearley as a late addition] shall be made without the consent of two thirds of the members present.*

Finally, after giving the president the power to demand reports in writing from any of his cabinet officers, Brearley concluded by enumerating the grounds for impeachment of the president:

> *He shall be removed from his office on impeachment by the House of Representatives, and conviction by the Senate, for Treason, or bribery, and in case of his removal as aforesaid, death, absence, resignation or inability to discharge the powers or duties of his office, the vice-president shall exercise those powers and duties until another president be chosen, or until the inability of the President be removed.*[15]

When he had finished, Brearley strode to the front of the room and handed the report to William Jackson, the convention secretary, who then read it aloud again.[16] The contents of the Brearley committee report may not have come as a surprise to the gathered delegates, each of whom had a colleague representing his state on the Committee on Postponed Matters. Nevertheless, the breadth and sweep of the recommendations — read aloud twice in succession — undoubtedly excited the same mixture of exhilaration and trepidation that greeted Randolph when he unveiled the Virginia Plan more than three months before.

The delegates launched into what would prove to be a five-day debate over the electoral college, presidential and congressional powers, the need for a vice-president, and the impeachment process.

"The complexity of the scheme, as every delegate surely

understood, stemmed in part from the Convention's rejection of such simpler methods as direct election of the President by the people or by a joint session of Congress," William Peters noted in his bicentennial analysis, *A More Perfect Union.* "But the Committee on Postponed Matters had also attempted, by involving the Senate, to steer a political course midway between the interests of the large and the small states."[17]

Winton U. Solberg, in his 1958 study *The Federal Constitution and the Formation of the Union of the American States*, noted that "the settlement from the Committee of Eleven contained something for everyone.... The new method of selecting a President conciliated republicans who feared aristocracy in the election of an executive, while awarding small states an advantage in the composition of presidential electors and in case the ballot went to" the Senate, where each state had equal votes.[18]

Brearley's hand can clearly be seen in the small-state/large-state compromise that gave New Jersey and Delaware three times the voice in the selection of the president and vice-president that they would have received based strictly on population in 1787.

But that point of relative unfairness had already been debated and resolved in the minds of most delegates during the July debate in which they had agreed to a more egregiously disproportionate power-sharing in the Senate as the price for keeping the small states in the union. Paterson, in fact, had suggested earlier that summer that the executive should be chosen by electors selected by each state according to a ratio that gave one elector to the smallest states and three to the largest.[19]

The debate over the electoral college focused not on "one man, one vote" issues of electoral fairness, but on what would happen when the electoral college inevitably failed to give a majority to any candidate.[20]

While it was tacitly understood that the man who chaired

their debate, George Washington, would be elected overwhelmingly as the first president, the delegates failed to foresee the rise of national political parties and therefore failed to see how any candidate other than Washington could muster the national support needed to win a majority in the electoral college.

Brearley's committee assumed that electors from the large states, in particular, would vote for "favorite son" candidates. In fact, the office of the vice-president had been created not to ensure proper succession, but was "introduced only as a valuable mode of election which required two to be chosen at the same time," Williamson, the committee member from North Carolina, acknowledged. By requiring electors to vote for at least one candidate from another state, the Brearley committee hoped at least one candidate would win a majority and be elected President independent of the Congress – which was the purpose in creating the electoral college in the first place.[21]

Gouverneur Morris defended the new system on behalf of the committee, citing "the indispensable necessity of making the Executive independent of the Legislature," and Baldwin, the committee member from Georgia, asserted that "increasing intercourse among the people of the States, would render important characters less & less unknown; and the Senate would be less & less likely to have the eventual appointment thrown into their hands."

Many delegates were not convinced, however. "Nineteen times in twenty," Mason predicted during the first day of debate, "the President would be chosen by the Senate, an improper body for the purpose."[22]

That evening, after a full day of Convention debate, the Brearley committee met for a final time to wrap up its work. Brearley opened the Wednesday session as he had the Tuesday session by reading his committee's report, then handing it to the secretary for a second reading.

The committee added to the Senate power "to declare war" the right to "grant letters of marque and reprisal" to American privateers; authorized Congress to appropriate funds "to raise and support armies" for up to two years, rather than one year; established a patent system for authors and inventors; and gave the national government authority over forts, dockyards, other military installations, and up to a ten-mile-square cession of territory for a new national capital that Brearley hoped would be situated in Trenton.

The most important new provision, Brearley believed, was intended as a concession to the larger states, whose delegates had raised the most questions about the compromises developed by the Committee on Postponed Matters the day before:

> All bills for raising revenue shall originate in the House of Representatives, and shall be subject to alterations and amendments in the Senate. No money shall be drawn from the Treasury, but in consequence of appropriations made by law.[23]

The new provision gave the large states, which would be paying the bulk of the taxes, control over how their taxes would be spent. But it did little to tone down the debate over the election of the president.

"We have in some revolutions of this plan made a bold stroke for monarchy," Virginia's Randolph warned, referring to the proposal to allow the president to serve consecutive four-year terms, rather than being limited to one seven-year term, as the convention had tentatively agreed to do in July. "We are now in doing the same for an aristocracy," he said, arguing that giving the Senate the power to elect the president would "convert that body into a real and dangerous Aristocracy."

Mason and two influential South Carolina delegates, John

Rutledge and Charles Pinckney, all agreed that the Senate would be too powerful, with Mason saying he "would prefer the Government of Prussia to one which will put all power into the hands of seven or eight men, and fix an Aristocracy worse than absolute monarchy."[24]

Maryland's James McHenry aptly summarized Wednesday's debate in a single sentence in his journal: "The greatest part of the day spent in desultory conversation on that part of the report respecting the mode of chusing the President – adjourned without coming to a conclusion –"[25]

James Wilson of Pennsylvania focused Thursday's debate with a long speech in which he argued that the net effect of the Brearley committee's recommendations was to create "a dangerous tendency to aristocracy" and to throw "a dangerous power into the hands of the Senate." Wilson noted that the Senate would not only have the power to elect the president if the electoral college failed to achieve a majority, but also to rule on appointments of cabinet officers and judges, to make treaties, and to be the court of impeachments. The Brearley committee had actually taken away the power of the Senate to make executive and judicial appointments unilaterally and given the power to nominate candidates to the president, but the convention was clearly determined to place further limitations on the power of the Senate.

It was Roger Sherman, who had originally suggested the creation of the Brearley committee, who came up with the critical compromise, suggesting that the power to select a president be shifted from the Senate to the House of Representatives, but with each state having one vote. The motion passed 10-1, with only Delaware in opposition.[26]

Friday's debate focused on the Brearley committee's second major surprise: the creation of the office of the vice-presidency. Gerry, Mason, and Randolph once again were the principal objectors, arguing that making the vice-president serve as president of the Senate, with the power to break tie votes, was an unacceptable executive branch encroachment on the powers of the legislature.

"We might as well put the President himself at the head of the Legislature," Gerry said. "The close intimacy that must subsist between the President & vice-president makes it absolutely improper."

"The vice president then will be the first heir apparent that ever loved his father," Gouverneur Morris shot back. "If there should be no vice president, the President of the Senate would be the temporary successor, which would amount to the same thing."

The Brearley committee's creation of the vice-presidency survived, as did the president's power to nominate and the Senate's power to confirm executive and judicial appointments, the Senate's power to make treaties, the impeachment process, and the House of Representatives' power to initiate tax and appropriations measures.[27]

By the end of Saturday's session, a five-member Committee of Revision was appointed to make a final version of the Constitution, which, thanks to the recommendations of Brearley's committee, now included a president and vice-president who would serve four-year terms and be eligible for reelection, a presidency strengthened by the power to nominate cabinet officers and judges, and an electoral college that balanced the interests of large and small states in the election of the president.[28]

The following day, on Sunday, September 9, Jonathan Dayton was able to write to his father, Elias:

> We have happily so far finished our business, as to be employed in giving it its last polish and preparing it for the public inspection. This, I conclude, may be done in three or four days, at which time the public

*curiousity and our desire of returning to our respective homes, will equally be gratified.*[29]

As with every piece of convention business, the final polish also took longer than promised.

The convention continued to debate potential changes, vote again on proposals that had been voted down before, and go over language submitted by the Committee of Revision on Monday, Wednesday, Thursday, Friday, and Saturday of the following week.

One of the language changes that Brearley and the New Jersey delegation found most satisfying was the explicit strengthening of Article 1, Section 10, to read: "No State shall, without the consent of Congress lay imposts or duties on imports or exports."[30]

Finally, on Monday, September 17, the convention met for the last time. Brearley, Livingston, and Dayton were in their usual chairs, and Paterson, who had done so much to push the New Jersey Plan, had returned for the signing.

James Wilson read a long speech written by Franklin, aimed clearly at those delegates who remained dissatisfied with the compromises contained in the new Constitution, two copies of which sat in the front of the room. Franklin was ailing, but his words were strong:

> ... I agree to this Constitution with all its faults, if they are such; because I think a general Government necessary for us, and there is no form of Government but what may be a blessing to the people if well administered, and believe farther that this is likely to be well administered for a course of years ... I doubt too whether any other Convention we can obtain may be able to make a better Constitution. For when you

*assemble a number of men to have the advantage of their joint wisdom, you inevitably assemble with those men, all their prejudices, their passions, their errors of opinion, their local interests, and their selfish views. From such an Assembly, can a perfect production be expected? It therefore astonishes me, Sir, to find this system approaching so near to perfection as it does ...*

Franklin then suggested that the Constitution be signed by each of the members as representing "the unanimous consent of the States," in the hopes that this would enable dissenting members to affix their names to the document.[31] Franklin's hopes were quickly dashed, however, first by Randolph, then by Gerry, and finally by Mason.

Randolph said that "in refusing to sign the Constitution, he took a step which might be the most awful of his life, but it was dictated by his conscience, and it was not possible for him to hesitate, much less, to change." He repeated his contention that asking state conventions to ratify the Constitution as is, without making provisions for amendments, was an invitation to "anarchy & civil convulsions."

"Nine States will fail to ratify the plan, and confusion must ensue," Randolph predicted. He said he would keep an open mind about whether to oppose the Constitution publicly.[32]

Gerry and Mason left no doubt where they would stand publicly. Gerry warned:

*A Civil war may result from the present crisis of the U.S.— In Massachusetts particularly he saw the danger of this calamitous event — In that State there are two parties, one devoted to Democracy, the worst he thought of all political evils, the other as violent in the opposite extreme. From the collision of these in opposing and resisting the Constitution, confusion was greatly to be feared.*[33]

While the opposition of Gerry, Randolph and Mason portended a difficult ratification fight ahead, particularly in their home states of Massachusetts and Virginia, Brearley and his fellow New Jersey delegates had no such qualms. They signed the Constitution, like Franklin, with the conviction that they were looking toward "a rising and not a setting Sun."

# CHAPTER TEN

# The Patriotic State

## Steering New Jersey's Ratification Convention

*"A correspondent informs us that, notwithstanding the dispatch of the Convention, many supposed exceptions were agitated, but that the Honorable Judge Brearley, with a perspicuity of argument and persuasive eloquence which carried conviction with it, bore down all opposition."*

— New Jersey Journal, December 26, 1787 [1]

Reaction to the proposed Constitution in New Jersey was almost uniformly favorable, even from influential officials who had served in Congress under the Articles of Confederation.

Elias Boudinot, President of the Confederation Congress in 1782-83, wrote to his son-in-law, Pennsylvania Attorney General William Bradford Jr., that he "rejoiced" to hear that Pennsylvania was likely to approve the new Constitution, which Boudinot personally supported:

*I am clear in it that some government is better than none and believe with you that there is now no alternative; but indeed when I consider the difficulty of reconciling thirteen jarring interests, and that in points of such essential consequence, I confess it is better than I expected. It will not meet with any opposition in this state, but it gives universal satisfaction as far as I can judge. The field for abilities and usefulness opens wide, and even ambition has its temptation.[2]*

Lambert Cadwalader, a New Jersey delegate to the Confederation Congress and cousin of John Dickinson, the Pennsylvanian who served on Brearley's Committee on Postponed Matters, wrote to George Mitchell, a member of the Delaware House of Assembly:

*... when I reflect that the smaller states are admitted to an equal representation in the Senate with the larger, it appears to me a circumstance much more favorable than I could have expected and ought to satisfy your state in particular. .... New Jersey I expect will be unanimous [in supporting ratification]...[3]*

Indeed, the *Pennsylvania Gazette* reported on October 10 that "A gentleman who lately travelled through New Jersey assured us that among many hundred persons with whom he conversed about the federal government, he met but one man who was opposed to it, and he was a citizen of Pennsylvania and an intimate friend of the head of the Antifederal Junto."[4]

Petitions were sent to the state Legislature by groups of citizens in Gloucester, Burlington, Salem, and Middlesex counties urging quick ratification of the new Constitution. The thirty-three signers of one of the Salem petitions averred: "We are convinced, after the most serious and unprejudiced examination of the different articles and sections of articles of this Constitution, that nothing but the immediate adoption of it can save the United States in general, and this state in particular, from absolute ruin."[5]

Formal county meetings were held in Burlington and Somerset counties on October 9 and in Essex County on October 15 to endorse the new Constitution and instruct their county delegations in the Council and General Assembly to push for a ratification convention.[6]

New Jersey's three principal newspapers, the *Trenton Mercury*, the *Brunswick Gazette*, and the *New Jersey Journal*, carried less about the debate over the Constitution than New York and Pennsylvania papers. For the most part, the New Jersey papers reprinted a slew of Federalist commentaries by proponents like James Wilson, Roger Sherman, and Oliver Ellsworth that had appeared in other newspapers, and only three out-of-state anti-Federalist tracts, including the objections of George Mason and Elbridge Gerry, two of the three delegates who had refused to sign the Constitution. Overall, however, the New Jersey newspapers carried a steady stream of news items "which created the impression that the Constitution would be ratified in other states with little difficulty."[7]

Four commentaries by New Jersey Federalists praised the Constitution. "A Jerseyman: To the Citizens of New Jersey" reminded his fellow citizens that the new Constitution provided the critical changes in the regulation and taxation of trade that New Jersey had been seeking since 1778 and which had been the cause of the New Jersey Legislature's refusal to pay the Confederation Congress' 1785 requisition:

> ... *the imposts on all foreign merchandise imported into America would still effectually aid our Continental treasury. This power has been heretofore held back by*

*some states on narrow and mistaken principles. The*
*amount of the duties, since the peace, would probably by*
*this time have nearly paid our national debt.*[8]

Writing as "A Farmer of New Jersey," John Stevens Jr.,
who served as state treasurer under Livingston from 1776 to
1783, noted: "When we consider the multiplicity of jarring
interests, which mutual concession alone could reconcile, it
really becomes matter of astonishment that a system of legislation
could have been effected in which so few imperfections arc to be
found."[9] Stevens suggested several amendments, but
acknowledged in a December 9 letter to his father, John Steven
Sr., who would be chosen president of the state ratification
convention two days later, that the "Constitution must either be
wholly received or wholly rejected. It is in vain to expect that any
kind of federal government can ever take place if the state
conventions are to make amendments."[10]

On Friday morning, October 25, Brearley joined Livingston
and Dayton at the Statehouse in Trenton to formally deliver a
printed copy of the new Constitution and accompanying
documents first to the Council and then to the Assembly. In a formal document also signed by William C. Houston, who was too
ill to come to Trenton, the commissioners reported that:

> *... in pursuance of their appointment, they met the*
> *commissioners of eleven of the other states in Union at*
> *Philadelphia and thereupon ... did, after long and serious*
> *deliberation, and with no small difficulty, finally agree*
> *upon a plan for the government of the said United*
> *States.*[11]

Meeting again on Saturday, and then from Monday through
Thursday the following week, the Council and the Assembly

made New Jersey the first state to approve legislation calling a "Convention of Delegates" to ratify the new Constitution.[12]

Livingston was delighted, as he wrote in a letter to Jedidiah Moore, a Congregational minister at Yale, on November 1, the day the legislation was approved:

> As to news in this part of the terraquaneous globe, I can inform you of one fact which gives me great pleasure. It is that both the branches of our Legislature were unanimous in laying before the people the constitution planned by the late Convention, & I hope & doubt not that the citizens of Connecticut will be as ready to adopt it, as I have reason to think we shall: & then I think we shall soon make my native Country, New York, a little sickish of their opposition to it.[13]

New York Governor George Clinton's opposition to the new Constitution was a matter of considerable public discussion, some of it scurrilous. As the Pennsylvania Journal on December 19 alleged,

> By a gentleman from New York and New Jersey, we are informed that it is reported in those states, that a Governor (George Clinton of New York) not one hundred miles from the seat of Congress still sets his face against the new Constitution of the United States, and has gone so far, it is said, as to proffer, thro a person of considerable weight in Jersey, one-half of the impost of his state to Jersey if they would reject the new Constitution.[14]

The "person of considerable weight" is presumed to be Abraham Clark, the congressman who had declined to serve as a delegate to the convention and who emerged as the only New Jersey opponent of the Constitution of any consequence. Clark would withdraw his objections once a Bill of Rights was added.[15]

New Jersey's ratification convention legislation specifically authorized the state's thirteen counties to hold meetings on the fourth Tuesday in November "to choose three suitable Persons as Delegates from each County in a State Convention" in Trenton on December 11.[16] The delegates would be paid "the Sum of Ten Shillings lawful Money of this State per Day, for each day he shall have attended."[17]

Procedures for electing delegates varied from county to county, following the system used to elect candidates for the state Assembly. Voting was restricted to adults with a net worth of £50 in proclamation money and who had been county residents for at least one year.

Voting would be by secret ballot in only five of the thirteen counties; in the other eight, voting was *viva voce*. Five counties had only one authorized polling place, presumably the courthouse, while eight counties had several authorized sites where elections could be held over the course of several days at the discretion of the county sheriff.[18] Joseph Lewis, who served as Morris County's clerk for the ratification convention election, reported supervising elections at the courthouse in Morristown on November 27 and 28, at Troy on the 29th, at Howell's Tavern in Rockaway on the 30th, and finally closing the balloting back at the courthouse on Saturday evening, December 1st.[19]

On the surface, New Jersey's election was a high-minded affair, particularly in contrast to neighboring Pennsylvania's November 6 vote in which forty-six committed Federalists and twenty-three avowed anti-Federalists were elected after bitter campaigns. However, considerable politicking also took place before the New Jersey election and undoubtedly at the election sites themselves.

Typical of the maneuvering was the letter that Robert Morris, Brearley's predecessor as Supreme Court Chief Justice and a lawyer in New Brunswick, wrote to Peter Wilson, a state Assembly representative from Bergen County, the week before the election. Morris reported that an anti-Federalist from New Brunswick had traveled to Bergen County to speak against the Constitution and that "a candidate in some measure under his influence" was one of those nominated as a potential delegate for the upcoming Convention:

> Now, sir, tho I think there will be no danger but the Jersey Convention will adopt the proposed Constitution, yet I consider its ratification [words crossed out] it as a matter of so much consequence to New Jersey and the other smaller State(s) [words crossed out] that no avoidable hazard ought to be risked.... Besides standing a candidate yourself, I think you ought to hold up [Assemblyman John] Outwater and [Assemblyman Adam] Boyd or some other Federal characters as [former Assemblyman] Isaac Blanch, if he is not poisoned, who have sufficient interest to carry an election against an opposition, which I conceive to be apprehended if the aforesaid Antifederal gentleman has had any success in his machinations.... Nicholls [presumably Assemblyman Isaac Nicoll] ought not to be trusted on this question nor any man whose connections in this state are in the opposition as is supposed to be the case with his.[20]

Similar behind-the-scenes machinations undoubtedly took place in other counties. There is no record of David Brearley's activities during this period; he had stopped making entries in his almanac the previous year. But it is difficult to imagine such a committed Federalist not taking an active role in the delegate selection process.

When Hunterdon County tallied its votes, Brearley, John Stevens Sr., and Joshua Corshon were chosen as its three delegates. Robert Livingston, New York State's chancellor, wrote to Stevens, his father-in-law, on December 8 that he was "very glad to hear the choice your county has made of members for the Convention, and hope from the general complexion of your state that you will have the honor of being the first in acceding to the new Constitution."[21] He did not know that Delaware had become "The First State" the previous day, but New Jersey's actions would still be closely watched.

Brearley was the only member of New Jersey's delegation to the Constitutional Convention elected to serve as a delegate to the state ratification convention. The thirty-nine delegates

> ... were almost without exception 'early Whigs' who had held either civil or military offices during the Revolution and who occupied positions of respect in their local communities. Almost all of them had been active in the militia, on revolutionary committees, or in the Provincial Congresses ... Nine had helped draft the state constitution in 1776, fifteen had been in the Assembly, eleven had been councilors, and seven had served in the Continental Congress.[22]

Only sixteen delegates — less than half — had no legislative experience, although Cape May County was the only county to elect current legislators, Assemblyman Matthew Whilldin and Councillor Jeremiah Eldridge.[23]

The delegation included both of New Jersey's college presidents, four lawyers, four ministers, two doctors, and four from the iron industry, with most of the rest classified as farmers or landowners. Businessman John Neilson, who declined his appointment as one of the four original New Jersey delegates to the Philadelphia convention, was one of the wealthier delegates to the state Ratification Convention. But the wealthiest by far was John Stevens Sr., whose land was valued that year at £62,500 and whose New Jersey loan office certificates totaled more than £20,000.[24]

On Tuesday, December 11, the Ratification Convention met at the Blazing Star Tavern at the corner of King and Second streets (now Warren and State streets). The largest building in Trenton, the Blazing Star had been known as the French Arms Tavern when the Continental Congress met there in November 1784. At the time, the tavern's Long Room had been repapered, recarpeted and equipped with forty-eight new Windsor chairs and thirteen new tables covered with green cloth — the perfect number not only for the thirteen states, but also for the thirteen counties that would now be sending delegates to the Ratification Convention.[25]

The following day, the credentials of the thirty-eight delegates in attendance were certified — Dr. Samuel Dick, the Salem County surrogate, did not attend because of family illness.[26] Stevens, fittingly, was elected president of the Convention. First elected to the New Jersey Assembly in 1751, he had been one of the most prominent members of the colonial government to cast his lot with the Revolution. Stevens' son-in-law, Samuel Witham Stockton, who was not a delegate, was selected to serve as Convention secretary.

But while Stevens wielded the gavel, it was Brearley who was the dominant force during the nine-day convention.

On the second day, Brearley, Neilson and Jacob Hardenbergh of Somerset County were chosen to draw up rules for the governance of the Convention, which were presented to the delegates the following morning.[27] The fifteen "Rules for conducting business in the Convention of New Jersey" were straightforward:

1. The Convention shall be opened every morning with prayers.

2. When the President assumes the chair, the members shall take their seats.

3. The minutes of the preceding day shall be read, and, if necessary, may be corrected.

4. Every petition, memorial, letter, or other thing of the like kind read in the Convention shall be deemed as lying on the table for further consideration unless any special order be moved thereon.

5. A motion made and seconded shall be repeated by the President; a motion shall be reduced to writing if the President or any two members require it; a motion may be withdrawn by the member making it before any decision is had thereon.

6. A motion of postponement or amendment shall always be in order and considered as the previous question.

7. If a question under debate contains several points, any member may have it divided.

8. No member speaking shall be interrupted but by a call to order by the President or by a member through the President.

9. No member shall be referred to in debate by name.

10. Every member, when he chooses to speak, shall rise and address the President; when two members chance to rise at the same time, the President shall name the person who is to speak first.

11. Every member shall conduct himself with decency and decorum. The President himself or by request

*may call to order any member who shall transgress the rule; if the disorder be continued or repeated, the President may refer to him by name; the Convention may then examine and censure the member's conduct, he being allowed to extenuate or justify himself.*

12. *Every member shall be in his place at the time the Convention stands adjourned to, or within half an hour thereafter.*

13. *No member shall speak more than once in a debate until every member who chooses shall have spoken on the same.*

14. *The "yeas" and "nays" may be called and entered on the minutes when any two members require it.*

15. *A motion to adjourn may be made at any time and shall always be in order. The question thereon shall be put without any debate.*[28]

The Pennsylvania Convention earlier that month had rejected delegate Benjamin Rush's effort to open its proceedings with prayers, but the New Jersey delegates had no objection.[29] In fact, the Reverend James Francis Armstrong, pastor of the Presbyterian Church, was asked to open each day's proceedings with prayers even before the Brearley rules calling for morning prayers could be discussed.

In addition to the rules of procedure, the delegates approved motions calling for the Convention to meet from ten in the morning until three o'clock daily, and for the Constitution to be read, discussed and voted upon section by section, with a final vote to be taken at the end on the general question: "Whether the Convention, in the name and in behalf of the people of this state, do ratify and confirm the said Constitution?"

For the next three meeting days, Friday, December 14,

Saturday, December 15, and Monday, December 17, the delegates "proceeded to consider and deliberate upon the said Constitution by sections," as Secretary Stockton's sparse Convention Proceedings reported.[30]

The apparent intentional confidentiality of the Ratification Convention's proceedings was in keeping with the secrecy of the Constitutional Convention in Philadelphia, whose debates only became public thirty years after the Convention when Secretary of State John Quincy Adams published Madison's extensive notes and other documents. No comparable notes have been found for the New Jersey Ratification Convention.

The *Trenton Mercury*, in its December 25 account of the convention proceedings, noted that: "Our correspondent observes that it must give every real friend of his country great pleasure, when he hears of the entire cordiality and unanimity which prevailed in the councils of our Honorable Convention."[31]

But the *New Jersey Journal* the next day carried a much different report: "A correspondent informs us that, notwithstanding the dispatch of the Convention, many supposed exceptions were agitated, but that the Honorable Judge (David) Brearley, with a perspicuity of argument and persuasive eloquence which carried conviction with it, bore down all opposition."[32]

"Unitas" commented in the *Trenton Mercury* of January 1, 1788, and the *Pennsylvania Mercury* of January 5 that:

> *The propriety of electing one or more members for the Convention of each state who had been in the Federal Convention must have struck every person of reflection. It must be supposed that men of equal abilities who had served in the General Convention of the United States would have superior advantages over those who had not, when we consider the various and*

extensive source of information which were opened by means of a delegation from TWELVE states. There the local interest of each state was held up to the view of the others, and, after being completely sifted, it settled down and mixed with the foundation of the general government of the whole Union. The prudence of the measure was apparent in our late Convention for this state [New Jersey], where objections to the proposed Constitution were made and enforced. Doubts and difficulties were raised, although ably combated; but many embarrassments would perhaps have remained in the minds of some of our representatives had not the necessary information been given with respect to the separate interests of the different states. The reasons which preponderated in that united representation to fix general principles, which were, in a certain degree, accommodated to all the states; and the necessity of yielding up local and partial rights and privileges in order to frame the plan and system of federal liberty.

This state is therefore obliged to the county of Hunterdon for furnishing such information through an honorable member (David Brearley), who served in the General Convention held at Philadelphia, and which cleared up the doubts in many minds to the entire satisfaction of those who heard him. I have noticed in the returns of those states who have already finished their elections for the state conventions that they have almost invariably followed the same rule, and which, I am confident, will be attended with good consequences.[33]

In fact, each of the twelve states represented in Philadelphia elected at least one delegate to its state ratification convention[34]

On Tuesday morning, December 18, after three days of

section-by-section deliberations, the Convention moved on to consideration of the overall document. "Several well-connected, sensible, and learned speeches were made on the subject in which a general review was taken of all the different articles in their relation to each other," the *Trenton Mercury* reported of that morning's proceedings.[35] Following the speeches, the Convention voted unanimously to ratify the new Constitution.

Brearley was then appointed to chair the committee "for drawing up the Form of the Ratification of the proposed Constitution, on the part of the state." The blue-ribbon panel also included the Reverend John Witherspoon, president of The College of New Jersey and a signer of the Declaration of Independence; John Beatty, who had worried two years earlier as a member of the Confederation Congress that New Jersey's defiance of Congress' requisition might tear the union apart; John Neilson, one of the New Jersey investors in Alexander Hamilton's Society for Useful Manufacture, which would found an industrial city named after Brearley's Convention colleague, William Paterson; and Andrew Hunter of Gloucester County. The Convention then adjourned for the afternoon to give the Brearley committee time to work.

When the Convention reconvened at six o'clock, Brearley reported that the committee had drafted a simple, but eloquent, Form of Ratification that included not only the provisions of the new Constitution, but also the congressional resolution of September 27 transmitting the Constitution to the states for ratification, the New Jersey Legislature's October 29 resolutions, and the November 1 law authorizing the state Convention. The Form concluded by emphasizing the democratic basis for the Convention's authority:

> Now be it known that we, the Delegates of the State
> of New Jersey, chosen by the People thereof for the

*purposes aforesaid having maturely deliberated on and considered the aforesaid proposed Constitution, do hereby for and on behalf of the People of the said State of New Jersey, agree to, ratify and confirm the same and every part thereof.*

*Done in Convention, by the unanimous consent of the members present, this eighteenth day of December in the Year of our Lord One Thousand Seven Hundred and Eighty-Seven, and of the Independence of the United States of America the twelfth. In witness whereof we have hereunto subscribed our names.*[36]

On Wednesday morning, December 19, Secretary Stockton laid out two copies of the Federal Constitution and the Form for Ratification, engrossed on parchment, for the delegates' signatures. For the second time in three months, David Brearley signed his name in neat script on official documents authorizing the Constitution on which he had worked so hard.[37]

The Convention then voted to march in procession to the Hunterdon County Courthouse in Trenton, where Brearley had spent so many hours, to read the Form of the Ratification to the residents of the city. As the *Trenton Mercury* reported,

*The Convention accordingly at one o'clock went in procession from the place of their sitting to the courthouse, preceded by Captain [Bernard] O'Hanlon's well-disciplined light infantry company, completely uniformed and accoutred, and joined by the judges of the supreme and inferior courts, and other magistrates, the attorney general, and the gentlemen of the town and vicinity; where, after proclamation made, the Ratification of the new Constitution was read by the secretary amidst the acclamations and huzzas of the people. After which, fifteen rounds were fired by Captain Hanlon's company, thirteen of which were for the United States of America, and a volunteer for each of the states of Delaware and Pennsylvania, they being the only states which, with this state, have as yet ratified the new Federal Constitution.*[38]

The *Pennsylvania Mercury*, in its report of the proceedings, noted wryly:

*It was observed by a spectator on Wednesday that the third line of fire given by the light infantry, which was a broken one, surprised him, being so badly executed by so complete and well-disciplined a body of men. O, sir (replied the officer), the design was to represent the shattered condition of the State of Rhode Island.*[39]

Rhode Island was the only state that did not send any delegates to the Constitutional Convention in Philadelphia and was widely expected to be the last state to ratify.

The Convention marched back to the Blazing Star in the same order in which it had marched to the courthouse and reconvened at six that evening. Stockton was directed to deliver the duplicate copy of the Form of the Ratification to Governor Livingston, and Brearley and George Anderson of Burlington County were appointed as a committee to review and revise the minutes of the Convention.[40]

When the Convention convened for the last time on the morning of Thursday, December 20, the delegates voted to recommend "that the State of New Jersey should offer a cession to Congress of a district, not exceeding ten miles square, for the seat of the government of the United States over which they may exercise exclusive legislation." The Legislature would follow up on this resolution with an act approved September 9, 1788, making such an offer, but New Jersey's hopes that Trenton would be the nation's capital would be sacrificed in a Madison-Hamilton legislative swap. The Convention also voted to authorize expenses to be paid by the state, including:

> To Samuel-Witham Stockton ... fourteen shillings per day for each day he shall have attended during the sitting of the Convention, and the sum of four pence per sheet, reckoning ninety words to the sheet, for entering the Minutes of the proceedings of the Convention fair in the Journals ...
>
> To Francis Witt, for the use of a room and for firewood during the sitting of the Convention, the sume of four pounds two shillings.
>
> To William Rogers, for his attendance as doorkeeper to the Convention, the sum of two pounds ten shillings.[41]

Stevens expressed his thanks to his fellow delegates for the honor of electing him president of the convention and invited the delegates to join him at Joseph Vandergrift's Tavern for dinner.

"After dinner," the *Trenton Mercury* reported, "the following toasts were drank" by the assembled delegates and guests:

1. The new Constitution.
2. The United States in Congress.
3. The President and members of the late Federal Convention.
4. The Governor and State of New Jersey.
5. The states of Delaware and Pennsylvania.

6. May the independence of the Union, reared on the basis of the new Constitution, be perpetual.

7. The princes and states in alliance with the United States.

8. May the interest of each state be ever deemed the interest of each state.

9. Religion, learning, agriculture, arts, manufactures, and commerce, in harmony and mutual subserviency to each other.

10. The memory and posterity of those who have fallen in the late war.

11. May the gratitude of the American Citizens be equal to the value and patriotism of the American Soldiery.

12. The daughters of America.

13. May the United States be the asylum of invaded liberty.

Volunteer: May the American drums soon beat reveille to the dawn of the new government and tattoo to anarchy and confusion.

Ditto: Universal liberty, justice and peace.[42]

Similar celebrations prevailed elsewhere in the state. The *Pennsylvania Mercury* reported that upon the return of one of the Burlington County delegates on December 22, the citizens of Burlington gathered at the courthouse to hear the Form of the Ratification of the Federal Constitution, as adopted by the state convention, read aloud. As in Trenton:

Thirteen cannon were fired for the United States, besides one for the State of Delaware and one for the State of Pennsylvania, which preceded us in this important business. A number of the persons present then adjourned to the house of Colonel [Oakey] Hoagland, where all parties joined in mutual congratulations on the occasion and in wishing success to a system of government which, by its principles of union and public justice, lays a solid foundation for the happiness of our wide-extended empire, and for a grandeur and national importance which will gain respect and secure us peace with all the world.[43]

New Jersey's unanimous ratification, in comparison to Pennsylvania's bitter convention and 46-23 ratification vote, was cited repeatedly by proponents of the new Constitution as evidence of its value. The *Pennsylvania Packet*, in a December 21 item that was reprinted thirty-one times throughout the country over the next two months, stated:

A correspondent hopes that the unanimous ratification of the federal government, by the State of New Jersey, will satisfy the friends of the minority in Pennsylvania that there is no despotism in the new Constitution. The yeomanry of New Jersey love liberty. Nearly every field in that state has been dyed with the blood of its militia, shed in the cause of freedom, and nearly every farm in the state has been plundered by the British army during the late war. Certainly a people who have sacrificed so much for liberty could not have surrendered it by an unanimous vote. No commercial influence, no terror of an applauding gallery, no legal sophistry had any weight in the Convention of that patriotic state in producing the ratification. The men who pretend to love liberty more than the citizens of New Jersey must show that they have done half as much in its defense before they can be believed.[44]

The *Massachusetts Centinel*, which carried the *Packet* commentary on January 2, 1788, under the title, "A SCRAP–Worthy to be Written in Letters of Gold," noted on January 5 that the New Jersey delegation consisted of "accomplished civilians, able judges, experienced generals, and honest farmers."[45]

Governor Livingston notified his fellow governors of New Jersey's ratification by letter in early January,[46] while responsibility for official notification of Congress, which was meeting in New York City, fell upon Stevens, as president of the convention. Stockton, the state convention's secretary, sent him copies of the *Trenton Mercury* from December 18 and December 25. Stockton was not above altering the official minutes:

> I remember, after your answer to the resolution of thanks which was read to you in Convention, you asked me, in a whisper, if your compliment to the Convention "of never having known an instance of such good order," etc., did not too strongly imply a reflection on all the other public bodies you had been in. I have therefore, as you will see, qualified it a little in the publication which I sent to the printer, by saying, you had "known but few instances in public bodies," etc., which alteration I hope will be agreeable to you.[47]

Representatives of only four states were present, however, in late December, and it was not until February 1 that he was able to present New Jersey's ratification to the assembled Congress. Cyrus Griffin, president of Congress, told Stevens he thought New Jersey's Form of the Ratification "the most ample of any that had been delivered to Congress and, in particular, the Convention reciting the powers by which they were convened," Stevens reported in a letter to Brearley.[48]

New Jersey's Form of the Ratification was one of five delivered to Congress that day. In addition to Delaware and

Pennsylvania, Georgia had ratified January 2 and Connecticut on January 9.

However, New Jersey, Delaware and Georgia would prove to be the only states to ratify the Constitution unanimously, reflecting the understanding of the smaller states that they had fared well with the Great Compromise preserving equality of votes in the Senate and the extra weight given to them in the electoral college.

Ratification of the new Constitution was by no means assured, Brearley and Stevens knew. While months of deliberation and compromise led all but three delegates to the Constitutional Convention to sign the document, those who refused to do so included Edmund Randolph of Virginia, one of the driving forces both in the creation of the Convention and in the development of the Virginia Plan, and fellow Virginian George Mason. Elbridge Gerry of Massachusetts would lead the anti-Federalist opposition in his state. New York's two anti-Federalists had gone home, leaving Alexander Hamilton alone and New York without a vote on the final two months of amendments.

While ratification by nine states was required, it was understood that rejection by any of the four large states — Massachusetts, New York, Pennsylvania or Virginia — would effectively defeat the plan.

On February 7, Massachusetts, still reeling in the aftermath of Shays Rebellion, ratified by a narrow 187-168 vote, but only after John Hancock came up with the idea of adding a series of suggested amendments to the document to assuage delegate fears that the new Constitution would take away individual rights.

It was not until April 28 that Maryland followed by a 63-11 vote. South Carolina ratified, 149 to 73, on May 23. Ironically, it was New Hampshire, whose delegates almost didn't make it to Philadelphia for the Convention, that provided the ninth — and conclusive — vote ensuring that the new form of government would be adopted. New Hampshire originally had been scheduled to meet in convention on February 13, the week after Massachusetts' ratification, but so many delegates had been elected with binding instructions to vote against the new Constitution that leading Federalists sought and won a postponement to June. On June 21, New Hampshire voted 57-47 for ratification, following Massachusetts' lead in suggesting twelve amendments.[49]

Brearley, Livingston, and other New Jersey leaders learned of New Hampshire's action and Virginia's subsequent June 26 ratification by a narrow 89-79 vote in time to celebrate together on July 4, the nation's twelfth Independence Day. Brearley and the Order of the Cincinnati, the *New Jersey Journal* reported,

> ... convened in Elizabeth Town for their annual meeting, listened to a sermon by the Reverend Mr. Austin on the appropriate text, "The Lord reigneth, let the earth rejoice," saw Governor Livingston review a "handsome legionary corps" under the command of General Ogden, and then convened at the convivial board to toast the union.[50]

Livingston's desire to see his native state "a little sickish of their opposition" was satisfied three weeks later when New York ratified the Constitution by a narrow 30-27 vote. As with Virginia, the New York delegates, when faced with a choice of "Union or no Union," chose to remain part of the new federal system. It was not until November 21 that North Carolina ratified the Constitution, 194-77, and recalcitrant Rhode Island waited until the following May — two months after George Washington took the oath of office as the first president by a vote of the electoral college that he and Brearley and their fellow delegates had created.

For Livingston, Paterson, and Brearley, their satisfaction was complete. Livingston, as he wrote in a February 7, 1787, letter to Elijah Clark, had regarded the nation to be "in eminent danger of lossing the great & important blessings to be expected" from independence for "want of an efficient national Government.... But from the Constitution now adopted, we have reason to hope for the reestablishment of public faith & private credit, of being respected abroad & revered at home."[51] In his August 29, 1788, message to the Legislature, Livingston reflected with pride on New Jersey's role in the approval of the new Constitution:

> It affords me great pleasure that New Jersey has the honour of so early and so unanimously agreeing to that form of national Government which has been so generally approved of by the other States. We are now arrived at that auspicious Era, which, I confess, I have most earnestly wished to see. Thanks to God that I have lived to see it.[52]

Years later, writing essays under the pseudonym "Aurelius," Paterson would note the "wonderful change" brought about by the new federal government. "Money became plentiful, confidence was restored, and credit placed on its proper basis; for contracts were rendered sacred by the constitution, and paper-money was forever interdicted."[53]

As for Brearley, the chief justice commented at the July 4 Society of the Cincinnati celebration that through the new Constitution, he could foresee "the honor of the union vindicated, and America, from her reproach among the nations, rise into an empire of strength, beauty, and wide-extended renown."[54]

# CHAPTER ELEVEN

# The First Electoral College

## A Final Duty, A Death 'Much Regretted'

*"Dear Sir: I have the pleasure to inform you that I have so much recovered as to be able to ride. I shall therefore set out for Brunswick on Monday next, and hope that I shall not be the occasion of any further delay to the operations of the district court.."*

— David Brearley to W. Dayton, December 17, 1789[1]

With the new Constitution ratified by the required number of states, the electoral college and the office of the vice-presidency — the "ingenious" mechanisms that Brearley's Committee on Postponed Matters had created to select a president — would now be put to the test.

Eleven states, all except for North Carolina and Rhode Island, had approved the new Constitution when Congress met on September 13, 1788, and adopted a resolution directing each ratifying state to appoint members of the first electoral college on the first Wednesday in January 1789. The electors were to assemble in their respective states on the first Wednesday in February 1789 to vote for the first president and vice president. Congress would then commence proceedings under the new federal government system on March 4, 1789.[2]

Livingston had trusted Brearley to guide the new Constitution through New Jersey's Ratification Convention, and the chief justice had won wide acclaim for his political deftness in guiding the document through with a unanimous vote. Therefore, it came as no surprise when Livingston and the Legislature turned to Brearley again to lead New Jersey's delegation to the electoral college that he had helped to create.

On January 13, 1789, Livingston issued the following proclamation:

> BE IT MADE KNOWN, That on this day, the honorable DAVID BREARLEY, JAMES KINSEY, JOHN NEILSON, DAVID MOORE, JOHN RUTHERFORD, and MATTHIAS OGDEN, Esquires, were duly appointed by the Governor and Council of this state, according to an act of the Legislature thereof, Electors on behalf of this state, for the purpose of choosing a President and Vice-President of the United States, agreeably to the Constitution of the said United States.[3]

For Brearley, it would be a welcome reunion with his former commander, Matthias Ogden. Neilson, who had been one of New Jersey's four original appointees to the Constitutional Convention before declining the duty, had served with Brearley at New Jersey's Ratification Convention.

There was no question that Washington would be elected president, possibly unanimously, and John Adams was the favorite for the vice-presidency, although Alexander Hamilton was publicly urging some electors to withhold their votes from Adams in order to ensure that he did not end up tied with Washington. This was an eventuality that the delegates to the Constitutional Convention had not really considered in their preoccupation with the possibility that no candidate would get a majority and that the selection would invariably be thrown into the House of Representatives.[4]

On February 4, the electors from New Jersey and eleven other states — Rhode Island would not ratify the Constitution for another two months — gathered in their respective capitals to cast two votes each for the leaders of the new executive branch. Brearley and his fellow electors cast their ballots in secret; no one would know the results of the election until Congress counted the votes.

Congress convened in New York on March 4, 1789, but it was not until April 1 and April 6 that quorums were achieved in the House and Senate, respectively. The first order of business on April 6 was to count the ballots from the electoral college. As expected, Washington was named on every ballot and elected unanimously, and Adams was elected vice-president. Adams received thirty-four votes, just one vote shy of a majority of the sixty-nine electors, but his plurality far outdistanced the nine votes received by John Jay, the New York diplomat who had been serving as secretary of foreign affairs in the weak Articles of Confederation government.[5]

Jay's nine votes included five of the six from New Jersey and all three from Delaware — the two states whose delegations had made common cause in pushing the "New Jersey Plan" at the Constitutional Convention to ensure that the interests of the small states would not be drowned out. Adams received the sixth New Jersey vote. While Brearley left no record of his vote, it is most likely that he exercised his influence to lead New Jersey's delegation in support of Jay. If Brearley had supported Adams, it is difficult to believe that he would have been unable to persuade any of his fellow New Jersey electors to join his position.

The other candidates received six or fewer votes each, but the fears voiced by so many Constitutional Convention delegates about electors voting for "favorite sons" from their own states proved to be somewhat well-founded in this first election. Adams received all ten electoral votes from Massachusetts, Robert N. Harrison all six of Maryland's votes, and John Rutledge six out of seven votes from South Carolina.[6]

Adams was to assume his duties as vice-president on April 21, and Washington was to be inaugurated as president on April 30, 1789. Washington's trip from Mount Vernon to New York turned into a triumphal procession, as he was greeted by crowds and feted with dinners in Alexandria, Virginia; Baltimore; Chester, Pennsylvania, and Philadelphia. On April 21, he was ferried across the Delaware River — about nine miles south from the location of his famous Christmas 1776 crossing — to Trenton, where Brearley and Livingston were among the official welcoming committee.[7] At the bridge over the Assunpink Creek, where Washington's troops had fought the Second Battle of Trenton on January 2, 1777, Washington passed under an arch of laurels and flowers that bore the inscription, "The Defender of the Mothers Will Be the Protector of the Daughters." He spent the following night in Princeton with the Reverend John Witherspoon, whose son had died fighting with Brearley's New Jersey Brigade at the Battle of Germantown, before traveling on to New York to deliver his Inaugural Address.[8]

The new Congress already had begun work on legislation that would create a new federal government according to the strictures set forth under the new Constitution. The Constitution established a strong Supreme Court, but left the size, jurisdiction, and powers of lower federal courts up to Congress, which delegated the task to a six-member Senate Judicial Committee. Paterson and Oliver Ellsworth of Connecticut, the former Princeton schoolmates who had worked together so closely as delegates to the Constitutional Convention, quickly emerged as the leading proponents of a strong federal court system.[9]

While Senator William Maclay of Pennsylvania wanted to preserve the supremacy of state courts by restricting the new federal courts to admiralty and maritime cases, Ellsworth and Paterson succeeding in pushing through legislation that created a strong system of federal courts with the power to decide all cases brought under federal law.

The Judiciary Act adopted that summer created a Supreme Court with a chief justice and five associate justices, and thirteen federal district courts, each with its own judge, district attorney, and federal marshal. The thirteen states were divided into three circuit courts to handle equity cases involving more than $500, disputes involving foreign nationals, cases involving citizens from more than one state, and appeals from district court rulings. Two Supreme Court justices and a district court judge would make up each circuit court panel.[10]

For Washington, the staffing of the executive and judicial branches offered an opportunity not only to create a government comprised of men of high character and talent, but one whose appointments would instill a confidence in the new national government that the Confederation government so sorely lacked. He and Vice President Adams were inundated with letters from job seekers and their supporters.

General Elias Dayton, with whom Brearley served in the New Jersey Brigade, wrote to Washington on August 17 strongly endorsing Brearley for appointment as New Jersey's first federal district court judge:

*You, sir, I presume, were not unacquainted with him during his services in the late war – The reputation which he brought with him into the army – the very great propriety & manliness of his conduct when in it – and the credit with which he retired from the service in obedience to the pressing calls of his state, to preside over the administration of justice therein, are facts, of which you, sir, in all probability are not ignorant. His uniform, firm & avowed attachment to the cause of his country strongly manifested by the manly & decisive part which he acted from the earliest stages of the revolution to its final accomplishment, is not unknown & should not be unnoticed.*

*For the last nine years, during which time he has officiated in the quality of Chief Justice, he has discharged the duties thereof with approved ability & to very general satisfaction. I may say in short, that, I believe, there is no one to whom the people of this district or state will so naturally look, or whom they will so earnestly wish, to be honored by the President with the appointment in question.[11]*

Brearley clearly wanted to be New Jersey's first district court judge, and by all standards was clearly entitled to the post, not only because of his superior credentials as New Jersey's Supreme Court chief justice for ten years, but also because of the major contributions he made to the Constitutional Convention and New Jersey's ratification. His close ally, Paterson, who would vote on Washington's nominations in the Senate, wanted Brearley to have the post,[12] and Washington, who undoubtedly consulted with Paterson on the appointment, was favorably disposed toward men like Brearley who had served in the Continental Army in the bleak winters before the French arrived.

But Brearley was worried. James Kinsey, who was a close friend of Elisha Boudinot, an influential Elizabethtown lawyer, also was lobbying for the appointment, and had reportedly promised the clerkship to Boudinot if he won it. Like Brearley, Kinsey also had served as a presidential elector, although his political career had suffered a setback in 1778 when he had declined to sign the loyalty oath that Brearley and the officers of the New Jersey Brigade had signed at Valley Forge. Nevertheless, Brearley wrote to Jonathan Dayton, his fellow delegate on September 24, "I think it is not impossible that he [Kinsey] will succeed."[13]

By the time Brearley's letter arrived, however, the issue was moot. One day after Brearley put his fears to paper, President Washington, exercising the power of nomination given to him by Brearley's Committee on Postponed Matters, submitted to the "Gentlemen of the Senate" a one-page "Nomination of Judge Attorneys and Marshalls for the districts of New York and New Jersey, of the Secretary of State, Attorney General of the United States and Post-Master General."

David Brearley was nominated as the first federal judge for the District of New Jersey, with Richard Stockton Jr., son of the late signer of the Declaration, as the state's first United States attorney, and Thomas Lowry, an Irish-born merchant who supervised quartermaster duties as a colonel in the New Jersey militia, as the state's first marshal.

Ironically, Brearley's chief adversary in the Constitutional Convention, Edmund Randolph, was nominated as Washington's first attorney general. The most notable name on the list was the selection of Thomas Jefferson as secretary of state.[14]

Brearley resigned his post as chief justice on November 20, 1789 and was succeeded, ironically, by James Kinsey, his erstwhile rival for the district court judgeship.[15] Brearley chose Jonathan Dayton, his young colleague at the Constitutional

Convention, as the district court's first clerk; Houston, who would undoubtedly have been his first choice, had died the previous year.[16]

As federal judge, Brearley continued to take the same wide-ranging interest in public affairs that he had as chief justice of the Supreme Court.

When the newly elected New Jersey Legislature locked in debate for more than a month to decide what to do about the state's paper money crisis in the wake of the new federal Constitution, Brearley took a particular interest. "Every Statesman, every Lawyer, every man of information and reflection, must now be sensible that the Tender for more than the real and current value of the bills, can no longer be supported," Brearley wrote to Jonathan Dayton, a member of the Legislature's Council. He added his judgment that the federal courts, of which he was now New Jersey's first judge, would be "against the Tender for the nominal value."[17]

But Brearley was not well. "A severe illness has confined me to my room nearly three months," he wrote.[18] Brearley's illness delayed the opening of the Federal District Court for New Jersey, and he was still sick when he wrote to his friend, the "Honble" W. Dayton, on December 17, 1789, from Trenton:

> Dear Sir:
>
> I have the pleasure to inform you that I have so much recovered as to be able to ride. I shall therefore set out for Brunswick on Monday next, and hope that I shall not be the occasion of any further delay to the operations of the district court.
>
> I am most respectfully,
> dear Sir,
> your obedient humble servant
> David Brearley[19]

Brearley made it to New Brunswick to preside over the first session of the United States District Court for the District of New Jersey on December 22, 1789,[20] then returned home for Christmas. In a January 11 letter to a creditor, he described himself as still "recovering" from his long illness.[21]

A few months later, on April 2, 1790, Brearley joined U.S. Supreme Court Justice James C. Wilson, with whom he had sparred so often during the Constitutional Convention two years before, in opening the first session of the Circuit Court for the District of New Jersey in Trenton. The "suitable charge" that Wilson delivered to a "respectable Grand Jury" has not been found, and the court adjourned after a one-day session.[22]

In early August 1790, while presiding over his fifth District Court session, Brearley decided the first case argued by the United States Attorney for the District of New Jersey. Henry Guest had petitioned for relief from paying the customs duties on shoes and leather transported on a ship captained by Edward Yard. Richard Stockton, the United States attorney, contended that the district court did not have jurisdiction over the claim. Brearley agreed and dismissed the case.[23] The modest decision would be the ailing Brearley's last ruling.

Less than two weeks later, on August 16, David Brearley died in Trenton. He was just forty-five years old.

Brearley was buried with full military and Masonic honors in St. Michael's Episcopal churchyard in Trenton after a funeral "attended by the largest and most respectable collection of Masons and Citizens ever known on the like occasion", the *Burlington Advertiser* reported. An obituary in the newspaper, which failed to reveal the cause of death, read: "Ever remarkable for gentleness of manner, humanity and probity, he conciliated the affection, friendship, and confidence of all who knew him. The unavailing sorrow of his widow and seven children, and the sighs of his friends and neighbors, particularly the poor, will remain the best and most lasting monuments of his character in private life."[24]

Brearley's tombstone in the St. Michael's graveyard reads:

> Sacred to the memory of Hon. David Brearley, Trenton, and Colonel in the army of the United States, a member of the state and federal conventions, nine years Chief Justice of New Jersey. As a soldier, he was cool, determined and brave; as a judge, intelligent and upright, as a citizen, an early decided and faithful patriot; in private and social life, irreproachable. He died much regretted, 16th Aug. 1790, in the 45th year of his age.[25]

In 1924, more than a century and a third after his death, the Grand Lodge of the Masonic Order of New Jersey marked his grave with a granite slab, which reads:

> In Memory of David Brearley, First Worshipful Grand Master of Masons in New Jersey. Born June 11, 1745. Died August 16, 1790. Practiced law in Allentown, New Jersey. Lieutenant-colonel in the U.S. Army during the War of the Revolution. Member of the first State and Federal Constitutional Conventions. Chief Justice of the Supreme Court of New Jersey.
>
> An ardent patriot; brave soldier; upright judge; and beloved Mason.[26]

A month after Brearley's death, the Honorable Elisha Lawrence affixed the Prerogative Seal of the State of New Jersey to an official document stating that Brearley's last will and testament had been proved before Surrogate Richard Throckmorton and that trustees Joseph Brearley, James Mott, and Joseph Bloomfield were authorized to dispose of all assets.[27] The will, dated August 13, 1790 — just three days before his death — left the following:

> Son, William, £5. Wife, Elizabeth, 1/2 of the real and personal estate. Son, Joseph, my small sword. Son, David, my Scotch pistols, inlaid with silver. Daughters, Elizabeth Brearley and Esther Brearley, and my sons, Joseph, David and George, rest of estate. Real and personal estate to be sold. Brother-in-law, Joseph Higbee, to be Guardian of my sons. Executors — brother, Joseph, and my friends, James Mott and Joseph Bloomfield. Witnesses — Aaron Dunham, George Woodruff, Ephraim Olden.[28]

The September 18 inventory by James Ewing and Charles Axford valued the estate at £1,350.12.8 Listed were "3 muskets and 2 bayonets, surveyor's compass, library, McMurray's York Town map." They also found: "One month and 16 days pay due the Testator at the time of his decease, as Judge, £ 47.18.4"

It was not a lot of money, and Brearley, whose personal correspondence is filled with letters from creditors demanding payment, left many unpaid bills. His widow, Elizabeth, and children moved in with her father, Joseph Higbee, who served as the children's guardian until they reached adulthood. The house was rented to Elias Boudinot, and Brearley's extensive library of 532 volumes, mostly on law, history, and politics, was sold to friends, lawyers, and political leaders for more than £250 to raise money.[29]

Breaeley's estranged oldest son, William, heard about his £5 bequest while on shore leave in Worcester, Massachusetts, and made arrangements to collect the money. Years afterward, his half-brother, George, saw William, now crippled by a fall from a mast, while their ships were exchanging papers at sea, but he did not identify himself. Of Brearley's three daughters by his first marriage, Elizabeth and Mary both married and each had two sons, while Hettie died unmarried. One of Elizabeth's sons, Edward Potts, served in the Louisiana Legislature.

David Brearley, the oldest son of Brearley and Elizabeth Higbee, held his father's membership in the Society of the Cincinnati until his death in Alabama in 1820. His two brothers, George and Joseph, both died young and unmarried.[30]

As for Harriett Luttrell, she went off in search of her father, Henry Lawes Luttrell, now the Earl of Carhampton, as soon as her husband, James Rogers, died in 1790. Headstrong like her mother, Elizabeth Mullen, Harriett survived a shipwreck off the Irish coast in 1791, and finally met her father at the ancestral estate in Luttrells town near Dublin. He embraced the daughter he had fathered out of wedlock:

> Harriet was the guest of her father at his elegant estate at Paine's Hill, Surrey , England. She was the recipient of many substantial marks of his favor, and continued during her life to be the object of his warm affection and solicitous care, being his only offspring. He settled upon her a considerable estate.... That this was her chief object in life is plainly shown by the inscription on her gravestone, which totally ignored both of her husbands and gives prominence only to the fact of her birth. It reads as follows: "Sacred to the memory of Harriet Luttrell, daughter of Henry Lawes Luttrell, Earl of Carhampton. Died January 2nd, 1819 in her 59th year."

The gravestone in Bordentown does not mention her mother or the stepfather who raised her, David Brearley.[31]

# The Legacy of David Brearley

## Shaping the Federal System

*"... the honor of the union vindicated, and America, from her reproach among the nations, rise into an empire of strength, beauty, and wide-extended renown."*

— David Brearley, at ceremony
marking the ratification of the Constitution

When David Brearley died at the age of forty-five, he was arguably second only to William Paterson in prominence, respect, and connections among New Jersey Federalists. Governor Livingston's death one month before Brearley's cleared the way for Paterson's election as New Jersey's second governor since independence. Brearley was already in ill health and would not have been considered for the post. William Paterson, who was the same age as Brearley, would go on to serve four years as governor and twelve years as associate justice of the

United States Supreme Court before his death in 1806 at the age of sixty-one.

During Paterson's tenure on the court, Richard Howell, who served as a major with Brearley in the New Jersey Brigade, and Joseph Bloomfield, Brearley's lawyer friend and executor of his estate, served as Governor. Aaron Ogden, who served under Brearley in the First Regiment, was elected New Jersey's fifth governor a few years after Paterson's death.

Had he lived, Brearley, not Howell, would most likely have been in line to succeed Paterson as governor, unless, of course, his service on the Federal District Court put him in contention for the U.S. Supreme Court judgeship that went to Paterson. Washington's personal relationship with Brearley was stronger than his tie to Paterson.

Brearley would have relished the opportunity that his ascension to the governorship, the Supreme Court or even a long career on the Federal District Court would have given him to further shape the new federal republic he had helped to create. It also would have assured preservation of more of his personal papers, which would have aided historians — many of whom concluded that he had left too little documentary evidence to support a full biography.

But Brearley's legacy, even in a short forty-five years, is substantial.

Brearley's courageous decision as a first-year New Jersey Supreme Court chief justice in *Holmes v. Walton* elevated the importance of the judicial branch of government by insisting upon the power of judges to overturn laws they deemed unconstitutional. The principle underlying Brearley's groundbreaking 1780 ruling was already accepted as an integral part of the checks and balances in the American system of government when the delegates to the Constitutional Convention gathered in Philadelphia in 1787.

Together, Brearley and Paterson, through their determined opposition to the Virginia Plan, did more than any other two delegates to ensure that the new nation would be a federal system, with states represented as equals in the Senate and the people represented equally in the House of Representatives.

When the convention seemed on the brink of collapse, Brearley exercised critical leadership as chairman of the Committee on Postponed Matters. Brearley's committee strengthened the presidency, invented the vice-presidency, enhanced the independence of the judiciary, and created the electoral college, the "ingenious mechanism" that has shaped American politics for more than two centuries.

Brearley personally steered the Constitution through the New Jersey ratification convention by a unanimous vote that was critical in the wake of Pennsylvania's bitter ratification convention and was widely cited by proponents as the new Constitution slowly won approval, state by state.

Born a "son of treason," David Brearley soldiered on the battlefields of New Jersey and Pennsylvania, then dedicated his judicial and political career to creating a governmental system that would protect the personal freedoms for which he and his father had fought so ardently.

Two hundred and fifteen years later, his legacy survives.

# The Road To The Constitution:

## A Documentary History

## A. The Articles of Confederation

*The Articles of Confederation — which were approved by Congress in 1777 and took effect in after ratification by Maryland in 1781 — provided the most important intellectual and political context for the Constitutional Convention in 1787. The Articles of Confederation provided for an equality of states in a Congress of one house, in which states could be represented by two to seven delegates, but each state delegation would have a single vote (Article V). While most major decisions by Congress required the approval of nine states (Articles IX and X), amendment of the Articles of Confederation required the approval of Congress and all 13 state legislatures (Article XIII), which enabled Rhode Island to block a plan to impose a critically needed tariff that was supported by every other state. Taxes were to be levied on the basis of the estimated property value in each state, but it was left up to state legislatures to raise the levy (Article VIII). New Jersey's refusal to raise its assigned levy in 1785 led directly to the Annapolis Convention, and thus to the Constitutional Convention. The Articles of Confederation provided for no executive* branch and no  federal courts except for admiralty cases (Article IX). Disputes between states were to be decided by multi-state tribunals, such as the one chaired by David Brearley that decided a land dispute between Pennsylvania and Connecticut (Article IX). Excerpts from the Articles of Confederation follow; the full Articles can be found on-line through the Avalon Project at Yale Law School.[1]

Articles of Confederation and perpetual Union between the states of New Hampshire, Massachusetts-bay Rhode Island and Providence Plantations, Connecticut, New York, New Jersey, Pennsylvania, Delaware, Maryland, Virginia, North Carolina, South Carolina and Georgia.

I.   The Stile of this Confederacy shall be "The United States of America".

II.  Each state retains its sovereignty, freedom, and independence, and every power, jurisdiction, and right, which is not by this Confederation expressly delegated to the United States, in Congress assembled.

III. The said States hereby severally enter into a firm league of friendship with each other, for their common defense, the security of their liberties, and their mutual and general welfare, binding themselves to assist each other, against all force offered to, or attacks made upon them, or any of them, on account of religion, sovereignty, trade, or any other pretense whatever.

IV.  The better to secure and perpetuate mutual friendship and intercourse among the people of the different States in this Union, the free inhabitants of each of these States, paupers, vagabonds, and fugitives from justice excepted, shall be entitled to all privileges and immunities of free citizens in the several States; and the people of each State shall free ingress and regress to and from any other State, and shall enjoy therein all the privileges of trade and commerce, subject to the same duties, impositions, and restrictions as the inhabitants thereof respectively, provided that such restrictions shall not extend so far as to prevent the removal of property imported into any State, to any other State, of which the owner is an inhabitant; provided also that no imposition, duties or restriction shall be laid by any State, on the property of the United States, or either of them.

If any person guilty of, or charged with, treason, felony, or other high misdemeanor in any State, shall flee from justice, and be found in any of the United States, he shall, upon demand of the Governor or executive power of the State from which he fled, be delivered up and removed to the State having jurisdiction of his offense.

Full faith and credit shall be given in each of these States to the records, acts, and judicial proceedings of the courts and magistrates of every other State.

V.    For the most convenient management of the general interests of the United States, delegates shall be annually appointed in such manner as the legislatures of each State shall direct, to meet in Congress on the first Monday in November, in every year, with a power reserved to each State to recall its delegates, or any of them, at any time within the year, and to send others in their stead for the remainder of the year.

No State shall be represented in Congress by less than two, nor more than seven members; and no person shall be capable of being a delegate for more than three years in any term of six years; nor shall any person, being a delegate, be capable of holding any office under the United States, for which he, or another for his benefit, receives any salary, fees or emolument of any kind.

Each State shall maintain its own delegates in a meeting of the States, and while they act as members of the committee of the States.

In determining questions in the United States in Congress assembled, each State shall have one vote.

Freedom of speech and debate in Congress shall not be impeached or questioned in any court or place out of Congress, and the members of Congress shall be protected in their persons from arrests or imprisonments, during the time of their going to and from, and attendence on Congress, except for treason, felony, or breach of the peace.

VI.    ... No two or more States shall enter into any treaty, confederation or alliance whatever between them, without the consent of the United States in Congress assembled, specifying accurately the purposes for which the same is to be entered into, and how long it shall continue.

No State shall lay any imposts or duties, which may

interfere with any stipulations in treaties, entered into by the United States in Congress assembled, with any King, Prince or State ...

VII. When land forces are raised by any State for the common defense, all officers of or under the rank of colonel, shall be appointed by the legislature of each State respectively, by whom such forces shall be raised, or in such manner as such State shall direct, and all vacancies shall be filled up by the State which first made the appointment.

VIII. All charges of war, and all other expenses that shall be incurred for the common defense or general welfare, and allowed by the United States in Congress assembled, shall be defrayed out of a common treasury, which shall be supplied by the several States in    proportion to the value of all land within each State, granted or surveyed for any person, as such land and the buildings and improvements thereon shall be estimated according to such mode as the United States in Congress assembled, shall from time to time direct and appoint.

The taxes for paying that proportion shall be laid and levied by the authority and direction of the legislatures of the several States within the time agreed upon by the United States in Congress assembled.

IX. The United States in Congress assembled, shall have the sole and exclusive right and power of determining on peace and war, except in the cases mentioned in the sixth article — of sending and receiving ambassadors — entering into treaties and alliances, provided that no treaty of commerce shall be made whereby the legislative power of the respective States shall be restrained from imposing such imposts and duties on foreigners, as their own people are subjected to, or from prohibiting the exportation or importation of any species of goods or commodities whatsoever — of establishing rules for deciding in all cases, what captures on land or water shall be legal, and in what manner prizes taken by land or naval forces in the service of the United States shall be divided or appropriated — of granting letters of marque and reprisal in times of peace — appointing courts for the trial of piracies and felonies commited on the high seas and establishing courts for receiving and determining finally appeals in all cases of captures, provided that no member of Congress shall be appointed a judge of any of the said courts.

The United States in Congress assembled shall also be the last resort on appeal in all disputes and differences now subsisting or that hereafter may arise between two or more States concerning boundary, jurisdiction or any other causes whatever; which authority shall always be exercised in the manner following. Whenever the legislative or executive authority or lawful agent of any State in controversy with another shall present a petition to Congress stating the matter in question and praying for a hearing, notice thereof shall be given by order of Congress to the legislative or executive authority of the other State in controversy, and a day assigned for the appearance of the parties by their lawful agents, who shall then be directed to appoint by joint consent, commissioners or judges to constitute a court for hearing and determining the matter in question: but if they cannot agree, Congress shall name three persons out of each of the United States, and from the list of such persons each party shall alternately strike out one, the petitioners beginning, until the number shall be reduced to thirteen; and from that number not less than seven, nor more than nine names as Congress shall direct, shall in the presence of Congress be drawn out by lot, and the persons whose names shall be so drawn or any five of them, shall be commissioners or judges, to hear and finally determine the controversy, so always as a major part of the judges who shall hear the cause shall agree in the determination: and if either party shall neglect to attend at the day appointed, without showing reasons, which Congress shall judge sufficient, or being present shall refuse to strike, the Congress shall proceed to nominate three persons out of each State, and the secretary of Congress shall strike in behalf of such party absent or refusing; and the judgement and sentence of the court to be appointed, in the manner before prescribed, shall be final and conclusive; and if any of the parties shall refuse to submit to the authority of such court, or to appear or defend their claim or cause, the court shall nevertheless proceed to pronounce sentence, or judgement, which shall in like manner be final and decisive, the judgement or sentence and other proceedings being in either case transmitted to Congress, and lodged among the acts of Congress for the security of the parties concerned: provided that every commissioner, before he sits in judgement, shall take an oath to be administered by one of the judges of the supreme or superior court of the State, where the cause shall be tried, "well and truly to hear and determine the matter in question, according to the best of his judgement, without favor, affection or hope of reward": provided also, that no State shall be deprived of territory for the benefit of the United States.

All controversies concerning the private right of soil claimed under different grants of two or more States, whose jurisdictions as they may respect such lands, and the States which passed such grants are adjusted, the said grants or either of them being at the same time claimed to have originated antecedent to such settlement of jurisdiction, shall on the petition of either party to the Congress of the United States, be finally determined as near as may be in the same manner as is before prescribed for deciding disputes respecting territorial jurisdiction between different States.

The United States in Congress assembled shall also have the sole and exclusive right and power of regulating the alloy and value of coin struck by their own authority, or by that of the respective States — fixing the standards of weights and measures throughout the United States — regulating the trade and managing all affairs with the Indians, not members of any of the States, provided that the legislative right of any State within its own limits be not infringed or violated — establishing or regulating post offices from one State to another, throughout all the United States, and exacting such postage on the papers passing through the same as may be requisite to defray the expenses of the said office — appointing all officers of the land forces, in the service of the United States, excepting regimental officers — appointing all the officers of the naval forces, and commissioning all officers whatever in the service of the United States — making rules for the government and regulation of the said land and naval forces, and directing their operations.

The United States in Congress assembled shall have authority to appoint a committee, to sit in the recess of Congress, to be denominated "A Committee of the States", and to consist of one delegate from each State; and to appoint such other committees and civil officers as may be necessary for managing the general affairs of the United States under their direction — to appoint one of their members to preside, provided that no person be allowed to serve in the office of president more than one year in any term of three years; to ascertain the necessary sums of money to be raised for the service of the United States, and to appropriate and apply the same for defraying the public expenses — to borrow money, or emit bills on the credit of the United States, transmitting every half-year to the respective States an account of the sums of money so borrowed or emitted — to build and equip a navy — to agree upon the number of land forces, and to make requisitions from each State for its quota, in proportion to the number of white inhabitants in such State; which requisition shall be binding, and thereupon the legislature of each State shall appoint the regimental officers, raise the men and cloath, arm and equip them in a solid-like manner, at the expense of the United States; and the officers and men so cloathed, armed and equipped shall march to the place appointed, and within the time agreed on by the United States in Congress assembled. ...

The United States in Congress assembled shall never engage in a war, nor grant letters of marque or reprisal in time of peace, nor enter into any treaties or alliances, nor coin money, nor regulate the value thereof, nor ascertain the sums and expenses necessary for the defense and welfare of the United States, or any of them, nor emit bills, nor borrow money on the credit of the United States, nor appropriate money, nor agree upon the number of vessels of war, to be built or purchased, or the number of land or sea forces to be raised, nor appoint a commander in chief of the army or navy, unless nine States assent to the same: nor shall a question on any other point, except for adjourning from day to day be determined, unless by the votes of the majority of the United States in Congress assembled. ...

X.      The Committee of the States, or any nine of them, shall be authorized to execute, in the recess of Congress, such of the powers of Congress as the United States in Congress assembled, by the consent of the nine States, shall from time to time think expedient to vest them with; provided that no power be delegated to the said Committee, for the exercise of which, by the Articles of Confederation, the voice of nine States in the Congress of the United States assembled be requisite. ...

XII.      All bills of credit emitted, monies borrowed, and debts contracted by, or under the authority of Congress, before the assembling of the United States, in pursuance of the present confederation, shall be deemed and considered as a charge against the United States, for payment and satisfaction whereof the said United States, and the public faith are hereby solemnly pleged.

XIII. Every State shall abide by the determination of the United States in Congress assembled, on all questions which by this confederation are submitted to them. And the Articles of this Confederation shall be inviolably observed by every State, and the Union shall be perpetual; nor shall any alteration at any time hereafter be made in any of them; unless such alteration be agreed to in a Congress of the United States, and be afterwards confirmed by the legislatures of every State....[2]

# B. The Virginia Resolution Proposing the Annapolis Convention

*The General Assembly of Virginia, on January 21, 1786, proposed a convention of commissioners from each state to recommend a new federal system for regulating — and implicitly, for taxing — trade in the wake of the failure of 13 states to approve a national tariff and New Jersey's subsequent decision to impose its own tax levy to pay off its own state's creditors instead of paying the national tax.*

Resolved, That Edmund Randolph, James Madison, jun. Walter Jones, Saint George Tucker and Meriwether Smith, Esquires, be appointed commissioners, who, or any three of whom, shall meet such commissioners as may be appointed by the other States in the Union, at a time and place to be agreed on, to take into consideration the trade of the United States; to examine the relative situations and trade of the said States; to consider how far a uniform system in their commercial regulations may be necessary to their common interest and their permanent harmony; and to report to the several States, such an act relative to this great object, as, when unanimously ratified by them, will enable the United States in Congress, effectually to provide for the same.[3]

# C. New Jersey Resolution Appointing Delegates to Annapolis Convention

*In appointing delegates to the Annapolis Convention, New Jersey authorized its three commissioners to consider not only trade, but any "other important matters" necessary for the "common Interest" of the United States — an open invitation by a frustrated legislature to expand the scope of the convention to consider major changes in the Articles of Confederation.*

... to take into Consideration the Trade of the United States; to examine the relative Situation and Trade of the said States; to consider how far a uniform System in their commercial Regulations and other important matters may be necessary to their common Interest and permanent Harmony; and to report to the several States Such an Act relative to this grand Object, as when unanimously ratified by them will enable the United States in Congress assembled effectually to provide for the Exigencies of the Union ... [4]

# D. Report of the Annapolis Convention

*The 13 delegates from Virginia, New Jersey, Pennsylvania, New York, and Delaware who met at the Annapolis Convention seized upon the "other important matters" clause of New Jersey's charge to its delegates to propose a full Constitutional Convention to revamp the Articles of Confederation the following year.*

To the Honorable, the Legislatures of Virginia, Delaware, Pennsylvania, New Jersey, and New York — The Commissioners from the said States, respectively assembled at Annapolis, humbly beg leave to report.

That, pursuant to their several appointments, they met, at Annapolis in the State of Maryland, on the eleventh day of September Instant, and having proceeded to a Communication of their powers; they found that the States of New York, Pennsylvania, and Virginia, had, in substance, and nearly in the same terms, authorised their respective Commissioners "to meet such Commissioners as were, or might be, appointed by the other States in the Union, at such time and place, as should be agreed upon by the said Commissioners to take into consideration the trade and Commerce of the United States, to consider how far an uniform system in their commercial intercourse and regulations might be necessary to their common interest and permanent harmony, and to report to the several States such an Act, relative to this great object, as when unanimously ratified by them would enable the United States in Congress assembled effectually to provide for the same."

That the State of Delaware, had given similar powers to their Commissioners, with this difference only, that the Act to be framed in virtue of those powers, is required to be reported "to the United States in Congress assembled, to be agreed to by them, and confirmed by the Legislatures of every State."

That the State of New Jersey had enlarged the object of their appointment, empowering their Commissioners, "to consider how far an uniform system in their commercial regulations and other important matters, might be necessary to the common interest and permanent harmony of the several States," and to report such an Act on the subject, as when ratified by them "would enable the United States in Congress assembled, effectually to provide for the exigencies of the Union."

That appointments of Commissioners have also been made by the States of New Hampshire, Massachusetts, Rhode Island, and North Carolina, none of whom however have attended; but that no information has been received by your Commissioners, of any appointment having been made by the States of Connecticut, Maryland, South Carolina or Georgia.

That the express terms of the powers to your Commissioners supposing a deputation from all the States, and having for object the Trade and Commerce of the United States, Your Commissioners did not conceive it advisable to proceed on the business of their mission, under the Circumstance of so partial and defective a representation.

Deeply impressed however with the magnitude and importance of the object confided to them on this occasion, your Commissioners cannot forbear to indulge an expression of their earnest and unanimous wish, that speedy measures may be taken, to effect a general meeting, of the States, in a future Convention, for the same, and such other purposes, as the situation of public affairs, may be found to require.

If in expressing this wish, or in intimating any other sentiment, your Commissioners should seem to exceed the strict bounds of their appointment, they entertain a full confidence, that a conduct, dictated by an anxiety for the welfare, of the United States, will not fail to receive an indulgent construction.

In this persuasion, your Commissioners submit an opinion, that the Idea of extending the powers of their Deputies, to other objects, than those of Commerce, which has been adopted by the State of New Jersey, was an improvement on the original plan, and will de serve to be incorporated into that of a future Convention; they are the more naturally led to this conclusion, as in the course of their reflections on the subject, they have been induced to think, that the power of regulating trade is of such comprehensive extent, and will enter so far into the general System of the federal government, that to give it efficacy, and to obviate questions and doubts concerning its precise nature and limits, may require a correspondent adjustment of other parts of the Federal System.

That there are important defects in the system of the Federal Government is acknowledged by the Acts of all those States, which have concurred in the present Meeting; That the defects, upon a closer examination, may be found greater and more numerous, than even these acts imply, is at least so far probable, from the embarrassments which characterize the present State of our national affairs, foreign and domestic, as may reasonably be supposed to merit a deliberate and candid discussion, in some mode, which will unite the Sentiments and Council's of all the States. In the choice of the mode, your Commissioners are of opinion, that a Convention of Deputies from the different States, for the special and sole purpose of entering into this investigation, and digesting a plan for supplying such defects as may be discovered to exist, will be entitled to a preference from considerations, which will occur, without being particularized.

Your Commissioners decline an enumeration of those national circumstances on which their opinion respecting the propriety of a future Convention, with more enlarged powers, is founded; as it would be an useless intrusion of facts and observations, most of which have been frequently the subject of public discussion, and none of which can have escaped the penetration of those to whom they would in this instance be addressed. They are however of a nature so serious, as, in the view of your Commissioners to render the situation of the United States delicate and critical, calling for an exertion of the united virtue and wisdom of all the members of the Confederacy.

Under this impression, Your Commissioners, with the most respectful deference, beg leave to suggest their unanimous conviction, that it may essentially tend to advance the interests of the union, if the States, by whom they have been respectively delegated, would themselves concur, and use their endeavours to procure the concurrence of the other States, in the appointment of Commissioners, to meet at Philadelphia on the second Monday in May next, to take into consideration the situation of the United States, to devise such further provisions as shall appear to them necessary to render the constitution of the Federal Government adequate to the exigencies of the Union; and to report such an Act for that purpose to the United States in Congress assembled, as when agreed to, by them, and afterwards confirmed by the Legislatures of every State, will effectually provide for the same.

Though your Commissioners could not with propriety address these observations and sentiments to any but the States they have the honor to Represent, they have nevertheless concluded from motives of respect, to transmit Copies of this Report to the United States in Congress assembled, and to the executives of the other States.[5]

# E. The Virginia Plan

*The "Virginia Plan" presented by Governor Edmund Randolph to the Constitutional Convention on May 29, 1787, proposed sweeping changes in the Articles of Confederation. The most controversial proposal was the creation of a two-house National Legislature in which votes were to be apportioned based on population or tax contribution, rather than giving each state an equal vote; this proposal would mark a fundamental change in the balance of political power that prevailed under the Articles of Confederation. The Virginia Plan also called for the election of a National Executive by the National Legislature and for the creation of supreme and inferior national courts. By developing the Virginia Plan in a series of closed meetings prior to the formal opening of the convention, Madison, Randolph, and the rest of the Virginia delegation seized control of the scope of the debate within the Constitutional Convention. Instead of an open-ended discussion of the defects in the Articles of Confederation, the debate immediately focused on the strengths and weaknesses of Virginia's preferred alternative.*

1.  Resolved that the Articles of Confederation ought to be so corrected & enlarged as to accomplish the objects proposed by their institution; namely, "common defence, security of liberty and general welfare."

2.  Resd therefore that the rights of suffrage in the National Legislature ought to be proportioned to the Quotas of contribution, or to the number of free inhabitants, as the one or the other rule may seem best in different cases.

3.  Resd that the National Legislature ought to consist of two branches.

4.     Resd that the members of the first branch of the National Legislature ought to be elected by the people of the several States every _____ for the term of _____ ; to be of the age of years at least, to receive liberal stipends by which they may be compensated for the devotion of their time to public service; to be ineligible to any office established by a particular State, or under the authority of the United States, except those peculiarly belonging to the functions of the first branch, during the term of service, and for the space of after its expiration; to be incapable of reelection for the space of after the expiration of their term of service, and to be subject to recall.

5.     Resold that the members of the second branch of the National Legislature ought to be elected by those of the first, out of a proper number of persons nominated by the individual Legislatures, to be of the age of \_\_\_\_\_ years at least; to hold their offices for a term sufficient to ensure their independency; to receive liberal stipends, by which they may be compensated for the devotion of their time to public service; and to be ineligible to any office established by a particular State, or under the authority of the United States, except those peculiarly belonging to the functions of the second branch, during the term of service, and for the space of \_\_\_\_\_ after the expiration thereof.

6.     Resolved that each branch ought to possess the right of originating Acts; that the National Legislature ought to be impowered to enjoy the Legislative Rights vested in Congress bar the Confederation & moreover to legislate in all cases to which the separate States are incompetent, or in which the harmony of the United States may be interrupted by the exercise of individual Legislation; to negative all laws passed by the several States, contravening in the opinion of the National Legislature the articles of Union; and to call forth the force of the Union agst any member of the Union failing to fulfill its duty under the articles thereof.

7.     Resd that a National Executive be instituted; to be chosen by the National Legislature for the term of \_\_\_\_\_ years, to receive punctually at stated times, a fixed compensation for the services rendered, in which no increase or diminution shall be made so as to affect the Magistracy, existing at the time of increase or diminution, and to be ineligible a second time; and that besides a general authority to execute the National laws, it ought to enjoy the Executive rights vested in Congress by the Confederation.

8.     Resd that the Executive and a convenient number of the National Judiciary, ought to compose a Council of revision with authority

to examine every act of the National Legislature before it shall operate, & every act of a particular Legislature before a Negative thereon shall be final; and that the dissent of the said Council shall amount to a rejection, unless the Act of the National Legislature be again passed, or that of a particular Legislature be again negatived by of the members of each branch.

9.     Resd that a National Judiciary be established to consist of one or more supreme tribunals, and of inferior tribunals to be chosen by the National Legislature, to hold their offices during good behaviour; and to receive punctually at stated times fixed compensation for their services, in which no increase or diminution shall be made so as to affect the persons actually in office at the time of such increase or diminution. that the jurisdiction of the inferior tribunals shall be to hear & determine in the first instance, and of the supreme tribunal to hear and determine in the dernier resort, all piracies & felonies on the high seas, captures from an enemy; cases in which foreigners or citizens of other States applying to such jurisdictions may be interested, or which respect the collection of the National revenue; impeachments of any National officers, and questions which may involve the national peace and harmony.

10.    Resolvd that provision ought to be made for the admission of States lawfully arising within the limits of the United States, whether from a voluntary junction of Government & Territory on otherwise, with the consent of a number of voices in the National legislature less than the whole.

11.    Resd that a Republican Government & the territory of each State, except in the instance of a voluntary junction of Government & territory, ought to be guarantied by the United States to each State.

12.    Resd that provision ought to be made for the continuance of Congress and their authorities and privileges, until a given day after the reform of the articles of Union shall be adopted, and for the completion of all their engagements.

13.    Resd that provision ought to be made for the amendment of the Articles of Union whensoever it shall seem necessary, and that the assent of the National Legislature ought not to be required thereto.

14.    Resd that the Legislative Executive & Judiciary powers within the several States ought to be bound by oath to support the articles of Union.

15. Resd that the amendments which shall be offered to the Confederation, by the Convention ought at a proper time, or times, after the approbation of Congress to be submitted to an assembly or assemblies of Representatives, recommended by the several Legislatures to be expressly chosen by the people, to consider & decide thereon.[6]

# F. Charles Pinckney's Plan: The "Three-Fifths" Rule

*South Carolina delegate Charles Pinckney's plan, presented to the Constitutional Convention on May 29, 1787 — the same day as the Virginia Plan — introduced the concept that representation in both the Senate and the House of Delegates should be determined on the basis of population, with each slave counting as "three-fifths" of a person. Madison and the Virginians quickly embraced the concept.*

Outline of the Plan.

1. A Confederation between the free and independent States of N.H. etc. is hereby solemnly made uniting them together under one general superintending Government for their common Benefit and for their Defense and Security against all Designs and Leagues that may be injurious to their Interests and against all Forc[e] [?] and Attacks offered to or made upon them or any of them.

2. The Stile

3. Mutual Intercourse — Community of Privileges — Surrender of Criminals-Faith to Proceedings etc.

4. Two Branches of the Legislature — Senate — House of Delegates — together the U. S. in Congress assembled

   H. D. to consist of one Member for every thousand Inhabitants 3/5 of Blacks included

   Senate to be elected from four Districts — to serve by Rotation of four years — to be elected by the H. D. either from among themselves or the People at large

5. The Senate and H. D. shall by joint Ballot annually chuse the Presidt U. S. from among themselves or the People at large. — In

the Presdt the executive authority of the U. S. shall be vested. — His Powers and Duties — He shall have a Right to advise with the Heads of the different Departments as his Council

6. Council of Revision, consisting of the Presidt S. for for. Affairs, S. of War, Heads of the Departments of Treasury and Admiralty or any two of them togr wt the Presidt.

7. The Members of S. and H. D. shall each have one Vote, and shall be paid out of the common Treasury.

8. The Time of the Election of the Members of the H. D. and of the Meeting of U. S. in C. assembled.

9. No State to make Treaties — lay interfering Duties — keep a naval or land Force Militia excepted to be disciplined etc. according to the Regulations of the U. S.

10. Each State retains its Rights not expressly delegated — But no Bill of the Legislature of any State shall become a law till it shall have been laid before S. and H. D. in C. assembled and received their Approbation.

11. The exclusive Power of S. and H. D. in C. Assembled.

12. The S. and H. D. in C. ass. shall have exclusive Power of regulating trade and levying Imposts — Each State may lay Embargoes in Times of Scarcity.

13. — -of establishing Post-Offices

14. S. and H. D. in C. ass. shall be the last Resort on Appeal in Disputes between two or more States; which Authority shall be exercised in the following Manner etc

15. S. and H. D. in C. ass. shall institute offices and appoint officers for the Departments of for. Affairs, War, Treasury and Admiralty.

They shall have the exclusive Power of declaring what shall be Treason and Misp. of Treason agt U. S. — and of instituting a federal judicial Court, to which an Appeal shall be allowed from the judicial Courts of the several States in all Causes wherein Questions shall arise on the Construction of Treaties made by U. S. — or on the Laws of Nations — or on the Regulations of U. S. concerning Trade and Revenue — or wherein U. S. shall be a Party — The Court shall consist of Judges to be appointed during good Behaviour — S and H. D. in C. ass. shall have the exclusive Right of instituting in each State a Court of Admiralty and appointing the Judges etc of the same for all maritime Causes which may arise therein respectively.

16. S and H. D. in C. Ass shall have the exclusive Right of coining Money-regulating its Alloy and Value — fixing the Standard of Weights and Measures throughout U. S.

I7. Points in which the Assent of more than a bare Majority shall be necessary.

18. Impeachments shall be by the H. D. before the Senate and the Judges of the Federeal judicial Court.

19. S. and H. D. in C. ass. shall regulate the Militia thro' the U.S.

20. Means of enforcing and compelling the Payment of the Quota of each State.

21. Manner and Conditions of admitting new States.

22. Power of dividing annexing and consolidating States, on the Consent and Petition of such States.

23. The assent of the Legislature of States shall be sufficient to invest future additional Powers in U. S. in C. ass. and shall bind the whole Confederacy.

24. The Articles of Confederation shall be inviolably observed, and the Union shall be perpetual: unless altered as before directed

25. The said States of N. H. etc guarrantee mutually each other and their Rights against all other Powers and against all Rebellion etc.[7]

# G. David Brearley's June 9 Speech Criticizing the Virginia Plan

*David Brearley's speech of June 9 and the subsequent address by William Paterson marked the first comprehensive attack on the Virginia Plan and its core assumption that the United States should have a national government with representation in both houses of the national legislature determined on the basis of population or tax contribution, not on an equality of states. Most of our knowledge of the debates that shaped the Constitution comes from the notes made during sessions and in the evenings by various delegates, particularly James Madison, who took notes on every session far superior to the indifferent work of William Jackson, the convention secretary. Other delegates whose notes survive include Rufus King of Massachusetts, Robert Yates and John Lansing Jr. of New York, and James*

*McHenry of Maryland. William Paterson and David Brearley Jr. of New Jersey took some notes and provided important drafts of the New Jersey Plan and various representation formulas. The variation in note-taking can be seen from the following accounts left by Madison, King, Yates, Lansing, and Paterson of Brearley's speech. Paterson's notes are particularly brief because he was planning to speak next and he already knew what Brearley was going to say. In fact, he was planning to deliver much the same speech.*

**Madison:** "He [Brearley]was sorry he said that any question on this point was brought into view. It had been much agitated in Congs. at the time of forming the Confederation and was then rightly settled by allowing to each sovereign State an equal vote. Otherwise the smaller Sttes must have been destroyed instead of being saved. The substitution of a ratio, he admitted carried fairness on the face of it; but on a deeper examination was unfair and unjust. Judging of the disparity of the States by the quota of Congs. Virga. would have 16 votes, and Georgia but one. A like proportion to the others will make the whole number ninity. (Brearley's numbers taken from identical run of numbers that exists in both Paterson and Brearly papers). There will be 3. large states and 10 small ones. The large States by which he meant Massts. Pena. & Virga. will carry every thing before them. It had been admitted, and was known to him from facts within N. Jersey that where large and small counties were united into a district for electing representatives for their district, the large counties always carried their point, and Consequently that the large States would do so. Virga. with her sixteen votes will be a solid column indeed, a formidable phalanx. While Georgia with her Solitary vote, and the other little States will be obliged to throw themselves constantly into the scale of some larger one, in order to have any weight at all. He had come to the convention with a view of being as useful as he could in giving energy and stability to the Federal Government. When the proposition for destroying the equality of votes came forward, he was astonished, he was alarmed. Is it fair then it will be asked that Georgia should have an equal vote with Virga.? He would not say it was. What remedy then? One only, that a map of the U.S. be spread out, that all the existing boundaries be erased, and that a new partition of the whole be made into 13 equal parts."[8]

**Yates:** "The present question is an important one. On the principle that each state in the union was sovereign, congress, in the articles of confederation, determined that each state in the public councils had <u>one</u> vote. If the states remain sovereign, the form of the present resolve is founded on principles of injustice. He then stated the comparative weight of each state — the number of votes 90. Georgia would be 1, Virginia 16, and so of the rest. This vote must defeat itself, or end in despotism. If we must have a national government, what is the remedy? Lay the map of the confederation on the table, and extinguish the present boundary lines of the respective state jurisdictions, and make a new division so that each state is equal — then a government on the present system will be just."[9]

**King:** "Brearly. opposes the equality of Representation, alledges that although it is numerically equal, yet in its operation it will be unequal — illustrates by saying there will be two divisions in the States thus represented, the one made up of Mass. Penn. & Virgin. the other including the Ten other states — when Georga. sends one member, Virginia will send sixteen — These 16 members are united, the members of three or four other small States although equal in number are not capable of combination, the influence of the 16 members of Virginia will be different, for these Reasons, from those from three or four small States — I agree that the Rule of confedn. is unequal — I shall be willing to take the map of the U.S. and divide it into 13 equal parts — this being done there may fairly be an equality in the representation of the States —"[10]

**Lansing:** "Brearly — This Mode of Representation just if all considered as one Nation — but if State Distinctions still obtain — if Measures are pursued to perpetuate their seperate Interests — let the whole be divided into Districts of nearly equal Size and Numbers of Inhabitants — but in our present Situation the Interests of the Smaller States must be sacraficed. He had made a calculation of the relative Representation which had been repeatedly hinted at which need only be read to enable us to determine the probable Consequence — this was on Number of free Inhabitants.

| | | | |
|---|---|---|---|
| Georgia | 1 | South Carolina | 6 |
| Deleware | 1 | North Carolina | 6 |
| Rhode Island | 2 | New York | 8 |
| New Hampshire | 3 | Connecticut | 8 |
| New Jersey | 5 | Maryland | 6 |
| | Massachusetts | 14 | |
| | Pennsylvania | 12 | |
| | Virginia | 16 | |

He was appointed to give foederal Powers — but these too extensive.[11]

**Paterson:** "Mr. Brearley. unfair; because of the Combination of the Parts.
 Districts —
 Equalize the States —"[12]


# H. Roger Sherman's Proposals for Inclusion in the New Jersey Plan

*Roger Sherman's papers included the following series of propositions, which Max Farrand, editor of The Records of the Federal Constitution of 1787, believes to be the ideas presented by the Connecticut delegation for consideration during the development of the New Jersey Plan.*[12] *Sherman's proposals open with a strong provision giving the national legislature the power to regulate commerce and tax trade, which was the original purpose of the Annapolis Convention. It also includes strong state's rights language in its second provision, perhaps reflecting the nervousness of the Connecticut delegation over giving too much power to a national legislature that would be dominated by the larger states. Sherman's proposals do not address the issue of how to determine representation in the national legislature. Sherman's suggestion that each state have equal votes in the Senate in exchange for determining representation by population in the House of Representation would ultimately be adopted as the so-called "Connecticut Compromise."*


1. That, in addition to the legislative powers vested in congress by the articles of confederation, the legislature of the United States be authorised to make laws to regulate the commerce of the United States with foreign nations, and among the several states in the union; to impose duties on foreign goods and commodities imported into the United States, and on papers passing through the post office, for raising a revenue, and to regulate the collection thereof, and apply the same to the payment of the debts due from the United States, and for supporting the government, and other necessary charges of the Union.

To make laws binding on the people of the United States, and on the courts of law, and other magistrates and officers, civil and military, within the several states, in all cases which concern the common interests of the United States: but not to interfere with the government of the individual states, in matters of internal police which respect the government of such states only, and wherein the general welfare of the

United States is not affected.

That the laws of the United States ought, as far as may be consistent with the common interests of the Union, to be carried into execution by the judiciary and executive officers of the respective states, wherein the execution thereof is required.

That the legislature of the United States be authorised to institute one supreme tribunal, and such other tribunals as they may judge necessary for the purpose aforesaid, and ascertain their respective powers and jurisdictions.

That the legislature of the individual states ought not to possess a right to emit bills of credit for a currency, or to make any tender laws for the payment or discharge of debts or contracts, in any manner different from the agreement of the parties, unless for payment of the value of the thing contracted for, in current money, agreeable to the standard that shall be allowed by the legislature of the United States, or in any manner to obstruct or impede the recovery of debts, whereby the interests of foreigners, or the citizens of any other state, may be affected.

That the eighth article of the confederation ought to be amended, agreeably to the recommendation of Congress of the [18th] day of [April, 1783].

That, if any state shall refuse or neglect to furnish its quota of supplies, upon requisition made by the legislature of the United States, agreeably to the articles of the Union, that the said legislature be authorised to order the same to be levied and collected of the inhabitants of such state, and to make such rules and orders as may be necessary for that purpose.

That the legislature of the United States have power to make laws calling forth such aid from the people, from time to time, as may be necessary to assist the civil officers in the execution of the laws of the United States; and annex suitable penalties to be inflicted in case of disobedience.

That no person shall be liable to be tried for any criminal offence committed within any of the United States, in any other state than that wherein the offence shall be committed, nor be deprived of the privilege of trial by a jury, by virtue of any law of the United States.[13]

# I. William Paterson's Notes Used in Preparation of the New Jersey Plan (June 13-15)

William Paterson's "preliminary sketches" of the New Jersey Plan, as Max Farrand characterized the following notes found among the Paterson Papers,[14] are notable not only for the provisions that made their way ultimately into the New Jersey Plan presented to the Convention, but also for what did not. Both sets of Paterson notes envision the creation of a "federal" system of united states, rather than the more truly national government that the Virginia Plan sought. The power to regulate and tax trade, which is clearly laid out in the fifth clause of the first document, became the second clause of the New Jersey Plan presented to the Convention. The second document eloquently argues that "representation in the supreme Legislature ought to be by States, otherwise some of the States in the Union will possess a greater Share of Sovereignty, Freedom, and Independance than others," which also became a centerpiece of the New Jersey Plan. Paterson's notes conclude with a provision to implement the idea he and Brearley developed prior to their June 9 speech to divide the states into thirteen equal districts, but that idea apparently was abandoned midway through the process of developing the New Jersey Plan. The idea is not mentioned in Brearley's or Paterson's final eleven-resolution drafts of the New Jersey Plan or even in Maryland delegate Luther Martin's earlier draft of sixteen resolutions that were under consideration.

I

1. Resolved, That a union of the States merely federal ought to be the sole Object of the Exercise of the Powers vested in this Convention.

2. Resolved, That the Articles of the Confederation ought to be so revised, corrected, and enlarged as to render the federal Constitution adequate to the Exigencies of Government, and the Preservation of the Union —

3. Resolved, That the federal Government of the United States ought to consist of a Supreme Legislative, Executive, and Judiciary —

4. Resolved, That the Powers of Legislation ought to be vested in Congress.

5.  Resolved, That in Addition to the Powers vested in the United States in Congress by the present existing Articles of Confederation, they be authorized to pass Acts for levying a Duty or Duties on all Goods and Merchandize of foreign Growth or Manufacture imported into any Part of the United States not exceeding — per Cent. ad Valorem to be applied to such federal Purposes as they shall deem proper and expedient, and to make Rules and Regulations for the Collection thereof; and the same from Time to Time to alter and amend in such Manner as they shall think proper. Provided, That all Punishments, Fines, Forfeitures, and Penalties to be incurred for contravening such Rules and Regulations shall be adjudged and decided upon by the Judiciaries of the State in which any Offence contrary to the true Intent and Meaning of such Rules and Regulations shall be committed or perpetrated; subject nevertheless to an Appeal for the Correction of any Errors in rendering Judgment to the Judiciary of the United States.

    That the United States in Congress be also authorized to pass Acts for the Regulation of Trade as well with foreign Nations as with each other, and for laying such Prohibitions, *[in margin:* Imposts Excise — Stamps — Post-Office — Poll-Tax — *]* and such Imposts and Duties upon Imports as may be necessary for the Purpose; Provided, That the Legislatures of the several States shall not be restrained from laying Embargoes in Times of Scarcity; and provided further that such Imposts and Duties so far forth as the same shall exceed ... per Centum ad Valorem on the Imports shall accrue to the Use of the State in which the same may be collected.

## II

1.  Resolved, That the articles of the confederation ought to be so revised, corrected, and enlarged as to render the federal constitution adequate to the exigencies of government, and the preservation of the union —

2.  Resolved, That the alterations, additions, and provisions made in and to the articles of the confederation shall be reported to the united states in congress and to the individual states composing the union, agreeably to the 13th. article of the confederation —

3.  Resolved, That the federal government of the united states ought to consist of a supreme legislative, executive, and judiciary —

4.  Resolved, That the powers of legislation be vested in Congress-

5.      ------------------------------------------------

6.      ------------------------------------------------

7.      ------------------------------------------------

Resolved, That every State in the Union as a State possesses an equal Right to, and Share of, Sovereignty, Freedom, and Independance —

Resolved, therefore, that the Representation in the supreme Legislature ought to be by States, otherwise some of the States in the Union will possess a greater Share of Sovereignty, Freedom, and Independance than others —

Whereas it is necessary in Order to form the People of the U. S. of America into a Nation, that the States should be consolidated, by which Means all the Citizens thereof will become equally intitled to and will equally participate in the same Privileges and Rights, and in all waste, uncultivated, and back Territory and Lands; it is therefore resolved, that all the Lands contained within the Limits of each State individually, and of the U. S. generally be considered as constituting one Body or Mass, and be divided into thirteen or more integral Parts.

Resolved, That such Divisions or integral Parts shall be styled Districts.[14]

## J. Luther Martin's Version of the New Jersey Plan

*Luther Martin's draft of 16 resolutions that were considered by the working group of delegates from New Jersey, Connecticut, Delaware, Maryland, and New York who developed the New Jersey Plan was similar to Paterson's early draft notes in a number of resolutions. But by the time Martin wrote his draft, the Brearley-Paterson proposal to redraw state lines to create 13 equal states was no longer under consideration.*

1.      Resolved, that an union of the states, merely federal, ought to be the sole object of the exercise of the powers vested in this convention.

2.      Resolved, that the articles of the confederation ought to be so revised, corrected, and enlarged, as to render the federal consti-

tution adequate to the exigencies of government, and the preservation of the union.

3.  Resolved, that in addition to the powers vested in the united states in congress, by the present existing articles of confederation, they be authorized to pass acts for raising a revenue by laying a duty or duties on all goods and merchandise of foreign growth or manufacture, imported into any part of the united states; by imposing stamps on paper, parchment, and vellum; and by a postage on all letters and packages passing through the general post office, to be applied to such federal purposes, as they shall deem proper and expedient; to make rules and regulations for the collection thereof; and the same from time to time to alter and amend in such manner as they shall think proper: provided that all punishments, fines, forfeitures, and penalties, to be incurred for contravening such rules and regulations, shall be adjudged by the common law judiciaries of the state in which any offense, contrary to the true intent and meaning of such rules or regulations, shall be committed or perpetrated; with liberty of commencing all suits or prosecutions for that purpose, in the first instance, in the supreme common law judiciary of such state-subject, nevertheless, to an appeal in the last resort, for the correction of errors, both of law and fact, in rendering judgment, to the judiciary of the united states; and that the united states shall have authority to pass acts for the regulation of trade and commerce, as well with foreign nations, as with each other.

4.  Resolved, that should requisitions be necessary, instead of the present rule, the united states in congress be authorized to make such requisitions in proportion to the whole number of white and other free citizens and inhabitants, of every age, sex, and condition, including those bound to servitude for a term of years, and three-fifths of all other persons, not comprehended in the foregoing descriptions (except Indians not paying taxes.)

5.  Resolved, that if such requisitions be not complied with, in the time specified therein, the united states in congress shall have power to direct the collection thereof in the non-complying states; and for that purpose to devise and pass acts directing and authorising the same: provided that none of the powers hereby vested in the united states in congress shall be exercised without the consent of at least _____ states; and in that proportion, should the number of confederated states hereafter be increased or diminished.

6.     Resolved, that the united states in congress, shall be authorised to elect a federal executive, to consist of _____ person or persons, to continue in office for the term of _____ years, to receive punctually, at stated times, a fixed compensation for the services by him or them to be rendered, in which no increase or diminution shall be made, so as to affect the executive in office, at the time of such increase or diminution, to be paid out of the federal treasury; to be incapable of holding any other office or appointment during the time of service, and for _____ years after; to be ineligible a second time, and removable on impeachment and conviction for mar-practice, corrupt conduct, and neglect of duty.

7.     Resolved, that the executive, besides a general authority to execute the federal acts, ought to appoint all federal officers, not otherwise provided for, and to direct all military operations; provided that the executive shall not on any occasion take command of any troops, so as personally to conduct any military enterprise as general, or in any other capacity.

8.     Resolved, that the legislative acts of the united states, made under and in pursuance to the articles of union, and all treaties made and ratified under the authority of the united states, shall be the supreme law of the respective states, as far as those acts or treaties shall relate to the said states or their citizens and inhabitants; and that the judiciaries of the several states shall be bound thereby in their decisions; any thing in the respective laws of the individual states to the contrary notwithstanding.

9.     Resolved, that if any state or body of men in any state, shall oppose or prevent the carrying into execution such acts or treaties, the federal executive shall be authorised to call forth the powers of the confederated states, or so much thereof as may be necessary to enforce and compel an obedience to such acts, or an observance of such treaties.

10.    Resolved, that a federal judiciary be established, to consist of a supreme tribunal; the judges of which to be appointed by the executive, and to hold their offices during good behaviour; to receive punctually, at stated times, a fixed compensation for their services, to be paid out of the federal treasury; in which no increase or diminution shall be made, so as to affect the persons actually in office, at the time of such increase of diminution. That the judiciary so established, shall have authority to hear and determine, in the first instance, on all impeachments of federal officers, and by way of appeal in the dernier resort in all cases touching the rights and privileges of ambassadors; in all cases of

captures from the enemy; in all cases of piracies and felonies committed on the high seas; in all cases in which foreigners may be interested in the construction of any treaty or treaties, or which may arise on any act or ordinance of congress for the regulation of trade, or the collection of the federal revenue; that none of the judiciary officers shall be capable of receiving or holding any other office or appointment, during the time they remain in office, or for ____ years afterwards.

11. Resolved, that the legislative, executive, and judiciary powers within the several states, ought to be bound by oath to support the articles of union.

12. Resolved, that provision ought to be made for hearing and deciding upon all disputes arising between the united states and an individual state, respecting territory.

13. Resolved, that provision ought to be made for the admission of new states into the union.

14. Resolved, that it is necessary to define what offenses, committed in any state, shall be deemed high treason against the united states.

15. Resolved, that the rule for naturalization ought to be the same in every state.

16. Resolved, that a citizen of one state, committing an offense in another state, shall be deemed guilty of the same offense, as if it had been committed by a citizen of the state, in which the offense was committed. [15]

# K. David Brearley's Copy of the New Jersey Plan

*David Brearley and William Paterson left identical copies of a near-final eleven-resolution "New Jersey Plan" that contained clauses strengthening the independence of both the executive and judicial branches that were not envisioned in Paterson's earlier notes (see Appendix I). The fourth resolution, like the Virginia Plan, calls for the Federal Executives to be elected by Congress, but the New Jersey Plan barred Congress from initiating impeachment proceedings without the support of a majority of the governors. The fifth resolution proposes that the new Supreme Court by appointed by the Executive, not by the Senate, as the Constitutional Convention had previously voted to do. The seventh resolution contains a "supremacy clause" that clearly* establishes the authority of the new national government over the states. Interestingly, the core issue underlying and driving the New Jersey Plan – the issue of how to determine representation in Congress – is not mentioned. By proposing no new method of election for Congress, the New Jersey Plan leaves in place the single-house Confederation Congress in which each state has one vote.

1.  Resolved, that the Articles of Confedern ought to be so revised, corrected, and enlarged as to render the federal Constitution adequate to the exigencies of Government, and the preservation of the Union.

2.  Resolved, that in addition to the Powers vested in the United States in Congress by the present existing Articles of Confederation, they be authorized to pass Acts for raising a Revenue by levying a Duty or Duties on all goods and Merchandise of foreign growth or manufacture imported into any part of the United States,-by Stamps on Paper Vellum or Parchment,- and by a Postage on all Letters and Packages passing through the general Post Office. To be applied to such federal purposes as they shall deem proper and expedient; to make rules and regulations for the collection thereof, and the same from time to time to alter and amend, in such manner as they shall think proper. To pass Acts for the regulation of Trade and Commerce, as well with foreign Nations, as with each other. Provided that all punishments, Fines Forfeitures and Penalties to be incurred for contravening such Rules, and regulations shall be adjudged by the common Law Judiciary of the States in which any offense contrary to the true intent and meaning of such Rules and regulations shall be committed or perpetrated; with liberty of commencing in the first instance all suits or prosecutions for that purpose in the Superior Common Law Judiciary of such State; subject Nevertheless to an Appeal for the Correction of all errors, both in Law in Fact, in rendering Judgment, to the Judiciary of the United States.

3.  Resolved, that whenever Requisitions shall be necessary, instead of the present Rule, the United States in Congress be authorized to make such Requisitions in proportion to the whole Number of White and other Free Citizens and Inhabitants of every age, sex and condition, including those bound to servitude for a Term of years, and three fifths of all other persons not comprehended in the foregoing description-(except Indians not paying Taxes): that if such Requisitions be not complied with, in the time to be spec-

ified therein, to direct the Collection thereof in the non complying States and for that purpose to devise and pass Acts directing and authorizing the same. Provided that none of the powers hereby vested in the United States in Congress shall be exercized without the Consent of at least _____ States, and in that proportion, if the number of confederated States should be hereafter encreased or diminished.

4.  Resolved, that the U. S. in Congress be authorized to elect a federal Executive to consist of _____ Persons, to continue in office for the Term of _____ years; to receive punctually at Stated times a fixed compensation for the services by them rendered, in which no increase or diminution shall be made, so as to affect the persons composing the Executive at the time of such encrease or diminution; to be paid out of the Federal Treasury; to be incapable of holding any other Office or appointment during their time of service, and for _____ years thereafter; to be ineligible a second time, and removable on impeachment and conviction for Mal practice or neglect of duty-by Congress on application by a Majority of the Executives of the several States. That the Executive, besides a general authority to execute the federal Acts, ought to appoint all federal Officers not other wise provided for, and to direct all Military operations; provided that none of the persons composing the federal Executive shall on any occasion take command of any Troops so as personally to conduct any Military enterprise as general ["Officer" stricken out] or in any other capacity.

5.  Resolved, that a federal Judiciary be established, to consist of a supreme Tribunal, the Judges of which to be appointed by the Executive, and to hold their Offices during good behavior; to receive punctually at stated times a fixed compensation for their services, in which no increase or diminution shall be made so as to effect the persons actually in Office at the time of such increase or diminution; - That the Judiciary so established shall have authority to hear and determine in the first instance on all impeachments of federal Officers, and by way of Appeal in the dernier resort in all cases touching the Rights and privileges of Embassadors; in all cases of captures from an Enemy; in all cases of Piricies and Felonies on the high Seas; in all cases in which Foreigners may be interested in the construction of any Treaty or Treaties, or which may arise on any Act or Ordinance of Congress for the regulation of Trade, or the collection of the Federal Revenue: that none of the Judiciary Officers shall during the time they remain in Office be capable of receiving or holding

any other Office or appointment during their time of service, or for thereafter.

6.    Resolved, that the Legislative, Executive, and Judiciary Powers within the several States ought to be bound by Oath to support the Articles of Union.

7.    Resolved, that all Acts of the United States in Congress Assembled, made by virtue and pursuance of the Powers hereby vested in them, and by the Articles of the Confederation, and all Treaties made and ratified under the authority of the United States, shall be the supreme Law of the respective States, as far as those Acts or Treaties shall relate to the said States or their [citizens "subjects" stricken out]; and that the Judiciaries of the several States shall be bound thereby in their decisions, anything in the respective Laws of the Individual States to the Contrary notwithstanding.

And if any State, or any body of Men in any State, shall oppose or prevent the carrying into Execution such Acts or Treaties, the federal Executive shall be authorized to call forth the Powers of the confederated States, or so much thereof as may be necessary to enforce and compel an obedience to such Acts or an observance of such Treaties.

8.    Resolved, that provision ought to be made for the admission of New States into the Union

9.    Resolved, that Provision ought to be made for hearing and deciding upon all disputes arising between the United States and an Individual State respecting Territory

10.   Resolved, that the Rule for Naturalization ought to be the same in every State.

11.   Resolved, that a Citizen of one State committing an Offence in another State, shall be deemed guilty of the same offense, as if it had been committed by a Citizen of the State in which the offense was committed.[16]

# L. The New Jersey Plan Presented to the Convention on June 16 (Madison's Notes)

*Madison's copy of the New Jersey Plan and the notes taken that day by convention secretary William Jackson are identical in listing nine resolutions. The sixth and ninth resolutions in the Brearley and Paterson copies of the New Jersey Plan are omitted from the Madison and Jackson notes, and there is no reason to believe that they were presented to the full convention. The missing resolutions called for state and federal officials to be bound by oath to support the new Constitution, and for a system to be set up for hearing and deciding disputes between the national government and individual states regarding territorial claims. Advocates of the New Jersey Plan may have decided to omit the clause pertaining to territorial disputes out of concern that it would anger delegates from Virginia and four of its voting allies, Pennsylvania, North and South Carolina, and Georgia, all of which had extensive western land claims.*

1.    Resd that the articles of Confederation ought to be so revised, corrected & enlarged, as to render the federal Constitution adequate to the exigencies of Government, & the preservation of the Union.

2.    Resd that in addition to the powers vested in the U. States in Congress, by the present existing articles of Confederation, they be authorized to pass acts for raising a revenue, by levying a duty or duties on all goods or merchandises of foreign growth or manufacture, imported into any part of the U. States, by Stamps on paper, vellum or parchment, and by a postage on all letters or packages passing through the general post-office, to be applied to such federal purposes as they shall deem proper & expedient; to make rules & regulations for the collection thereof; and the same from time to time, to alter & amend in such manner as they shall think proper: to pass Acts for the regulation of trade & commerce as well with foreign nations as with each other: provided that all punishments, fines, forfeitures & penalties to be incurred for contravening such acts rules and regulations shall be adjudged by the Common law Judiciaries of the State in which any offense contrary to the true intent & meaning of such Acts rules & regulations shall have been committed or perpetrated, with liberty of commencing in the first instance all suits & prosecutions for that purpose in the superior common law Judiciary in such State, subject nevertheless, for the correction of all errors, both in law & fact in rendering Judgment, to an appeal to the Judiciary of the U. States.

3.    Resd that whenever requisitions shall be necessary, instead of the rule for making requisitions mentioned in the articles of Confederation, the United States in Congs be authorized to make

such requisitions in proportion to the whole number of white & other free citizens & inhabitants of every age sex and condition including those bound to servitude for a term of years & three fifths of all other persons not comprehended in the foregoing description, except Indians not paying taxes; that if such requisitions be not complied with, in the time specified therein, to direct the collection thereof in the non complying States & for that purpose to devise and pass acts directing & authorizing the same; provided that none of the powers hereby vested in the U. States in Congs shall be exercised without the consent of at least States, and in that proportion if the number of Confederated States should hereafter be increased or diminished.

4.      Resd that the U. States in Congs be authorized to elect a federal Executive to consist of persons, to continue in office for the term of years, to receive punctually at stated times a fixed compensation for their services, in which no increase or diminution shall be made so as to affect the persons composing the Executive at the time of such increase or diminution, to be paid out of the federal treasury; to be incapable of holding any other office or appointment during their time of service and for years thereafter; to be ineligible a second time, & removeable by Congs on application by a majority of the Executives of the several States; that the Executives besides their general authority to execute the federal acts ought to appoint all federal officers not otherwise provided for, & to direct all military operations; provided that none of the persons composing the federal Executive shall on any occasion take command of any troops, so as personally to conduct any enterprise as General or in other capacity.

5.      Resd that a federal Judiciary be established to consist of a supreme Tribunal the Judges of which to be appointed by the Executive, & to hold their offices during good behaviour, to receive punctually at stated times a fixed compensation for their services in which no increase or diminution shall be made, so as to affect the persons actually in office at the time of such increase or diminution; that the Judiciary so established shall have authority to hear & determine in the first instance on all impeachments of federal officers, & by way of appeal in the dernier resort in all cases touchung the rights of Ambassadors, in all cases of captures from an enemy, in all cases of piracies & felonies on the high Seas, in all cases in which foreigners may be interested, in the construction of any treaty or treaties, or which may arise on any of the Acts for  regulation of trade, or the collection of the federal

Revenue: that none of the Judiciary shall during the time they remain in office be capable of receiving or holding any other office or appointment during their time of service, or for there-after.

6.    Resd that all Acts of the U. States in Congs made by virtue & in pursuance of the powers hereby & by the articles of Confederation vested in them, and all Treaties made & ratified under the authority of the U. States shall be the supreme law of the respective States so far forth as those Acts or Treaties shall relate to the said States or their Citizens, and that the Judiciary of the several States shall be bound thereby in their decisions, any thing in the respective laws of the Individual States to the contrary notwithstanding; and that if any State, or any body of men in any State shall oppose or prevent ye carrying into execution such acts or treaties, the federal Executive shall be authorized to call forth ye power of the Confederated States, or so much there-of as may be necessary to enforce and compel an obedience to such Acts, or an observance of such Treaties.

7.    Resd that provision be made for the admission of new States into the Union.

8.    Resd the rule for naturalization ought to be the same in every State.

9.    Rest a Citizen of one State committing an offense in another State of the Union, shall be deemed guilty of the same offense as if it had been committed by a Citizen of the State in which the offense was committed.[17]

# M. The Brearley Committee: Reports of the Committee on Postponed Matters

*On August 31, 1797, a deeply divided and pessimistic Convention referred all unresolved issues to a newly created Committee on Postponed Matters for resolution. Brearley was elected chairman of the new committee, which achieved consensus on all remaining issues in just four days. Brearley presented the committee's recommendations to the Convention on the mornings of September 1, September 4, and September 5. The recommendations of September 4 were breathtaking in their scope and innovation. On that day, Brearley presented the Convention with resolutions to create a strong president eligible to seek* reelection, to invent the office of the vice-presidency, and to elect both through an electoral college that balanced the interests of large states and small states in its apportionment of votes. Often overlooked is the first recommendation presented that day establishing the power of Congress to levy taxes and tariffs, which was the purpose of the Annapolis Convention and one of the centerpieces of the New Jersey Plan in all of its formulations. The Brearley Committee recommended impeachment of the president by the House of Representatives and conviction by the Senate, omitting the requirement in the New Jersey Plan for consent by a majority of the nation's governors. The most significant recommendation on September 5 was the proposal that all tax bills originate in the House of Representatives, which was designed to give greater control over revenue measures to the larger states who would pay the bulk of the taxes.

*(Saturday, September 1, 1787)*

Mr. Brearley from the Comme. of eleven to which were referred yesterday, the postponed part of the Constitution, & parts of reports not acted upon, made the following partial report,

Tht in lieu of the 9th sect: of art: 6. the words following be inserted viz "The members of each House shall be ineligible to any civil office under the authority of the U. S. during the time for which they shall respectively be elected, and no person holding an office under the U. S. shall be a member of either House during his continuance in office."[18]

*(Tuesday, September 4)*

Mr. Brearley from the Committee of eleven made a further partial Report as follows

"The Committee of Eleven to whom sundry resolutions &c were referred on the 31st. of August, report that in their opinion the following additions and alterations should be made to the Report before the Convention, viz

(1) The first clause of sect: I. art. 7 to read as follows — 'The Legislature shall have power to lay and collect taxes duties imposts & excises, to pay the debts and provide for the common defence & general welfare of the United States.

(2). At the end of 2nd clause of sect. I. art. 7. add 'and with the Indian tribes'.

(3) In the place of the 9th. art: Sect. I.to be inserted 'The Senate of the U—S— shall have power to try all impeachments; but no person shall be convicted without the concurrence of two thirds of the members present.

(4) After the word 'Excellency'in sect. I. art. 10 to be inserted: 'He shall hold his office during the term of four years, and together with the vice-President, chosen for the same term, be elected in the following manner, viz. Each State shall appoint in such manner as its Legislature may direct, a number of electors equal to the whole number of Senators and members of the House of Representatives, to which the State may be entitled in the Legislature. The Electors shall meet in their respective States, and vote by ballot for two persons, of whom one at least shall not be an inhabitant of the same State with themselves; and they shall make a list of all the persons voted for, and of the number of votes for each, which list they shall sign and certify and transmit sealed to the Seat of the. Genl. Government, directed to the President of the Senate — The President of the Senate shall in that House open all the certificates; and the votes shall be then & there counted. The Person having the greatest number of votes shall be the President, if such number be a majority of that of the electros; and if there be more than one who have such a majority, and have an equal number of votes, then the Senate shall immediately choose by ballot one of them for President: but if no person have a majority, then from the five highest on the list, the Senate shall choose by ballot the President. And in every case after the choice of the President, the person having the greatest number of votes shall be vice-president: but if there should remain two or more who have equal votes, the Senate shall choose from them the vice-President. The Legislature may determine the time of choosing and assembling the Electors, and the manner of certifying and transmitting their votes.'

(5) 'Sect. 2. No person except a natural born citizen or a Citizen of the U—S— at the time of the adoption of this Constitution shall be eligible to the office of President; nor shall any person be elected to that office, who shall be under the age of thirty five years, and who has not been in the whole, at least fourteen years a resident of within the U—S.

(6) 'Sect— 3— The vice-president shall be ex officio President of the Senate, except when they sit to try the impeachment of the President, in which case the Chief Justice shall preside, and excepting also when he shall exercise the powers and duties of President, in which case & in case of his absence, the Senate shall chuse a President pro tempore. — The vice President when acting as President of the Senate shall not have a vote unless the House be equally divided.'

(7) 'Sect— 4 The President by and with the advice and Consent of the Senate, shall have power to make Treaties; and he shall nominate and by and with the advice and consent of the Senate shall appoint ambassadors, and other public Ministers, Judges of the Supreme

Court, and all other Officers of the U—S—, whose appointments are not otherwise herein provided for. But no Treaty shall be made without the consent of two thirds of the members present.'

(8) After the words "into the service of the U S." in sect. 2. art: 10. add 'and may require the opinion in writing of the principal Officer in each of the Executive Departments, upon any subject relating to the duties of their respective offices.'

The latter part of Sect. 1. Art: 1. to read as follows:

(9) He shall be removed from his office on impeachment by the House of Representatives, and conviction by the Senate, for Treason, or bribery, and in case of his removal as aforesaid, death, absence, resignation or inability to discharge the powers or duties of his office, the vice-president shall exercise those powers and duties until another President be chosen, or until the inability of the President be removed.'[19]

*(Wednesday, September 5)*

Mr. Brearley from the Committee of Eleven made a farther report as follows,

(1) To add to the clause "to declare war" the words "and grant letters of marque and reprisal."

(2) To add to the clause "to raise and support armies" the words "but no appropriation of money to that use shall be for a longer term than two years"

(3) Instead of sect: 12. art. 6. say — "All bills for raising revenue shall originate in the House of Representatives, and shall be subject to alterations and amendments by the Senate: No money shall be drawn from the Treasury, but in consequence of appropriations made by law."

(4) Immediately before the last clause of Sect. 1. art. 7 — insert "To exercise exclusive legislation in all cases whatsoever over such district (not exceeding ten miles square) as may by Cession of particular States and the acceptance of the Legislature become the seate of the Government of the U—S— and to exercise like authority over all places purchased for the erection of Forts, Magazines, Arsenals, Dock-Yards, and other needful buildings"

(5) "To promote the progress of Science and useful arts for securing the limited times to authors & inventors, the exclusive right to their respective writings and discoveries"[20]

# N. The Constitution of the United States Adopted by the Constitutional Convention

*The Constitution adopted by the Convention on September 17, 1787, was signed by all but three delegates and ultimately ratified by all 13 states. The "Connecticut Compromise" basing representation in the House on population and providing each state equal votes in the Senate is embodied in Article I, Sections 2 and 3. The Brearley Committee can take credit for most of Article II, which creates the electoral college, defines the powers of the presidency, and provides for impeachment proceedings. An independent judiciary is created in Article III, although no mention is made of the power of judges to declare laws unconstitutional; the delegates regarded that power to be understood in the wake of Judge Brearley's Holmes v. Walton decision and similar cases in other states.*

We, the people of the United States, in order to form a more perfect Union, establish justice, insure domestic tranquility, provide for the common defense, promote the general welfare, and secure the blessings of liberty to ourselves and our posterity, do ordain and establish this Constitution for the United States of America.

## Article I

**Section 1** - Legislative powers; in whom vested
All legislative powers herein granted shall be vested in a Congress of the United States, which shall consist of a Senate and House of Representatives.

**Section 2** - House of Representatives, how and by whom chosen Qualifications of a Representative. Representatives and direct taxes, how apportioned. Enumeration. Vacancies to be filled. Power of choosing officers, and of impeachment.

1. The House of Representatives shall be composed of members chosen every second year by the people of the several States, and the elector in each State shall have the qualifications requisite for electors of the most numerous branch of the State Legislature.

2. No person shall be a Representative who shall not have attained the age of twenty-five years, and been seven years a Citizen of the United States, and who shall not, when elected, be an inhabitant of that State in which he shall be chosen.

3. Representatives and direct taxes shall be apportioned among the several States which may be included within this Union, according to their respective numbers, which shall be determined by adding the whole number of free persons, including those bound to service for a term of years, and excluding Indians not taxed, three-fifths of all other persons.(The previous sentence was superseded by Amendment XIV). The actual enumeration shall be made within three years after the first meeting of the Congress of the United States, and within every subsequent term of ten years, in such manner as they shall by law direct. The number of Representatives shall not exceed one for every thirty thousand, but each State shall have at least one Representative; and until such enumeration shall be made, the State of New Hampshire shall be entitled to choose three, Massachusetts eight, Rhode Island and Providence Plantations one, Connecticut five, New York six, New Jersey four, Pennsylvania eight, Delaware one, Maryland six, Virginia ten, North Carolina five, South Carolina five, and Georgia three.

4. When vacancies happen in the representation from any State, the Executive Authority thereof shall issue writs of election to fill such vacancies.

5. The House of Representatives shall choose their Speaker and other officers; and shall have the sole power of impeachment.

**Section 3** - Senators, how and by whom chosen. How classified. State Executive, when to make temporary appointments, in case, etc. Qualifications of a Senator. President of the Senate, his right to vote. President pro tem., and other officers of the Senate, how chosen. Power to try impeachments. When President is tried, Chief Justice to preside. Sentence.

1. The Senate of the United States shall be composed of two Senators from each State, (chosen by the Legislature thereof,) (The preceding five words were superseded by Amendment XVII) for six years; and each Senator shall have one vote.

2. Immediately after they shall be assembled in consequence of the first election, they shall be divided as equally as may be into three classes. The seats of the Senators of the first class shall be vacated at the expiration of the second year, of the second class at the expiration of the fourth year, and of the third class at the expiration of the sixth year, so that one-third may be chosen every second year; and if vacancies happen by resignation, or otherwise, during the recess of the Legislature of any State, the Executive thereof may make temporary appointments until the next meeting of the Legislature, which shall then fill such

vacancies. (The words in italics were superseded by Amendment XVII)

3. No person shall be a Senator who shall not have attained to the age of thirty years, and been nine years a Citizen of the United States, and who shall not, when elected, be an inhabitant of that State for which he shall be chosen.

4. The Vice-President of the United States shall be President of the Senate, but shall have no vote, unless they be equally divided.

5. The Senate shall choose their other officers, and also a President pro tempore, in the absence of the Vice President, or when he shall exercise the office of the President of the United States.

6. The Senate shall have the sole power to try all impeachments. When sitting for that purpose, they shall be on oath or affirmation. When the President of the United States is tried, the Chief Justice shall preside: and no person shall be convicted without the concurrence of two-thirds of the members present.

7. Judgement in cases of impeachment shall not extend further than to removal from office, and disqualification to hold and enjoy any office of honor, trust, or profit under the United States: but the party convicted shall nevertheless be liable and subject to indictment, trial, judgement and punishment, according to law.

**Section 4** - Times, etc., of holding elections, how prescribed. One session in each year.

1. The times, places and manner of holding elections for Senators and Representatives, shall be prescribed in each State by the Legislature thereof; but the Congress may at any time by law make or alter such regulations, except as to the places of choosing Senators.

2. The Congress shall assemble at least once in every year, and such meeting shall be on the first Monday in December,(The words in italics were superseded by Amendment XX) unless they by law appoint a different day.

**Section 5** - Membership, Quorum, Adjournments, Rules, Power to punish or expel. Journal. Time of adjournments, how limited, etc.

1. Each House shall be the judge of the elections, returns and qualifications of its own members, and a majority of each shall constitute a quorum to do business; but a smaller number may adjourn from day to day, and may be authorized to compel the attendance of absent members, in such manner, and under such penalties as each House may provide.

2. Each House may determine the rules of its proceedings, punish

its members for disorderly behavior, and, with the concurrence of two-thirds, expel a member.

3. Each House shall keep a journal of its proceedings, and from time to time publish the same, excepting such parts as may in their judgement require secrecy; and the yeas and nays of the members of either House on any question shall, at the desire of one-fifth of those present, be entered on the journal.

4. Neither House, during the session of Congress, shall, without the consent of the other, adjourn for more than three days, nor to any other place than that in which the two Houses shall be sitting.

**Section 6** - Compensation, Privileges, Disqualification in certain cases.

1. The Senators and Representatives shall receive a compensation for their services, to be ascertained by law, and paid out of the Treasury of the United States. They shall in all cases, except treason, felony and breach of the peace, be privileged from arrest during their attendance at the session of their respective Houses, and in going to and returning from the same; and for any speech or debate in either House, they shall not be questioned in any other place.

2. No Senator or Representative shall, during the time for which he was elected, be appointed to any civil office under the authority of the United States, which shall have increased during such time; and no person holding any office under the United States, shall be a member of either House during his continuance in office.

**Section 7** - House to originate all revenue bills. Veto. Bill may be passed by two-thirds of each House, notwithstanding, etc. Bill, not returned in ten days to become a law. Provisions as to orders, concurrent resolutions, etc.

1. All bills for raising revenue shall originate in the House of Representatives; but the Senate may propose or concur with amendments as on other bills.

2. Every bill which shall have passed the House of Representatives and the Senate, shall, before it become a law, be presented to the president of the United States; if he approve, he shall sign it, but if not, he shall return it, with his objections, to that house in which it shall have originated, who shall enter the objections at large on their journal, and proceed to reconsider it. If after such reconsideration, two thirds of that house shall agree to pass the bill, it shall be sent, together with the objections, to the other house, by which it shall likewise be reconsid-

ered, and if approved by two-thirds of that house, it shall become a law. But in all such cases the votes of both houses shall be determined by yeas and nays, and the names of the persons voting for and against the bill shall be entered on the journal of each house respectively. If any bill shall not be returned by the president within ten days (Sundays excepted) after it shall have been presented to him, the same shall be a law, in like manner as if he had signed it, unless the Congress by their adjournment prevent its return, in which case it shall not be a law.

3. Every order, resolution, or vote to which the concurrence of the Senate and House of Representatives may be necessary (except on a question of adjournment) shall be presented to the president of the United States; and before the same shall take effect, shall be approved by him, or, being disapproved by him, shall be re-passed by two-thirds of the Senate and House of Representatives, according to the rules and limitations prescribed in the case of a bill.

**Section 8** - Powers of Congress

The Congress shall have the power

1. To lay and collect taxes, duties, imposts and excises, to pay the debts and provide for the common defence and general welfare of the United States; but all duties, imposts and excises shall be uniform throughout the United States:

2. To borrow money on the credit of the United States:

3. To regulate commerce with foreign nations, and among the several states,and with the Indian tribes:

4. To establish an uniform rule of naturalization, and uniform laws on the subject of bankruptcies throughout the United States:

5. To coin money, regulate the value thereof, and of foreign coin, and fix the standard of weights and measures:

6. To provide for the punishment of counterfeiting the securities and current coin of the United States:

7. To establish post-offices and post-roads:

8. To promote the progress of science and useful arts, by securing for limited times to authors and inventors the exclusive right to their respective writings and discoveries:

9. To constitute tribunals inferior to the supreme court:

10. To define and punish piracies and felonies committed on the high seas, and offences against the law of nations:

11. To declare war, grant letters of marque and reprisal, and make

rules concerning captures on land and water:

12. To raise and support armies, but no appropriation of money to that use shall be for a longer term than two years:

13. To provide and maintain a navy:

14. To make rules for the government and regulation of the land and naval forces:

15. To provide for calling forth the militia to execute the laws of the union, suppress insurrections and repel invasions:

16. To provide for organizing, arming and disciplining the militia, and for governing such part of them as may be employed in the service of the United States, reserving to the states respectively, the appointment of the officers, and the authority of training the militia according to the discipline prescribed by Congress:

17. To exercise exclusive legislation in all cases whatsoever, over such district (not exceeding ten miles square) as may, by cession of particular states, and the acceptance of Congress, become the seat of the government of the United States, and to exercise like authority over all places purchased by the consent of the legislature of the state in which the same shall be, for the erection of forts, magazines, arsenals, dockyards, and other needful buildings: And,

18. To make all laws which shall be necessary and proper for carrying into execution the foregoing powers, and all other powers vested by this constitution in the government of the United States, or in any department or officer thereof.

**Section 9** - Provision as to migration or importation of certain persons. Habeas Corpus, Bills of attainder, etc. Taxes, how apportioned. No export duty. No commercial preference. Money, how drawn from Treasury, etc. No titular nobility. Officers not to receive presents, etc.

1. The migration or importation of such persons as any of the states now existing shall think proper to admit, shall not be prohibited by the Congress prior to the year 1808, but a tax or duty may be imposed on such importations, not exceeding 10 dollars for each person.

2. The privilege of the writ of habeas corpus shall not be suspended, unless when in cases of rebellion or invasion the public safety may require it.

3. No bill of attainder or ex post facto law shall be passed.

4. No capitation, or other direct tax shall be laid unless in proportion to the census or enumeration herein before directed to be taken.

(Modified by Amendement XVI)

5. No tax or duty shall be laid on articles exported from any state.

6. No preference shall be given by any regulation of commerce or revenue to the ports of one state over those of another: nor shall vessels bound to, or from one state, be obliged to enter, clear, or pay duties in another.

7. No money shall be drawn from the treasury but in consequence of appropriations made by law; and a regular statement and account of the receipts and expenditures of all public money shall be published from time to time.

8. No title of nobility shall be granted by the United States: And no person holding any office or profit or trust under them, shall, without the consent of the Congress, accept of any present, emolument, office, or title, of any kind whatever, from any king, prince, or foreign state.

**Section 10** - States prohibited from the exercise of certain powers.

1. No state shall enter into any treaty, alliance, or confederation; grant letters of marque and reprisal; coin money; emit bills of credit; make any thing but gold and silver coin a tender in payment of debts; pass any bill of attainder, ex post facto law, or law impairing the obligation of contracts, or grant any title of nobility.

2. No state shall, without the consent of the Congress, lay any imposts or duties on imports or exports, except what may be absolutely necessary for executing its inspection laws; and the net produce of all duties and imposts, laid by any state on imports or exports, shall be for the use of the treasury of the United States; and all such laws shall be subject to the revision and control of the Congress.

3. No state shall, without the consent of Congress, lay any duty of tonnage, keep troops, or ships of war in time of peace, enter into any agreement or compact with another state, or with a foreign power, or engage in a war, unless actually invaded, or in such imminent danger as will not admit of delay.

### Article II

**Section** 1- President: his term of office. Electors of President; number and how appointed. Electors to vote on same day. Qualification of President. On whom his duties devolve in case of his removal, death, etc. President's compensation. His oath of office.

1. The Executive power shall be vested in a President of the United States of America. He shall hold office during the term of four years, and together with the Vice President, chosen for the same term, be elected as follows:

2. Each State shall appoint, in such manner as the Legislature may direct, a number of electors, equal to the whole number of Senators and Representatives to which the State may be entitled in the Congress: but no Senator or Representative, or person holding an office of trust or profit under the United States, shall be appointed an elector. The electors shall meet in their respective States, and vote by ballot for two persons, of whom one at least shall not be an inhabitant of the same State with themselves. And they shall make a list of all the persons voted for each; which list they shall sign and certify, and transmit sealed to the seat of Government of the United States, directed to the President of the Senate. The President of the Senate shall, in the presence of the Senate and House of Representatives, open all the certificates, and the votes shall then be counted. The person having the greatest number of votes shall be the President, if such number be a majority of the whole number of electors appointed; and if there be more than one who have such majority, and have an equal number of votes, then the House of Representatives shall immediately choose by ballot one of them for President; and if no person have a majority, then from the five highest on the list the said House shall in like manner choose the President. But in choosing the President, the votes shall be taken by States, the representation from each State having one vote; a quorum for this purpose shall consist of a member or members from two-thirds of the States, and a majority of all the States shall be necessary to a choice. In every case, after the choice of the President, the person having the greatest number of votes of the electors shall be the Vice President. But if there should remain two or more who have equal votes, the Senate shall choose from them by ballot the Vice President.

3. The Congress may determine the time of choosing the electors, and the day on which they shall give their votes; which day shall be the same throughout the United States.

4. No person except a natural born Citizen, or a Citizen of the United States, at the time of the adoption of this Constitution, shall be eligible to the office of President; neither shall any person be eligible to that office who shall not have attained to the age of thirty-five years, and been fourteen years a resident within the United States.

5 . In case of the removal of the President from office, or of his death, resignation, or inability to discharge the powers and duties of the

said office, the same shall devolve on the Vice President, and the Congress may by law provide for the case of removal, death, resignation, or inability, both of the President and Vice President, declaring what officer shall then act as President, and such officer shall act accordingly, until the disability be removed, or a President shall be elected.

6. The President shall, at stated times, receive for his services, a compensation, which shall neither be increased nor diminished during the period for which he shall have been elected, and he shall not receive within that period any other emolument from the United States, or any of them.

7. Before he enter on the execution of his office, he shall take the following oath or affirmation:

"I do solemnly swear (or affirm) that I will faithfully execute the office of the President of the United States, and will to the best of my ability, preserve, protect and defend the Constitution of the United States."

**Section 2** - President to be Commander-in-Chief. He may require opinions of cabinet officers, etc., may pardon. Treaty-making power. Nomination of certain officers. When President may fill vacancies.

1. The President shall be Commander-in-Chief of the Army and Navy of the United States, and of the militia of the several States, when called into the actual service of the United States; he may require the opinion, in writing, of the principal officer in each of the executive departments, upon any subject relating to the duties of their respective offices, and he shall have power to grant reprieves and pardons for offenses against the United States, except in cases of impeachment.

2. He shall have power, by and with the advice and consent of the Senate, to make treaties, provided two-thirds of the Senators present concur; and he shall nominate, and by and with the advice and consent of the Senate, shall appoint ambassadors, other public ministers and consuls, judges of the Supreme Court, and all other officers of the United States, whose appointments are not herein otherwise provided for, and which shall be established by law: but the Congress may by law vest the appointment of such inferior officers, as they think proper, in the President alone, in the courts of law, or in the heads of departments.

3. The President shall have the power to fill up all vacancies that may happen during the recess of the Senate, by granting commissions, which shall expire at the end of their next session.

**Section 3** - President shall communicate to Congress. He may convene and adjourn Congress, in case of disagreement, etc. Shall receive ambassadors, execute laws, and commission officers.

He shall from time to time give to the Congress information of the state of the Union, and recommend to their consideration such measures as he shall judge necessary and expedient; he may, on extraordinary occasions, convene both Houses, or either of them, and in case of disagreement between them, with respect to the time of adjournment, he may adjourn them to such time as he shall think proper; he may receive ambassadors, and other public ministers; he shall take care that the laws be faithfully executed, and shall commission all the officers of the United States.

**Section 4** - All civil offices forfeited for certain crimes.

The President, Vice President, and all civil officers of the United States, shall be removed from office on impeachment for, and conviction of, treason, bribery, or other high crimes and misdemeanors.

**Article III**

**Section 1-** Judicial powers. Tenure. Compensation.

The judicial power of the United States, shall be vested in one supreme court, and in such inferior courts as the Congress may, from time to time, ordain and establish. The judges, both of the supreme and inferior courts, shall hold their offices during good behaviour, and shall, at stated times, receive for their services a compensation, which shall not be diminished during their continuance in office.

**Section 2** - Judicial power; to what cases it extends. Original jurisdiction of Supreme Court Appellate. Trial by Jury, etc. Trial, where

1. The judicial power shall extend to all cases, in law and equity, arising under this constitution, the laws of the United States, and treaties made, or which shall be made under their authority; to all cases affecting ambassadors, other public ministers and consuls; to all cases of admiralty and maritime jurisdiction; to controversies to which the United States shall be a party; to controversies between two or more states, between a state and Citizens of another state, between Citizens of different states, between Citizens of the same state, claiming lands under grants of different states, and between a state, or the Citizens thereof, and foreign states, Citizens or subjects.

2. In all cases affecting ambassadors, other public ministers and consuls, and those in which a state shall be a party, the supreme court shall have original jurisdiction. In all the other cases before-mentioned,

the supreme court shall have appellate jurisdiction, both as to law and fact, with such exceptions, and under such regulations as the Congress shall make.

3. The trial of all crimes, except in cases of impeachment, shall be by jury; and such trial shall be held in the state where the said crimes shall have been committed; but when not committed within any state, the trial shall be at such place or places as the Congress may by law have directed.

**Section 3** - Treason defined. Proof of. Punishment of.

1. Treason against the United States shall consist only in levying war against them, or in adhering to their enemies, giving them aid and comfort. No person shall be convicted of treason unless on the testimony of two witnesses to the same overt act, or on confession in open court.

2. The Congress shall have power to declare the punishment of treason, but no attainder of treason shall work corruption of blood, or forfeiture, except during the life of the person attainted.

### Article IV

**Section 1** - Each State to give credit to the public acts, etc. of every other State.

Full faith and credit shall be given in each state to the public acts, records and judicial proceedings of every other state. And the Congress may by general laws prescribe the manner in which such acts, records and proceedings shall be proved, and the effect thereof.

**Section 2** - Privileges of Citizens of each State. Fugitives from Justice to be delivered up. Persons held to service having escaped, to be delivered up.

1. The Citizens of each state shall be entitled to all privileges and immunities of Citizens in the several states.

2. A person charged in any state with treason, felony, or other crime, who shall flee justice, and be found in another state, shall, on demand of the executive authority of the state from which he fled, be delivered up, to be removed to the state having jurisdiction of the crime.

3. No person held to service or labour in one state, under the laws thereof, escaping into another, shall, in consequence of any law or regulation therein, be discharged from such service or labour, but shall be deliv-

ered up on claim of the party to whom such service or labour may be due.

**Section 3** - Admission of new States. Power of Congress over territory and other property.

1. New states may be admitted by the Congress into this union; but no new state shall be formed or erected within the jurisdiction of any other state, nor any state be formed by the junction of two or more states, without the consent of the legislatures of the states concerned, as well as of the Congress.

2. The Congress shall have power to dispose of and make all needful rules and regulations respecting the territory or other property belonging to the United States; and nothing in this constitution shall be so construed as to prejudice any claims of the United States, or of any particular state.

**Section 4** - Republican form of government guaranteed. Each State to be protected.

The United States shall guarantee to every state in this union, a republican form of government, and shall protect each of them against invasion; and on application of the legislature, or of the executive (when the legislature cannot be convened), against domestic violence.

### Article V

**Constitution:** how amended; proviso.

The Congress, whenever two-thirds of both houses shall deem it necessary, shall propose amendments to this constitution, or on the application of the legislatures of two-thirds of the several states, shall call a convention for proposing amendments, which , in either case, shall be valid to all intents and purposes, as part of this constitution, when ratified by the legislatures of three-fourths of the several states, or by conventions in three-fourths thereof, as the one or the other mode of ratification may be proposed by the Congress: Provided, that no amendment which may be made prior to the year 1808, shall in any manner affect the first and fourth clauses in the ninth section of the first article; and that no state, without its consent, shall be deprived of its equal suffrage in the Senate.

### Article VI

**Certain debts**, ect. declared valid, Supremacy of Constitution, treaties, and laws of the United States, Oath to support Constitution, by whom taken. No religious test.

1. All debts contracted and engagements entered into, before the adoption of this constitution, shall be as valid against the United States under this constitution, as under the confederation.

2. This constitution, and the laws of the United States which shall be made in pursuance thereof; and all treaties made, or which shall be made, under the authority of the United States shall be the supreme law of the land; and the judges in every state shall be bound thereby, any thing in the constitution or laws of any state to the contrary notwithstanding.

3. The senators and representatives before-mentioned, and the members of the several state legislatures, and all executive and judicial officers, both of the United States and of the several states, shall be bound by oath or affirmation, to support this constitution; but no religious test shall ever be required as a qualification to any office or public trust under the United States.

### Article VII

What ratification shall establish constitution.

The ratification of the conventions of nine states, shall be sufficient for the establishment of this constitution between the states so ratifying the same.[21]

# Large State, Small State

New Jersey ranked ninth in population and regarded itself as a small state when its delegation led a coalition of small- and mid-sized states in battling the giant states of Virginia, Massachusetts and Pennsylvania over how power would be apportioned in the new government. David Brearley and his fellow New Jersey delegates ultimately won equal votes for each state in the Senate and greater weight for the smaller states in the Electoral College. They did not foresee that two centuries later, New Jersey would be one of the larger states — third in population among the original 13 and ninth overall out of 50 — and that its political power, and that of the "blue states" with which it usually votes, would have been greater under the strict-population approach embodied in the Virginia Plan. If votes in the Electoral College were apportioned strictly on the basis of population, Democrat Al Gore would have been elected President over Republican George W. Bush in 2000.

| EstimatedPopulationof13OriginalStates During1787ConstitutionalConvention | | | Populationof13OriginalStates in 2000 U.S. Census | | |
|---|---|---|---|---|---|
| 1 Virginia | 420,000 | 16.4% | 1 New York | 18,976,457 | 22.8% |
| 2 Massachusetts | 352,000 | 13.8% | 2 Pennsylvania | 12,281,054 | 14.7% |
| 3 Pennsylvania | 341,000 | 13.3% | 4 New Jersey | 8,414,350 | 10.1% |
| 4 New York | 238,000 | 9.3% | 4 NorthCarolina | 8,049,313 | 9.7% |
| 5 Maryland | 222,000 | 8.7% | 5 Virginia | 7,078,515 | 8.5% |
| 6 Connecticut | 202,000 | 7.9% | 6 Georgia | 6,478,216 | 7.8% |
| 7 NorthCarolina | 200,000 | 7.8% | 7 Massachusetts | 6,349,097 | 7.6% |
| 8 SouthCarolina | 150,000 | 5.9% | 8 Maryland | 5,296,486 | 6.4% |
| 9 New Jersey | 145,000 | 5.7% | 9 SouthCarolina | 4,012,012 | 4.8% |
| 10 New Hampshire | 102,000 | 4.0% | 10 Connecticut | 3,405,565 | 4.1% |
| 11 Georgia | 90,000 | 3.5% | 11 New Hampshire | 1,235,786 | 1.5% |
| 12 RhodeIsland | 58,000 | 2.3% | 12 RhodeIsland | 1,048,319 | 1.3% |
| 13 Delaware | 37,000 | 1.4% | 13 Delaware | 783,600 | 0.9% |
| | 2,557,000 | | Total for 13 States | 83,408,770 | |
| | | | U.S.Total | 281,421,906 | |

SOURCES: The chart above uses South Carolina delegate Charles C. Pinckney's population estimates for Virginia, Maryland, the Carolinas, and Georgia, and Brearley's figures for the other eight states; Pinckney's estimate counts slaves as 3/5 based on the ratio

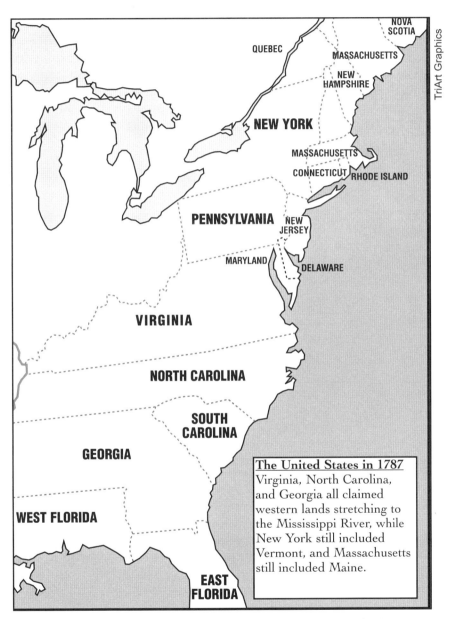

TriArt Graphics

QUEBEC

NOVA
SCOTIA

MASSACHUSETTS

NEW
HAMPSHIRE

NEW YORK

MASSACHUSETTS

CONNECTICUT RHODE ISLAND

PENNSYLVANIA NEW
JERSEY

MARYLAND DELAWARE

VIRGINIA

NORTH CAROLINA

SOUTH
CAROLINA

GEORGIA

**The United States in 1787**
Virginia, North Carolina,
and Georgia all claimed
western lands stretching to
the Mississippi River, while
New York still included
Vermont, and Massachusetts
still included Maine.

WEST FLORIDA

EAST
FLORIDA

agreed upon early in the Constitutional Convention. Brearley's
numbers for eight northern states count free inhabitants and slaves
equally because those states already had approved gradual emancipa-
tion laws. Figures for the year 2000 are drawn from the U.S. Census.

# BIBLIOGRAPHY

Abbot, W. W., and Dorothy Twohig, eds. *The Papers of George Washington, Confederation Series, Vols. 1-4 and 6.* Charlottesville, Va., and London: University Press of Virginia, 1992-1997.

— *The Papers of George Washington, Revolutionary War Series, Vols. 5, 12 and 14.* Charlottesville, Va., and London: University Press of Virginia, 1985-2003.

*Appleton's Cyclopaedia of American Biography.* "Brearley, David," in Volume 1. New York: D. Appleton and Company, 1888.

Avalon Project at Yale Law School, The. *Notes of William Paterson in the Federal Convention of 1787,* http://www.yale.edu/lawweb/avalon/const/patterson.htm.

Avery, Ron. "The Story of Valley Forge," http://www.ushistory. org/valley-forge/history/vstory.htm.

Bellot, Carla Vivian and Arthur T. Vanderbilt II. *Jersey Justice: 300 Years of the New Jersey Judiciary.* New Jersey: Institute for Continuing Legal Education, 1978.

Berkin, Carol. *A Brilliant Solution: Inventing the American Constitution.* New York: Harcourt, Inc., 2002.

Bernstein, David A. "William Livingston: The Role of the Executive in New Jersey's Revolutionary War," in Wright, William C., ed., *New Jersey in the American Revolution II. Papers Presented at the Fourth Annual New Jersey History Symposium, December 2, 1972.* Trenton, N.J.: New Jersey Historical Commission, 1973.

Bernstein, Richard B., with Kim Rice. *Are We To Be a Nation? The Making of the Constitution.* Cambridge, Mass.: Harvard University Press, 1987.

Bloom, Sol. "Questions and Answers Pertaining to the Constitution." National Archives and Records Administration, http://www.nara.gov/exhall/charters/constitution/conqa.html.

Bogin, Ruth. *Abraham Clark and the Quest for Equality in the Revolutionary Era, 1774-1794.* Rutherford, Madison, and Teaneck, N.J.: Fairleigh Dickinson University Press, 1982.

Boyd, Julian P., ed. "The Connecticut-Pennsylvania Territorial Dispute," in *The Papers of Thomas Jefferson. Volume 6. 21 May 1781 to 1 March 1784,* Princeton, N.J.: Princeton University Press, 1952.

Brearley, David. "Extracts from the Diary of Chief Justice David Brearley Jan. 1776-Dec. 1786," in N.J. State Archives, Division of Records Management Manuscript Collection, General William S. Stryker Papers.

Brearley, W. H. (William Henry). "Genealogical Chart of the American Branch of the Brearley Family." Detroit: Privately printed, March 1, 1886.

Brennan, Justice William J. Jr. "New Jersey's Ratified Copy of the Federal Constitution." *The Journal of the Rutgers University Library.* Vol. XXIII (1). New Brunswick, N.J.: December 1959.

Brown, Richard D. "Brearley, David." *World Book Online Americas Edition.* http://www.aolsvc.worldbook.aol.com/wbol/Wb Page/na/ar/co/75180.

Brown, Roger H. *Redeeming the Republic: Federalists, Taxation, and the Origins of the Constitution.* Baltimore and London: The Johns Hopkins University Press, 1993.

Casey, Monita. "Framer of few words: N.J.'s Brearley wasn't free with his speech," *The Times of Trenton,* September 8, 1987, 2.

Clevenger, William M. *The Courts of New Jersey: Their Origin, Composition, and Jurisdiction.* Plainfield, N.J.: New Jersey Law Journal Publishing Company, 1903.

Collier, Christopher. *All Politics Is Local: Family, Friends, and Provincial Interests in the Creation of the Constitution.* Hanover, N.H., and London: University Press of New England, 2003.

Common Pleas. *Elisha Walton v. John Holmes.* Monmouth County Archives, Freehold, N.J., 1789-1791.

Dayton, Hughes. "Elias Dayton, Brigadier General, Continental Line of New Jersey." Address to the Society of the Cincinnati, Atlantic City, N.J., July 4, 1901.

Dayton, William L. "Historical Sketch of the Trenton Academy, Speech read at the Centennial Anniversary of Its Foundation, February 10, 1881." Trenton, N.J.: John L. Murphy, Book and Job Printer, 1881.

DePauw, Linda Grant, ed. *Senate Executive Journal and Related Documents, Volume II.* Baltimore and London: The Johns Hopkins University Press, 1974.

Duer, William Alexander. *The Life of William Alexander, Erl of Stirling; Major General in the Army of the United States During the Revolution: With Selections from his Correspondence.* New York: Wiley & Putnam. Published for the New Jersey Historical Society, 1847.

Ellis, Franklin. *History of Monmouth County, New Jersey.* Philadelphia: R.T. Peck & Co., 1885.

Erdman, Charles R. Jr. *The New Jersey Constitution of 1776*. Princeton, N.J.: Princeton University Press, 1929.

Farrand, Max, ed., *The Records of the Federal Convention of 1787, Vols. I-III.* New Haven: Yale University Press, 1911.

Fitzpatrick, John C., ed. *The Writings of George Washington from the Original Manuscript Sources 1745-1799. Vols. 5-7, 9-12, 14, and 19.* Washington, DC: United States Government Printing Office, 1931-1944.

Fleming, Thomas. *1776: Year of Illusions.* New York: W. W. Norton & Company Inc., 1975.

Fliegel, Jonah. *William Paterson.* Master's thesis, Columbia University., New York City, n.d.

Fowler, David J., *Egregious Villains, Wood Rangers and London Traders: The Pine Robber Phenomenon During the Revolutionary War.* Ph.D. dissertation. University of Michigan, Ann Arbor, 1987.

Garrison, Ann, John Fabiano, and Alice Wikoff, ed. "Allen's Town, New Jersey: A Crossroads of the American Revolution 1775-1783." (Early Research Draft. March, 21, 2001, updated through 2005).

Gerlach, Larry R. *Prologue to Independence: New Jersey in the Coming of the American Revolution.* New Brunswick, N.J.: Rutgers University Press, 1976.

Glenn, Thomas Allen. *William Churchill Houston 1746-1788.* Norristown, Pa.: Privately printed, 1903.

Gudmundson, G. G. *Courts in New Jersey.* Elizabeth, N.J.: Thomas Jefferson High School, 1931.

Haskett, Richard C. *William Paterson, Counselor at Law.* PhD dissertation, Princeton University, Princeton, N.J., 1952.

Heaton, Ronald E. *Masonic Membership of the Signers of the Constitution of the United States.* Washington, D.C.: Masonic Service Association, 1962.

Historic Valley Forge. "Weather Report at Valley Forge 1775-1782." http://ushistory.org/valleyforge/history/weather.html.

Hodges, Graham. "New Jersey in the American Revolution," in Blanco, Richard L., ed., *The American Revolution 1775-1783: An Encyclopedia. Vol. II.* New York & London: Garland Publishing Inc., 1993.

Horowitz, Gary S. *New Jersey Land Riots, 1745-1755.* PhD dissertation, The Ohio State University, 1966.

Hutchinson, Esq., Charles R., "Allentown." Charles R. Hutchinson Collection, New Jersey Historical Society Archives, Newark, N.J., Family Records [Series 1], Book 4.

Jensen, Merrill, ed. *The Documentary History of the Ratification of the Constitution. Volume III. Ratification of the Constitution by the States Delaware New Jersey Georgia Connecticut.* Madison, Wis.: The State Historical Society of Wisconsin, 1978.

Jillson, Calvin C. *Constitution Making: Conflict and Consensus in the Federal Convention of 1787.* New York: Agathon Press Inc., 1988.

Johnson, Allen, ed. "David Brearly," in the *Dictionary of American Biography. Volume III.* New York: Charles Scribner's Sons, 1929.

Kahn, Lea. "Signer of U.S. Constitution was born here — but where?" in the *Lawrence Ledger,* February 10, 1987, 1.

Keasbey, Edward Quinton. *The Courts And Lawyers Of New Jersey, 1661–1912. Vol. II.* New York: Lewis Historical Publishing Company, 1912.

Kelly, C. Brian. "Battle of Long Island, New York (August 27, 1776)," in Blanco, Richard L., ed., *The American Revolution 1775-1783: An Encyclopedia. Vol. I.* New York & London: Garland Publishing Inc., 1993.

Lawrence Historical Society. "1761 Brearley House." Lawrence, N.J., 2000.

— "Brearley House History." Lawrence, N.J., 2000.

— "Lawrence Township Celebrates the Bicentennial of the Constitution." Exhibition Pamphlet for 200th Anniversary Observance, September 20, 1987. Lawrenceville, N.J.: Union Camp Corporation.

Lee, Francis B., ed. *Documents Relating To The Revolutionary History of the State of New Jersey Vol. II: Extracts From American Newspapers. Vol. II, 1778.* Trenton, N.J.: The John L. Murphy Publishing Company, 1903.

Lefkowitz, Arthur S. *The Long Retreat: The Calamitous Defense of New Jersey 1776.* Metuchen, N.J.: The Upland Press, 1998.

Lender, Mark Edward, and James K. Martin. *Citizen Soldier: The Revolutionary War Journal of Joseph Bloomfield.* Newark, N.J.: New Jersey Historical Society, 1982.

—*"This Honorable Court": A History of the United States District Court for the District of New Jersey* (working title). New Brunswick, N.J.: Rutgers University Press, 2005.

Library of Congress. *Journals of the Continental Congress 1774-1789. Volumes XIV, XXXIII and XXXIV.* Washington, DC: United States Government Printing Office, 1937.

— *The George Washington Papers.* Washington, DC: Manuscript Division, Reference Department, 1964.

Lurie, Maxine L. *New Jersey and the Ratification of the United States*

*Constitution: A Transcription of the Ratification Document, Biographies of the Signers, and Bibliography Sources.* New Brunswick, N.J.: Rutgers University Press, 1976.

— *New Jersey and the Ratification of the United States Constitution: An Exhibition Catalog.* New Brunswick, N.J.: Rutgers University Press, 1976.

Marcus, Maeva, ed. *The Documentary History of the Supreme Court of the United States, 1789-1800. Volume Two. The Justices on Circuit 1790-1794.* New York: Columbia University Press, 1988.

Martin, Joseph Plumb. *Private Yankee Doodle; being a narrative of some of the adventures, dangers, and sufferings of a Revolutionary soldier.* Edited by George F. Scheer. Boston: Little, Brown, 1962.

Masonic Service Association of the United States. *The Master Mason ...* Washington, D.C.: The Masonic Service Association of the United States, n.d.

McConville, Brendan. *Those Daring Disturbers of the Public Peace: The Struggle for Property and Power in Early New Jersey.* Ithaca, N.Y., and London: Cornell University Press, 1999.

McCormick, Richard. *Experiment in Independence: New Jersey in the Critical Period 1781-1789.* New Brunswick, N.J.: Rutgers University Press, 1950.

— *New Jersey from Colony to State.* New Brunswick, N.J.: Rutgers University Press, 1964.

— "The Unanimous State." *The Journal of the Rutgers University Library.* Vol. XXIII (1). New Brunswick, N.J.: December 1959.

McCullough, David. *John Adams.* New York: Simon & Schuster, 2001.

McGregor, David. "Historical Address on Early Free-masonry in New Jersey and Pennsylvania." The Annual Grand Communication of the Grand Lodge of Pennsylvania, Philadelphia, December 27, 1928.

— "Contributions to the Early History of Freemasonry in New Jersey," n.d.

*Minutes of the Provincial Congress and the Council of Safety of the State of New Jersey, 1775 and 1776.* Trenton, N.J.: Naar, Day & Naar, 1879.

Monmouth County Historical Association. *Cherry Hall Papers.* Collection of Revolutionary War-era documents in the archives of the MCHA in Freehold, N.J.

Mossman, Philip L. *Money of the American Colonies and Confederation.* New York: The American Numismatic Society. 1993.

Murrin, Mary R. *To Save This State From Ruin: New Jersey and the Creation of the United States Constitution 1776-1789.* Trenton, N.J.: New Jersey Historical Commission, Department of State, 1987.

Nash, Winona D., ed. *A History of Land Ownership, Lawrence (Maidenhead) Township, Mercer County, New Jersey, Circa 1776: Your Guide to Our Bicentennial Map.* Lawrenceville, N.J.: Lawrence Historic & Aesthetic Commission, 1977.

— "Brearley Genealogy." Lawrence Township Historical Society collection, n.d.

— (ed.) *Pictorial History of Lawrence Township, 1697–1997.* Lawrenceville, N.J.: The Township of Lawrence, 1997.

— (ed.) *Volume I of the Minutes of Lawrence (Maidenhead) Township, Mercer, County, New Jersey.* 2 vols. Lawrenceville, N.J.: Lawrence Historic and Aesthetic Commission, 1976.

— "Commentary on Research of W.H. Brearley." Unpublished. Lawrence Township Historical Society collection, 1999.

National Archives and Records Administration. "America's Founding Fathers: Delegates to the Constitutional Convention," http://www.archives.gov/national_archives_experience/charters/constitution_founding_fathers.html.

— "Electoral Votes for President and Vice President 1789-1793," http://nara.gov.fedreg/elctcoll/ecstats.html.

Neale, Isaac. *Cases Adjudged in the Supreme Court of New Jersey; Relative to the Manumission of Negros and Others Holden in Bondage.* Burlington, N.J.: The New Jersey Society for Promoting the Abolition of Slavery, 1794.

Nelson, William, ed. *Documents Relating to the Colonial History of the State of New Jersey Volume XII: I. Some Account of American Newspapers, Particularly of the Eighteenth Century, and Libraries in Which They May Be Found. II. Extracts from American Newspapers Relating to New Jersey. Vol. II.* Paterson, N.J.: The Call Printing and Publishing Co., 1895.

— ed. *Documents Relating to the Colonial History of the State of New Jersey Volume XXVI: Extracts From American Newspapers Relating To New Jersey Vol. VII, 1768-1769.* Paterson, N.J.: The Call Printing and Publishing Co., 1904.

— ed. *Documents Relating to the Colonial History of the State of New Jersey Volume XXVII: Extracts From American Newspapers, Relating to New Jersey Vol. VIII, 1770-1771.* Paterson, N.J.: The Press Printing and Publishing Co., 1905.

— ed. *Documents Relating to the Colonial History of the State of New Jersey Volume XXVIII: Extracts From American Newspapers Relating to New Jersey Vol. IX, 1772–1773.* Paterson, N.J.: The Call Printing and Publishing Co., 1916.

— ed. *Documents Relating to the Colonial History of the State of New Jersey Volume XXIX: Tenth Volume of Extracts From American Newspapers Relating to New Jersey 1773–1774.* Paterson, N.J.: The Call Printing and Publishing Co., 1917.

— ed. *Documents Relating to the Revolutionary History of the State of New Jersey Volume III: Extracts From American Newspapers Relating to New Jersey. Vol. III, 1779.* Trenton, N.J.: The John L Murphy Publishing Company, 1906.

— ed. *Documents Relating to the Revolutionary History of the State of New Jersey Volume IV: Extracts From American Newspapers Relating To New Jersey. November 1, 1779 to September 30, 1780.* Trenton, N.J.: State Gazette Publishing Company, 1914.

New Jersey State Archives, Book 15. Manuscript Collection, Reference Department, New Jersey State Archives, Trenton, N.J.

New Jersey Supreme Court. *John Holmes and Solomon Ketcham v. Elisha Walton*, Supreme Court case number 18354. New Jersey State Archives, Trenton, N.J.

— *Holmes v. Walton*, Supreme Court case number 44928. New Jersey State Archives, Trenton, N.J.

O'Connor, John E. *William Paterson: Lawyer and Statesman, 1745-1806.* New Brunswick, N.J.: Rutgers University Press, 1979.

Ogden, Aaron. *Autobiography ... An original document written by Col. Aaron Ogden for his children.* Paterson, N.J.: Press Printing & Publishing Company, 1893.

*Pennsylvania Gazette,* Numb. 2202, March 7, 1771 (short account of fire at Brearley home), August 13, 1777 (death notice of Elizabeth Brearley), and February 9, 1979 (American Philosophical Society).

*Pennsylvania Magazine of History and Biography.* "General Muhlenberg's Orderly Book, 1777," in Vol. 35, No. 1, 1911.

— "Letter of Colonel Israel Shreve, New Jersey Continental Line, To His Wife, 1778," in "Notes and Queries." Vol. 39, No. 3, 1915.

— "Orderly Book of General Edward Hand," in Vol. 41, No. 2, 1917.

— "Residents of Bucks County, Pa., 1677-1687," in Vol. 9, No. 2, 1885.

— "William Biles," in Vol. 26, No. 4, 1902.

Peters, William. *A More Perfect Union.* New York: Crown Publishers Inc., 1987.

Prince, Carl E. *William Livingston: New Jersey's First Governor.* Trenton, N.J.: The New Jersey Historical Commission, 1975.

Prince, Carl E., Mary Lou Lustig, David William Voorhees, and Robert J. Weiss, eds. *The Papers of William Livingston, Vols. 1-5*. Published for the New Jersey Historical Commission, Department of State, by Rutgers University Press, New Brunswick, N.J., and London, 1988.

Princeton University Online, "Princeton University in the American Revolution." http://www.Princeton.edu/pr/facts/revolution. html.

Rees, John U. "'One of the best in the army': An Overview of the 2nd New Jersey Regiment and General William Maxwell's Jersey Brigade." http://www.continentalline.org/articles/9801/ 980105.htm.

Richards, Louis, and George S. L. Ward. *Records Relating to Richards and Rogers Families Used in Preparation of a 'Sketch of Descendants of Owen Richards,' (1885) 'Memorial Tribute to the Late John Richards,' (1885) and a 'Sketch of Descendants of Samuel Rogers' (1888)*. Manuscript in the private collection of John Fabiano, Allentown, N.J.

Ricord, Frederick M., and William Nelson, eds. *Documents Relating to the Colonial History of the State of New Jersey. Volume XV. Journal of the Governor and Council. Vol. III, 1738-1748*. Trenton, N.J.: The John L. Murphy Publishing Co., 1891.

Rosenberg, Leonard Boyne. *The Political Thought of William Paterson*. PhD dissertation, New School for Social Research, New York City, 1967.

Rossiter, Clinton Lawrence. *1787: The Grand Convention*. New York: Macmillan, 1966.

Rutgers University Libraries, Special Collections and University Archives. "New Jersey's Three Constitutions: 1776, 1844, 1947. Exhibition Guidebook." January 27-June 30, 1998, Gallery 50, Special Collection and University Archives, Archibald Stevens Alexander Library. New Brunswick, N.J.: Rutgers University Press, 1998.

— "Jonathan Dayton Papers, 1783-1819 (inclusive)." Manuscript collection.

— "William Paterson Papers, 1766-1898." Manuscript collection.

Ryan, Dennis P. *New Jersey in the American Revolution, 1763-1783: A Chronology*. Trenton, N.J.: New Jersey Historical Commission, 1974.

Sanborn, Paul J. "Battle of Brandywine, Pennsylvania," "Battle of Germantown, Pennsylvania," and "Battle of Monmouth, New Jersey," in Blanco, Richard L., ed., *The American Revolution 1775-1783: An Encyclopedia. Vols. I and II*. New York & London: Garland Publishing Inc., 1993.

Schecter, Barnet. *The Battle for New York: The City at the Heart of the American Revolution*. New York: Walker and Company, 2002.

Schuyler, Hamilton. *A History of St. Michael's Church: Trenton - In the Diocese of New Jersey from its Foundation in the Year of Our Lord 1703 to 1926*. Princeton, N.J.: Princeton University Press, 1926.

Scott, Austin, ed. *Documents Relating to the Revolutionary History of the State of New Jersey Vol. V: Newspaper Extracts Relating to the New Jersey, October 1780–July 1782*. Trenton, N. J.: State Gazette Publishing Co., 1917.

— "Holmes vs. Walton: The New Jersey Precedent: A Chapter in the History of Judicial Power and Unconstitutional Legislation." *American Historical Review*, Vol. 4: 1899.

Second New Jersey Regiment Revolutionary War Research Library. "A Day in the Life of Camp." http://www.2nj.org/ camp.htm.

— "New Jersey Continentals and Militia." http://www.2nj.org/ nj_continentals.htm.

— "Officer Life." http://www.2nj.org/officers_life.htm

— "Soldier Life in Morristown." http://www.2nj.org/ soldiers_ life.htm.

— "The 1764 Manual Exercise." http://www.2nj.org/ 1764.htm.

*Selections from the Correspondence of the Executive of New Jersey, From 1776 to 1786*. Published by Order of the Legislature. N.J.: *Newark Daily Advertiser*, 1848.

Shaw, William H. *History of Essex and Hudson Counties, New Jersey*, Volume 1. Philadelphia: Everts & Peck, 1884.

Sheridan, Eugene R. *Lewis Morris 1671-1746: A Study in Early American Politics*. Syracuse, N.Y.: Syracuse University Press, 1981.

*The Shreve Papers, 1776-1792*. Emily Scott Evans Collection, University of Houston Libraries, 1967.

Shreve, John, "Personal Narrative of the Services of Lieut. John Shreve of the New Jersey Line of the Continental Army," in *Magazine of American History*, Vol. 3, Part 2, 1879.

Shriner, Charles. *William Paterson*. Paterson, N.J.: Paterson Industrial Commission, 1940.

Smith, Edward Y., Jr., Earl G. Gieser, George J. Goss, Frank Z. Kovach, and Stanford Lanterman. *History of Freemasonry in New Jersey Commemorating the Two Hundredth Anniversary of the Organization of the Grand Lodge of The Most Ancient and Honorable Society of Free and Accepted Masons for the State of New Jersey 1787-1987*. History Committee, New Jersey Masons, 1987.

Smith, Paul H., ed., and Ronald M. Gephardt, assoc. ed. *Letters of Delegates to Congress 1774-1789. Vols. 16, 19, and 24.* Washington, DC: Library of Congress, 1996.

*The Society of the Cincinnati in the State of New Jersey, With the Institution, Rules and Regulations of the Society, General Officers, Officers of the New Jersey Society, By-Laws, Roll of Members, Interesting Documents from the Archives of the Society, etc., etc.* Bethlehem, Pa.: Times Publishing Company, Inc., 1949.

Solberg, Winton U., ed. *The Constitutional Convention and the Formation of the Union.* 2d ed. Chicago: University of Illinois Press, 1990.

Stellhorn, Paul A., and Michael J. Birkner, ed. *The Governors of New Jersey 1664-1974: Biographical Essays.* Trenton, N.J.: New Jersey Historical Commission, 1982.

Stockton, Samuel Witham, Esq., Convention Secretary. *Minutes of the Convention of the State of New Jersey Holden at Trenton the 11th Day of December 1787.* Trenton, N.J.: Isaac Collins, Printer to the State, 1788.

Storms, F. Dean. *History of Allentown New Jersey.* Allentown, N.J.: Allentown Messenger, 1965.

Strayer, Joseph Reese, ed. *The Delegate From New York, or Proceedings of the Federal Convention of 1787 from the Notes of John Lansing Jr.* Princeton, N.J.: Princeton University Press, 1939.

Stryker, William S., ed. *Documents Relating to the Revolutionary History of the State of New Jersey Vol. I: Extracts From American Newspapers Vol. I, 1776–1777.* Trenton, N.J.: The John L. Murphy Publishing Co., 1903.

— *Official Register: Officers and Men of New Jersey In Revolutionary War.* Trenton, N.J.: William T. Nicholson & Company, 1872.

— *General Maxwell's Brigade of the New Jersey Continental Line in the expedition against the Indians in the year 1779.* Trenton, N.J.: W. S. Sharp, printer, 1885.

— *Washington's Reception by the People of New Jersey in 1789.* Trenton, N.J.: Naar, Day & Naar, 1882.

— *The Battles of Trenton and Princeton.* New York: Houghton, Mifflin and Company, 1898.

— *The Heroes in the Revolution: Address at the dinner of the State Society of the Cincinnati of Pennsylvania on the occasion of the unveiling of the Washington Monument, in Fairmount Park, Philadelphia, May 15, 1897.* Trenton, N.J.: The John L. Murphy Publishing Company, Printers, 1898

— *The Battle of Monmouth.* Edited by William Starr Myers. Princeton, N.J.: Princeton University Press, 1927.

Syrett, Harold C., ed. *The Papers of Alexander Hamilton. Volume XIII. November 1792–February 1793.* New York and London: Columbia University Press, 1967.

Tanner, Mary Nelson. "David Brearley, Soldier and Statesman," in Township of Lawrence, *Pictorial History of Lawrence Township 1697-1997. A Tricentennial Publication.* Succasunna, N.J.: Esposito Office, Jostens, 1997.

— "David Brearley, Soldier and Statesman," a September 20, 1787, slide address for the Lawrence Township bicentennial celebration of the Constitution of the United States.

— "Joseph Brearley and the Campaign to Conquer Canada." Unpublished manuscript.

—"Letters Home: Joseph Brearley and the Campaign to Conquer Canada," in *New Jersey Heritage*, Summer 2002, Vol. 1, No. 3, 32-41.

— Memo to the author reviewing early draft of David Brearley book, 2002.

Thompson, William V. *Israel Shreve: Revolutionary War Officer.* Ruston, La.: McGinty Trust Fund Publications, 1979.

United States Army. *David Brearley.* Part of the "Soldier-  statesmen of the Constitution" series. Washington, D.C.: U.S. Army Center of Military History, 1986.

United States Congress. *The Judiciary Act of 1789: "An Act to establish the Judicial Courts of the United States,"* September 24, 1789. http://air.fjc.gov/history/landmark/ 02a_bdy.html.

U.S. Constitution Online, The. "New Jersey's Ratification." http://www.usconstitution.net/rat_nj/html.

United States District Court: New Jersey History. "The Early History of the United States District Court for the District of New Jersey." http://pacer.njd.uscourts.gov.njdc.hist1.htm.

Von Steuben, Baron Frederick William. *Baron von Steuben's Revolutionary War Drill Manual: A Facsimile Reprint of the 1794 Edition.* New York: Dover Publications, Inc., 1985.

Walker, Edwin Robert, et. al. *A History of Trenton 1679-1929: Two Hundred and Fifty Years of a Notable Town with Links in Four Centuries.* Vol. 1. Princeton, N.J.: Princeton University Press, 1929.

Ward, George S. L., and Louis Richards. *A Sketch of Some of the Descendants of Samuel Rogers of Monmouth County, New Jersey.* Philadelphia: Collins Printing House, 1888.

Ward, Harry M. *General William Maxwell and the New Jersey Continentals.* Contributions in Military Studies, Number 168. Westport, Conn., and London: Greenwood Press, 1997.

Weedon, General George. *Valley Forge Orderly Book of General George Weedon of the Continental Army under Command of Genl George Washington, in the Campaign of 1777-8.* New York: Dodd, Mead and Company, 1902.

Whitehead, John. *The Judicial and Civil History of New Jersey.* Boston: The Boston History Company, Publishers, 1897.

Whitney, David C. *The Signers of the Constitution.* Text for a Limited Edition Collection of Philatelic Commemorative Covers Authorized by the United States Capitol Historical Society. Cheyenne, Wyo.: Fleetwood, 1978.

Williams, Robert F. "The New Jersey State Constitution Comes from Ridicule to Respect," in *Rutgers Law Journal,* Vol. 29, No. 4A, Summer 1998.

Wood, Gertrude Sceery. *William Paterson of New Jersey, 1745-1806.* Fair Lawn, N.J.: Fair Lawn Press, Inc., 1933.

Woodward, Major E. M., and John F. Hageman. *History of Burlington and Mercer Counties, New Jersey, with Biographical Sketches of Many of the Pioneers and Prominent Men.* Philadelphia: Everts & Peck, 1883.

Wright, Robert K., Jr., and Morris J. MacGregor, Jr. *Soldier-Statesmen of the Constitution.* Washington, D.C.: Center of Military History, 1987.

Yesenko, Michael R. *General William Maxwell and the New Jersey Brigade During the American Revolutionary War.* Union, N.J.: MRY Publishing Company, Inc., 1996.

# Endnotes

## Chapter I: Saving the Constitution
## David Brearley and the Creation
## of the Electoral College

1.  Virginia delegate James Madison's notes for September 4, 1787, in Farrand, Max, *The Records of the Federal Convention of 1787, Vol. II,* New Haven: Yale University Press, 1911, 497.

2.  Georgia delegate William Pierce's description of William Paterson is one of a series of of "Character Sketches of Delegates to the Federal Convention." Pierce was the only attendee at the Constitutional Convention to write short impressions of each of his fellow delegates. It is not known exactly when Pierce wrote the sketches, scholar Max Farrand notes. Pierce's comment about Paterson appears in Farrand, *Records of the Federal Convention Vol. III*, Appendix A, 90.

3.  *New Jersey Journal,* December 26, 1787, in Jensen, Merrill, ed. *The Documentary History of the Ratification of the Constitution. Volume III. Ratification of the Constitution by the States Delaware New Jersey Georgia Connecticut.* Madison, Wis.: The State Historical Society of Wisconsin, 1978, 194.

4.  "David Brearley to William Paterson, August 21, 1787," in Rutgers University Libraries, Special Collections and University Archives, "William Paterson Papers, 1766-1898." Manuscript collection.

5.  Madison's notes for August 31, 1787, in Farrand, *Records of the Federal Convention*, Vol. II, 475-479.

6.  Ibid., 481.

7.  Pierce's "Character Sketches of Delegates to the Federal Convention," in Farrand, *Records of the Federal Convention, Vol. III*, 90.

8.  Rossiter, Clinton Lawrence. *1787: The Grand Convention.* New York: Macmillan, 1966, 218.

9.  Journal of convention secretary William Jackson for September 4, 1787, in Farrand, *Records of the Federal Convention*, Vol. II, 493-495.

## Chapter II: Prelude to Revolution: David Brearley Sr., the Anti-Proprietary Committees, and the New Jersey Land Riots

1.  "Hunterdon County Sheriff David Martin to Governor Jonathan Belcher, December 7, 1747," New Jersey State Archives, Vol. 4, p. 86 (ref. no. 1651), *Proceedings of the Council of New Jersey*, Trenton, N.J.

2.  William Henry Brearley of Detroit, who compiled and published his "Genealogical Chart of the American Branch of the Brearley Family" (Detroit, Mich.: Privately printed, March 1, 1886) after four years of research with the assistance of Louisa Brearley, David Brearley's grand-niece, placed great stock in David Brearley's request to the Herald's College:

    *This matter of the coat of arms is of little importance, except as it assists us to establish our descent from James Brearley, for we know that Judge David Brearley, over 100 years ago, and while his father was living, obtained and used the same coat or arms that was granted to James Brearley. This, at present, is the single link of evidence to connect John (1), who was born about 1645, to James Brearley of York, England, who was born about 1515 [This James Brearley is presumably the grandfather of the James Brearley to whom the coat of arms was granted].*

    It is significant that David Brearley, whose library contained a number of books tracing the genealogy of the British nobility, sought the coat of arms granted in 1615 to James Brearley, rather other Brearley coats of arms that were available, such as those belonging to Sir John Brereleye or, more significantly, Christopher Brearly, who was both more prominent and a generation more recent.

    When David Brearley specifically sought James Brearley's coat of arms, he was reaching back just four generations, as his grandfather, John Brearley, who emigrated from Yorkshire in 1680, was most likely the grandson or at least the grand-nephew of the James Brearley upon whom the coat of arms was bestowed. While no documentary evidence has been uncovered, David's father, David Brearley Sr., presumably would have had direct knowledge of the family connection, as he was about 17 years old when his father, John Brearley, died.

    James Brearley's crest depicts a demi-lion rampant, rather than the wings and cross on the original crest, which "probably indicates the privilege of the younger sons, or another branch of the family," W. H. Brearley noted.

3.  Brearley, W. H. "Genealogical Chart."

4.  In September 1390, Richard de Brerelay of York was one of a gang of highwaymen who robbed poet Geoffrey Chaucer, author of the celebrated "Canterbury Tales." Trial records state that Chaucer and the guard or guards riding with him were robbed depredare (by force). The gang took Chaucer's horse and at least twenty pounds, six shillings, and eight pence that were the property of King Richard II (the equivalent of $4,880 today).

Richard de Brerelay was identified, brought to trial and pleaded not guilty, then decided to turn King's evidence against his fellow gang members, two of whom were sufficiently well-educated to be able to read Latin and claim the right to a trial by clergy.

De Brerelay also accused one Adam Clerk of taking part in a second robbery. Clerk denied the accusation and claimed his right under English law to judicial combat. On May 3, 1391, De Brerelay and Clerk fought a duel in front of a judge, and when de Brerelay was defeated, he was promptly ordered hanged.

The College of Heraldry reports that no direct connection can be established between the James Brearley who was born in 1515 and the notorious highwayman. Nor has any direct connection been established between the James Brearley line and Sir John Brereleye or Christopher Brearley.

5.  "Partial List of the Families Who Resided in Buck County, Pennsylvania, Prior to 1687, With the Date of Their Arrival," in *Pennsylvania Magazine of History and Biography*, Vol. 9, No. 2, 1885.

6   Brearley, W. H., "Genealogical Chart."

7.  "Nottingham Town Book," 1695. New Jersey State Archives, Trenton, N.J., No. 728.

8.  Nash, Winona D., ed. *Volume I of the Minutes of Lawrence (Maidenhead) Township, Mercer, County, New Jersey*. 2 vols. Lawrenceville, N.J.: Lawrence Historic and Aesthetic Commission, 1976, XVI.

9.  Ibid.

10. Hutchinson, Esq., Charles R., "Allentown." Charles R. Hutchinson Collection, New Jersey Historical Society Archives, Newark, N.J., Family Records [Series 1], Book 4. Also Nash, *Minutes of Lawrence*, XVI.

11. Hutchinson, "Allentown."

12. Nash, *Minutes of Lawrence*, XVI.

13. Tanner, Mary Nelson. Memo to the author on early draft of David Brearley book, 2002.

14. Nash, *Minutes of Lawrence*, X

15. Ibid., XXVI.

16. Ibid., X and XXXIII-XXXIV.

17. Ibid., XVI.

18. Brearley, W. H., "Genealogy Chart."

19. Nash, *Minutes of Lawrence*, January 1, 1712, 3-4.

20. Ibid., January 1, 1713, 5.

21. Ibid., January 1, 1712, 3.

22. Ibid., January 1, 1712, 4.

23. Ibid., January 1, 1718, and January 9, 1719, 6-8.

24. Tanner. Memo to the author.

25. Hutchinson, "Allentown."

26. Nash, *Minutes of Lawrence*, March 8, 1737 and March 9, 1742, 21-22.

27. Ibid., March 12, 1745, 26-27.

28. W. H. Brearley's 1888 "Genealogical Chart" states that all five of David Brearley Sr.'s children, beginning with Esther on May 1, 1739, were born at Spring Grove Farm. He evidently based his assertion on information provided by Louisa Brearley, the grand-niece of the chief justice. Her records evidently included the family bible because David Brearley Sr., his wife, and his four older children are the only branch of John Brearley's descendants for whom precise dates of birth are given.

29. Nash, Wynona D., "Commentary on Research of W H. Brearley." Unpublished, 1999, 1-3.

30. Brearley, W. H., "Genealogical Chart."

31. Tanner, Mary, "Joseph Brearley and the Campaign to Conquer Canada." Unpublished manuscript, 2.

32. Nash, *Minutes of Lawrence*, XVIII.

33. Stellhorn, Paul A., and Michael J. Birkner, ed. *The Governors of New Jersey 1664-1974: Biographical Essays*. Trenton, N.J.: New Jersey Historical Commission, 1982, 59-60. Also McCormick, Richard. *New Jersey from Colony to State*. New Brunswick, N.J.: Rutgers University Press, 1964.

34. McConville, Brendan. *Those Daring Disturbers of the Public Peace: The Struggle for Property and Power in Early New Jersey*. Ithaca, N.Y., and London: Cornell University Press, 1999. Also Horowitz, Gary S. *New Jersey Land Riots, 1745-1755*. Ph.D. dissertation, The Ohio State University, 1966.

35. Ricord, Frederick M., and William Nelson, eds. *Documents Relating to th*

*Colonial History of the State of New Jersey. Volume XV. Journal of the Governor and Council. Vol. III, 1738-1748.* Trenton, N.J.: The John L. Murphy Publishing Co., 1891, 628-629.

36. Ibid., 595.

37. McConville, *Those Daring Disturbers of the Public Peace,* 137.

38. Ricord and Nelson, *Documents Relating to the Colonial History,* 595-596.

39. Ibid., 550-552.

40. Ibid., 630.

41. Nash, *Minutes of Lawrence,* XVIII.

42. "Hunterdon County Sheriff David Martin to Governor Jonathan Belcher, December 7, 1747," *Proceedings of the Council of New Jersey.*

43. Ricord and Nelson, *Documents Relating to the Colonial History,* 554.

44. "Hunterdon County Sheriff David Martin to Governor Jonathan Belcher, December 7, 1747," *Proceedings of the Council of New Jersey.*

45. Stellhorn, *Governors of New Jersey,* 60.

46. Nash, *Minutes of Lawrence,* XVIII.

47. Stellhorn, *Governors of New Jersey,* 60.

48. Nash, *Minutes of Lawrence,* XVIX, 29-50.

49. Nash, *Minutes of Lawrence,* Meeting setting officers for May Term 1751 (31); May 1752 (33); March 9, 1756 (39); March 18, 1759 (44-45); March 10, 1761(47); March 12, 1761(50); March 11, 1766 (50-51); March 14, 1769 (53-54); March 13, 1770 (54-55); and March 12, 1771 (55).

50. McConville, *Those Daring Disturbers of the Public Peace,* 247

51. McCormick, *New Jersey from Colony to State,* 129

# Chapter III. Son of Treason: Law, Romance, and Revolution

1. *Pennsylvania Gazette,* Numb. 2202, March 7, 1771.

2. Tanner, Mary Nelson. "David Brearley, Soldier and Statesman," in Township of Lawrence, *Pictorial History of Lawrence Township 1697-1997. A Tricentennial Publication.* Succasunna, N.J.: Esposito Office, Jostens, 1997, 224.

3.    Brearley, W. H. "Genealogical Chart."

4.    Tanner, Mary Nelson, "Joseph Brearley and the Campaign to Conquer Canada." Unpublished manuscript, 3n.

5.    Tanner, Mary Nelson. Interview with the author on March 6, 2002, in Lawrenceville, New Jersey.

6.    www.nara.gov/exhall/charters/constitution/newjers.htm.

7.    Mary Nelson Tanner, in her biographical sketch of "David Brearley" in the *Pictorial History of Lawrence* (page 224) notes the failure of secondary sources to record with whom Brearley read law. John Fabiano, president of the Allentown-Upper Freehold Historical Society, suggests that it is possible that Brearley read law with Samuel Rogers Jr. of Allen's Town, where he later opened his law practice.

8.    www.nara.gov/exhall/charters/constitution/newjers.htm.

9.    Ryan, Dennis P. *New Jersey in the American Revolution, 1763-1783: A Chronology*. Trenton, N.J.: New Jersey Historical Commission, 1974, 10.

10.   Hutchinson, "Allentown," 163-165. Also, George S. L. Ward and Louis Richards. *A Sketch of Some of the Descendants of Samuel Rogers of Monmouth County, New Jersey*. Philadelphia: Collins Printing House, 1888, 13-14.

11.   Richards, Louis, and George S. L. Ward. "Statement of Miss Louisa Brearley," granddaughter of Joseph Brearley, to    Richards and Ward on May 5, 1882, in *Records Relating to Richards and Rogers Families Used in Preparation of a 'Sketch of Descendants of Owen Richards,' (1885) 'Memorial Tribute to the Late John Richards,' (1885) and a 'Sketch of Descendants of Samuel Rogers' (1888).*

12.   Hutchinson, "Allentown." Also Ward and Richards, *Descendants of Samuel Rogers*, and Richards and Ward. *Records Relating to Richards and Rogers Families*.

13.   Richards and Ward, *Records Relating to Richards and Rogers Families.*

14.   Ibid.

15.   "Statement of Miss Louisa Brearley," in Richards and Ward, *Records Relating to Richards and Rogers Families.*

16.   Ibid.

17.   Ward and Richards, *Descendants of Samuel Rogers.*

18.   Brearley, W. H. "Genealogical Chart."

19.   Richards and Ward, *Records Relating to Richards and Rogers Families.*

20.   Monmouth County Historical Association. *Cherry Hall Papers*. Box 1,

David Brearley File. Documents in the archives of the MCHA in Freehold, N.J.

21. Hutchinson, "Allentown," 37.

22. Ibid., "Stafford Family Notes," submitted by Sarah Smith Stafford, March 4, 1979, 111.

23. Nelson, William, ed. *Documents Relating to the Revolutionary History of the State of New Jersey Volume IV: Extracts From American Newspapers Relating To New Jersey. November 1, 1779 to September 30, 1780.* Trenton, N.J.: State Gazette Publishing Company, 1914, 83. Also Hutchinson, "Allentown," 32-33.

24. *Pennsylvania Evening Post,* March 29, 1777, cited in Ann Garrison, John Fabiano, and Alice Wikoff, ed. "Allen's Town, New Jersey: A Crossroads of the American Revolution 1775-1783." (Working paper, January 2005), 38-39.

25. *Pennsylvania Gazette,* Numb. 2202, March 7, 1771.

26. New Jersey State Archives, Manuscript Collection, Reference Department, NJSA, Trenton, N.J., Book 15, 164, 412.

27. Ryan, *New Jersey in the American Revolution,* 14.

28. Ellis, Franklin. *History of Monmouth County, New Jersey.* Philadelphia: R.T. Peck & Co., 1885, 117.

29. Ryan, *New Jersey in the American Revolution,* 16-17.

30. Ellis, *Monmouth County,* 120.

31. McCormick, *New Jersey from Colony to State,* 127.

32. Ibid., 129.

33. Brearley, W. H., "Genealogical Chart."

34. Hutchinson, "Allentown."

# Chapter IV. The Brearley Brothers Go to War: Retreat from Quebec, Retreat from Long Island, Victory in Trenton

1. "Extract from a Letter from Samuel Tucker, Esq., President of New Jersey, to Hon. John Hancock, July 6, 1776," *American Archives,* 5th series, 1:357, New Jersey State Archives, 1049.

2. Ellis, *Monmouth County,* 126.

3.   Stryker, William S. *Official Register: Officers and Men of New Jersey In Revolutionary War*. Trenton: William T. Nicholson & Company, 1872, 332.

4.   Ibid., 118.

5.   "Joseph Brearley to David Brearley, Albany, N.Y., February 18, 1776, " New Jersey State Archives, Manuscript Collection, Reference Division. "Revolutionary War Manuscripts," Office of the Adjutant General.

6.   "Joseph Brearley to David Brearley, Montreal, March 7, 1776," New Jersey State Archives, Manuscript Collection, Reference Division. "Revolutionary War Manuscripts," Office of the Adjutant General.

7.   Tanner, Mary, "Joseph Brearley and the Campaign to Conquer Canada."

8.   "David Brearley to Joseph Brearley, March 22, 1776," New Jersey State Archives, Manuscript Collection, Reference Division. "Revolutionary War Manuscripts," Office of the Adjutant General.

9.   "David Brearley to Samuel Tucker, January 31, 1776," New Jersey State Archives, Manuscript Collection, Reference Division. "Revolutionary War Manuscripts," Office of the Adjutant General, 1155.

10.  Stryker, William S. *General Maxwell's Brigade of the New Jersey Continental Line in the expedition against the Indians in the year 1779*. Trenton, N.J.: W. S. Sharp, printer, 1885, 11.

11.  "Notes from the Diary of Chief Justice David Brearley," January 1776-December 1786, are included in the General William S. Stryker Papers in the N.J. State Archives, Division of Records Management Manuscript Collection, DARM WSSB 216.

12.  December 2004 telephone interview with Scott Houting, curator at Valley Forge National Historic Park. The *Gaine's New York Pocket Almanac 1776-1777* (H. Gaine, publisher) in which David Brearley recorded entries from January 1776 to June 1786 is part of the John Reed Collection at Valley Forge National Historic Park.

13.  Stryker's "Notes from the diary of Chief Justice Brearley," 1.

14.  Fowler, David J., *Egregious Villains,Wood Rangers and Lond on Traders: The Pine Robber Phenomenon During the Revolutionary War*. Ph.D. dissertation. University of Michigan, Ann Arbor, 1987, 58.

15.  Hutchinson, "Allentown," 17.

16.  *Minutes of the Provincial Congress and the Council of Safety of the State of New Jersey, 1773 and 1776*. Trenton: Naar, Day & Naar, 1879, 451.

17.  "Extract from a Letter from Samuel Tucker, Esq., President of New

Jersey, to Hon. John Hancock, July 6, 1776," *American Archives*, 5th series, 1:357, New Jersey State Archives, 1049.

18.  Ellis, *Monmouth County*, 140.

19.  Stryker, *Official Register*, 334.

20.  Ellis, *Monmouth County*, 141.

21.  *Minutes of the Provincial Congress*, 551.

22.  Ibid., 461.

23.  Stryker's "Notes from the diary of Chief Justice Brearley," 1.

24.  "George Washington Order of July 14, 1776," in Abbot, W.W., and Dorothy Twohig, eds. *The Papers of George Washington, Revolutionary War Series, Vol. 6*, Charlottesville, Virginia, and London: University Press of Virginia, 301.

25.  "Joseph Brearley to David Brearley, Camp at Sorell, May 15, 1776," New Jersey State Archives, Manuscript Collection, Reference Division. "Revolutionary War Manuscripts," Office of the Adjutant General, No. 2322, May 15, 1775.

26.  "John Adams to Abigail Adams," in *Adams Papers*, 1: 38.

27.  Tanner, "Joseph Brearley and the Campaign to Conquer Canada."

28.  Schecter, Barnet. *The Battle for New York: The City at the Heart of the American Revolution*. New York: Walker and Company, 2002, 161-165.

29.  Stryker's "Notes from the diary of Chief Justice Brearley," 2. Also Lefkowitz, Arthur S. *The Long Retreat: The Calamitous Defense of New Jersey 1776*. Metuchen, N.J.: The Upland Press, 1998, 11-20.

30.  Lefkowitz, *The Long Retreat*, 22.

31.  Stryker's "Notes from the diary of Chief Justice Brearley," 2.

32.  Lefkowitz, *The Long Retreat*, 39-42. Also Stryker's "Notes from the diary of Chief Justice Brearley," 2.

33.  Stryker's "Notes from the diary of Chief Justice Brearley," 2.

34.  Lefkowitz, *The Long Retreat*, 92-93.

35.  Ibid., 75.

36.  Stryker's "Notes from the diary of Chief Justice Brearley," 2.

37.  Stryker, *Official Register*, 65.

38.  "Washington to Colonel Forman, Morris Town, Jan. 11, 1777," in Fitzpatrick, John C., ed. *The Writings of George Washington from the Original Manuscript Sources 1745-1799, Vol. 6*, Washington, D.C.: United States Government Printing Office, 494.

39. Fitzpatrick, *The Writings of George Washington, Vol. 6,* 494n.

40. Ellis, *Monmouth County,* 157.

41. "Pension Application of Rachel McClary Brearley,   December 7, 1836," New Jersey State Archives, Manuscript Collection, Reference Division. "Revolutionary War Manuscripts," Office of the Adjutant General, No. 5944.

42. Stryker, William S. *The Battles of Trenton and Princeton,* New York: Houghton, Mifflin and Company, 1898.

43. Stryker, *Official Register,* 31.

44. "Joseph Brearley to the Legislative Council of New Jersey, Maidenhead, January 22, 1777," New Jersey State Archives, Manuscript Collection, Reference Division. "Revolutionary War Manuscripts," Office of the Adjutant General, No. 2315.

45. "Pension Application of Rachel McClary Brearley,   December 7, 1836," New Jersey State Archives, Manuscript Collection, Reference Division. "Revolutionary War Manuscripts," Office of the Adjutant General, No. 5944.

46. "Statement of Miss Louisa Brearley," in Richards and Ward, *Records Relating to Richards and Rogers Families.*

# Chapter V. The New Jersey Brigade: Brandywine and Germantown, Valley Forge and Monmouth

1. "Colonel Isaac Shreve and Lt. Col. David Brearley to Governor Livingston and New Jersey Legislature, February 7, 1778," in New Jersey State Archives, Manuscript Collection, Reference Division. "Revolutionary War Manuscripts," Office of the Adjutant General.

2. Stryker, *Official Register,* 4

3. Ibid, 4.

4. Stryker, William S. *The Heroes in the Revolution: Address at the dinner of the State Society of the Cincinnati of Pennsylvania on the occasion of the unveiling of the Washington Monument, in Fairmount Park, Philadelphia, May 15, 1897.* Trenton, N.J.: The John L. Murphy Publishing Company, Printers, 1898, 4.

5. "George Washington to Morris, Clymer and Walton, February 13, 1777," in Abbot and Twohig, eds. *The Papers of George Washington, Revolutionary War Series, Vol. 7,* 143n.

6. Fowler, *Egregious Villains*, 72.

7. "Stafford Family Notes," in Hutchinson, "Allentown," 112.

8. "Will of Isaac Rogers," New Jersey State Archives, Manuscript Collection, Reference Department, NJSA, Trenton, N.J., Book 18, 180. No. 2330.

9. *Pennsylvania Evening Post*, March 29, 1777, in Stryker, ed., *Documents Relating to the Revolutionary History of the State of New Jersey Vol. I: Extracts From American Newspapers Vol. I, 1776–1777.* Trenton, N.J.: The John L. Murphy Publishing Co., 1903, 324.

10. Stryker's "Notes from the diary of Chief Justice Brearley," 2.

11. "From Colonel Brearley to Governor Livingston, Allens Town, N.J., May 19, 1777," in *Selections from the Correspondence of the Executive of New Jersey, From 1776 to 1786.* Published by Order of the Legislature. Newark, New Jersey: *Newark Daily Advertiser*, 1848, 60-61.

12. Garrison, Fabiano, and Wikoff, ed. "Allen's Town, New Jersey," 42-43.

13. Stryker's "Notes from the diary of Chief Justice Brearley," 2.

14. *Pennsylvania Gazette*, August 13, 1777, in Stryker, ed., *Documents Relating to the Revolutionary History, Vol. I*, 446.

15. Monmouth County Historical Association. *Cherry Hall Papers*, Box 1, David Brearley file.

16. "Robert Montgomery's Ledger A., found at Egleton in 1881," in New Jersey State Archives, Manuscript Collection, No. 785.

17. Stryker's "Notes from the diary of Chief Justice Brearley," 3.

18. Sanborn, Paul J. "Battle of Brandywine, Pennsylvania," in Blanco, Richard L., ed., *The American Revolution 1775-1783: An Encyclopedia. Vol. I.* New York & London: Garland Publishing Inc., 1993.

19. Shreve, John, "Personal Narrative of the Services of Lieut. John Shreve of the New Jersey Line of the Continental Army," in *Magazine of American History*, 3:2, 1879, 567.

20. Thompson, William V. *Israel Shreve: Revolutionary War Officer.* Ruston, La.: McGinty Trust Fund Publications, 1979, 35.

21. Lender, Mark E. *Citizen Soldier: The Revolutionary War Journal of Joseph Bloomfield.* Newark, N.J.: New Jersey Historical Society, 1982, 127.

22. Sanborn. "Battle of Brandywine," in Blanco, *The American Revolution.*

23. Ward, Harry M. *General William Maxwell and the New Jersey Continentals.* (Contributions in Military Studies, Number 168). Westport, Connecticut, and London: Greenwood Press, 1997, 77.

24. Yesenko, Michael R. *General William Maxwell and the New Jersey Brigade During the American Revolutionary War.* Union, N.J.: MRY Publishing Company, Inc., 1996, 7.

25. Ward, *General William Maxwell and the New Jersey Continentals,* 77.

26. Ibid., 77-78.

27. Sanborn, "Battle of Germantown, Pennsylvania," in Blanco, *The American Revolution.*

28. Ibid. Also Stryker, *Official Register,* 69.

29. Ward, *General William Maxwell and the New Jersey Continentals,* 80.

30. Ibid., 73.

31. Ibid., 68.

32. "General Muhlenberg's Orderly Book, 1777," in *Pennsylvania Magazine of History and Biography,* 35:1, 1911, 86.

33. "November 20th General Orders, White Marsh," in Abbot and Twohig, eds. *The Papers of George Washington, Revolutionary War Series,* 327.

34. Stryker's "Notes from the diary of Chief Justice Brearley," 3.

35. "Orders from White Marsh, November 5, 1777," in "General Muhlenberg's Orderly Book, 1777," in *Pennsylvania Magazine of History and Biography,* 35:1, 171.

36. "Head Quarters November 13th, 1777," in "General Muhlenberg's Orderly Book, 1777," in *Pennsylvania Magazine of History and Biography,* 35:1, 178.

37. Martin, Joseph Plumb. *Private Yankee Doodle; being a narrative of some of the adventures, dangers, and sufferings of a Revolutionary soldier.* Edited by George F. Scheer. Boston: Little, Brown, 1962.

38. Stryker's "Notes from the diary of Chief Justice Brearley," 3.

39. Avery, Ron, "The Story of Valley Forge" on http://www.ushistory.org/valleyforge/history/vstory.htm.

40. "Orderly Book of General Edward Hand," in *Pennsylvania Magazine of History and Biography,* 41:2, 1917, 217.

41. Ibid., 217.

42. Stryker's "Notes from the diary of Chief Justice Brearley," 4.

43. *American National Biography,* 448.

44. "Governor Livingston's Message to the Legislature, February 16, 1778," in Lee, Francis B., ed. *Documents Relating To The Revolutionary History of the State of New Jersey Vol. II: Extracts From American Newspapers. Vol. II, 1778,* 84.

45. "Letter of Colonel Israel Shreve, New Jersey Continental Line, To His Wife, 1778," in "Notes and Queries," *Pennsylvania Magazine of History and Biography*, 39:3, 1915.

46. *The Shreve Papers, 1776-1792.* Emily Scott Evans Collection, University of Houston Libraries, 1967, 3.

47. Ward, *General William Maxwell and the New Jersey Continentals*, 89-90.

48. Ibid.

48. "Washington to Colonel Elias Dayton, Valley Forge, March 8, 1778," in Abbot and Twohig, eds. *The Papers of George Washington, Revolutionary War Series.* Vol. 14, 101-102.

49. "Colonel Isaac Shreve to Washington, Valley Forge, March 10, 1778," in Abbot and Twohig, eds. *The Papers of George Washington, Revolutionary War Series.* Vol. 14, 102n.

50. Dayton, Hughes, "Elias Dayton, Brigadier General, Continental Line of New Jersey," Address to the Society of the Cincinnati, Atlantic City, N.J., July 4, 1901, 24-25.

51. Stryker, *Official Register*, 63.

52. Stryker's "Notes from the diary of Chief Justice Brearley," 4.

53. Ward, *General William Maxwell and the New Jersey Continentals*, 94.

54. Lender, *Citizen Soldier: Joseph Bloomfield*, 133.

55. Washington "To Lord Stirling, May 11, 1778," in Fitzpatrick, ed. *The Writings of George Washington from the Original Manuscript Sources 1745-1799*, 11:374.

56. Stryker, *Official Register*, 42.

57. Lender, *Citizen Soldier: Joseph Bloomfield*, 135.

58. Ibid., 136.

59. Dayton, Hughes, "Elias Dayton," 24.

60. Ellis, *Monmouth County*, 166.

61. Ibid., 167-175.

62. Stryker's "Notes from the diary of Chief Justice Brearley," 4.

63. "To Brigadier General William Maxwell, Head Quarters, August 8, 1778," in Fitzpatrick, ed. *The Writings of George Washington from the Original Manuscript Sources 1745-1799*, Vol. 12, 295.

64. "To Lieutenant Colonel John Laurens, Head Quarters, White Plains, August 8, 1778," in Fitzpatrick, ed. *The Writings of George Washington from the Original Manuscript Sources 1745-1799*, op. cit., Vol. 12, 296-297.

65. Stryker's "Notes from the diary of Chief Justice Brearley," 4.

66. Ibid.

67. "Statement of Miss Louisa Brearley," in Richards and Ward, *Records Relating to Richards and Rogers Families.*

68. Richards and Ward, *Records Relating to Richards and Rogers Families.*

69. Hutchinson, "Allentown," 16-19.

70. Ward and Richards, *Descendants of Samuel Rogers,* op. cit., and Richards and Ward, *Records Relating to Richards and Rogers Families.*

71. Stryker's "Notes from the diary of Chief Justice Brearley," 5.

72. Stryker, *General Maxwell's Brigade of the New Jersey Continental Line in the expedition against the Indians,* 1-4.

73. Stryker's "Notes from the diary of Chief Justice Brearley," 5.

74. "Robert Morris to William Livingston, June 1779," in Prince, Lustig, Voorhees, and Weiss, ed., *The Papers of William Livingston.*

75. *Pennsylvania Gazette,* June 16, 1779, in Nelson, ed., *Documents Relating to the Revolutionary History of the State of New Jersey Volume III: Extracts From American Newspapers Relating to New Jersey. Vol. III, 1779.* Trenton, N.J.: The John L. Murphy Publishing Company, 1906, 446.

76. "William Livingston to David Brearley, Chatham, June 30, 1779," in Prince, *The Papers of William Livingston,* 127-128.

77. Stryker, *General Maxwell's Brigade of the New Jersey Continental Line in the expedition against the Indians,* 15.

78. Whitehead, John. *The Judicial and Civil History of New Jersey.* Boston: The Boston History Company, Publishers, 1897.

79. Library of Congress. *Journals of the Continental Congress 1774-1789.* Washington, D.C.: United States Government Printing Office, 1937, 14:861.

80. Stryker, *Official Register,* 65-66.

81. "Head Quarters, July 17, 1780, To the Board of War," in Fitzpatrick, ed. *The Writings of George Washington from the Original Manuscript Sources 1745-1799,* 19:194.

82. "To the Board of War, Morris Town, May 1780," in Prince, Lustig, Voorhees, and Weiss, ed., *The Papers of William Livingston,* Vol. 3, 371.

83. "To David Brearley, Head Quarters near Passaick Falls, July 7, 1780," in Fitzpatrick, ed. *The Writings of George Washington from the Original Manuscript Sources 1745-1799,* Vol. 19, 141.

# Chapter VI. Chief Justice: Holmes v. Watson and the Principle of Judicial Review

1. Bellot, Carla Vivian and Arthur T. Vanderbilt II. *Jersey Justice: 300 Years of the New Jersey Judiciary*. New Jersey: Institute for Continuing Legal Education, 1978, 137.

2. Whitehead, *Judicial and Civil History of New Jersey*, 400-401.

3. Ibid., 402-403.

4. Stryker's "Notes from the diary of Chief Justice Brearley," 5.

5. Scott, Austin. "Holmes vs. Walton: The New Jersey Precedent: A Chapter in the History of Judicial Power and Unconstitutional Legislation." *American Historical Review*. Vol. 4, 1899, 456.

6. Stryker, *Official Register*, 370.

7. Scott, "Holmes vs. Walton," 457.

8. New Jersey Supreme Court. *John Holmes and Solomon Ketcham v. Elisha Walton*, Supreme Court case number 18354. New Jersey State Archives, Trenton, N.J.

9. Ibid.

10. Scott, "Holmes vs. Walton," 458.

11. Brearley, David. "Notes from the diary," 5.

12. New Jersey Supreme Court. *John Holmes and Solomon Ketcham v. Elisha Walton*.

13. Brearley, David. "Notes from the diary," 5.

14. Scott, "Holmes vs. Walton," 458.

15. Erdman, Charles R. Jr. *The New Jersey Constitution of 1776: A Dissertation Presented to the Faculty of Princeton University in Candidacy for the Degree of Doctor of Philosophy*. Princeton: Princeton University Press, 1929.

16. Scott, "Holmes vs. Walton," 458-459.

17. Ibid., 459.

18. Ibid., 459-460.

19. Ibid.

20. Prince, *The Papers of William Livingston*.

21. Scott, "Holmes vs. Walton," 460.

22. Ibid., 465.

23. Whitehead, *Judicial and Civil History of New Jersey.*

24. "Governor Livingston to the Assembly, June 7, 1782," in Scott, "Holmes vs. Walton," 465.

25. Keasbey, Edward Quinton. *The Courts And Lawyers Of New Jersey, 1661–1912. Vol. II.* New York: Lewis Historical Publishing Company, 1912, 685.

26. Bellot, *Jersey Justice,* 137.

27. Ibid., 134-135.

28. "David Brearley to William Livingston, February 6, 1781," in Prince, Lustig, Voorhees, and Weiss, ed., *The Papers of William Livingston,* 139-140.

29. "David Brearley to William Livingston, January 30, 1781," in Prince, *The Papers of William Livingston,* 135-136.

30. "Lt. Col. William Kline to Governor Livingston, February 8, 1781," in Prince, *The Papers of William Livingston,* 140.

31. Abbot, W.W., and Dorothy Twohig, eds. *The Papers of George Washington, Revolutionary War Series, Vols. 5, 12 and 14.* Charlottesville, Virginia, and London: University Press of Virginia, 1985-2003.

32. Duer, William Alexander. *The Life of William Alexander, Erl of Stirling; Major General in the Army of the United States During the Revolution: With Selections from his Correspondence.* New York: Wiley & Putnam. Published for the New Jersey Historical Society, 1847, 245-246.

33. "David Brearley to William Livingston, May 13, 1782," in Prince, Lustig, Voorhees, and Weiss, ed., *The Papers of William Livingston,*

34. Neale, Isaac. *Cases Adjudged in the Supreme Court of New Jersey; Relative to the Manumission of Negros and Others Holden in Bondage.* Burlington, N.J.: The New Jersey Society for Promoting the Abolition of Slavery, 1794.

35. Ibid..

35. Ibid., 6, 9.

37. Ibid., 10.

38. Ibid., 11-12.

39. Monmouth County Historical Association. *Cherry Hall Papers.* Box 1, David Brearley file.

40. Ibid.

41. Monmouth County Historical Association. *Cherry Hall Papers*, David Brearley file.

42. Stryker's "Notes from the diary of Chief Justice Brearley," 7.

43. Brearley, W. H. "Genealogical Chart." Also, George S. L. Ward and Louis Richards, *Descendants of Samuel Rogers*.

44. Dayton, William L. "Historical Sketch of the Trenton Academy, Speech read at the Centennial Anniversary of Its Foundation, February 10, 1881." Trenton, N.J.: John L. Murphy, Book and Job Printer, 1881.

45. "David Brearley to John Mehelm, Esq., November 22, 1781," in Monmouth County Historical Association, *Cherry Hall Papers*, David Brearley file.

46. Princeton University records, June 1781.

47. Stryker's "Notes from the diary of Chief Justice Brearley," 8.

48. Schuyler, Hamilton. *A History of St. Michael's Church: Trenton - In the Diocese of New Jersey from its Foundation in the Year of Our Lord 1703 to 1926.* Princeton, N.J.: Princeton University Press, 1926.

49. *The Society of the Cincinnati in the State of New Jersey, With the Institution, Rules and Regulations of the Society, General Officers, Officers of the New Jersey Society, By-Laws, Roll of Members, Interesting Documents from the Archives of the Society, etc., etc.* Bethlehem, Pa.: Times Publishing Company, Inc., 1949.

50. Ibid.

51. Smith, Edward Y., Jr., Earl G. Gieser, George J. Goss, Frank Z. Kovach, and Stanford Lanterman. *History of Freemasonry in New Jersey Commemorating the Two Hundredth Anniversary of the Organization of the Grand Lodge of The Most Ancient and Honorable Society of Free and Accepted Masons for the State of New Jersey 1787-1987.* History Committee, New Jersey Masons, 1987.

52. Ibid.

53. Ibid.

54. Stryker's "Notes from the diary of Chief Justice Brearley," 9.

55. Ibid., 9.

56. Ibid., 10-11.

57. Schuyler, *A History of St. Michael's Church.*

58. "Wil.; Livingston, Bowes Reed to David Brearley, William Churchill Houston, William Patterson and John Neilson Esquires, November 23, 1786," in Prince, *Papers of William Livingston, Vol. 5,* 263-264.

# Chapter VII. The New Jersey Idea: Taxation, Trade and the Challenge to the Confederation Government

1.  McCormick, Richard. *Experiment in Independence: New Jersey in the Critical Period 1781-1789.* New Brunswick, N.J.: Rutgers University Press, 1950, 254.

2.  "Edmund Randolph to William Livingston, Richmond, Virginia, February 19, 1786," in Prince, *The Papers of William Livingston, Vol. 5,* 242-243.

3.  McCormick, *Experiment in Independence,* 233-234.

4.  Currency sheets and individual notes signed by David Brearley and Philemon Dickinson are in the personal collection of Donald Scarinci, and examples are reproduced in the folio of color photographs. The best historical sources of information on colonial currency are Philip L. Mossman's *Money of the American Colonies and Confederation* (New York: The American Numismatic Society, 1993) and Eric P. Newman's *Early Paper Money of America: An Illustrated, Historical, and Descriptive Compilation of Data Relating to American Paper Currency from Its Inception in 1686 to the Year 1800* (Iola, Wis.: Krause Publications, 1990).

    Money was always a problem in colonial America. Since the time of the first settlers, the economy was based upon barter. What little money did circulate were bits of gold and silver     carried by settlers from their own countries. Spanish, French, Dutch, and English coins traded hands in the commercial centers of the American colonies based upon their weight and upon conversion tables maintained in trading houses.

    As a child, David Brearley would have remembered using small St. Patrick's copper pieces as halfpennies. Mark Newby, an English Quaker who settled in West Jersey, brought a bulk of these coppers from the Isle of Mann. Since New Jersey needed small change for simple transactions, the West Jersey Assembly in May 1682 authorized these small tokens to be used as legal tender. In 1690, Massachusetts Bay became the first colony to issue Bills of Credit, and New Jersey followed suit, authorizing its own paper currency on July 1, 1709.

    Beginning in 1775, the Continental Congress issued paper money that passed at par value for a year and a half so that Congress could use all available silver and gold to buy items needed for the war. The British engaged in economic warfare by encouraging counterfeiters and publishing advertisements in local newspapers that discouraged the public from using the Continental notes.

By the beginning of 1780, the Continental currency had depreciated to one fortieth of its face value, and Congress authorized states to use $1 of state money to redeem $40 in Continental currency. States who did so, including New Jersey, received credits against their tax quota for support of the war.

It was this issuance of $600,000 in notes that David Brearley, Philemon Dickinson, Moore Furman, John Imlay, Robert Neil, and Benjamin Smith were selected to sign. The Guarantee on the reverse of the notes was signed by Colonel Joseph Borden, whose revolutionary credentials dated back to 1774, when he served on the New Jersey Committee of Correspondence, and by Joseph Kirkbride.

Hall & Sellers of Philadelphia printed the notes on 12,000 uncut sheets of eight notes per page with one of each denomination: $1, $2, $3, $4, $5, $7, $8, and $20. The notes were printed on watermarked paper in black with the backs in red and black ink.

Presumably, each of the six signers received 4,000 sheets, each of which had to be signed eight times, once for each note. The sheets would have been signed from the top down, right to left, to avoid smudging the ink before it dried.

The 1781 issuance of £30,000 pounds was printed by Isaac Collins and Trenton. The paper was watermarked "New Jersey" rather than "united States" as on the 1780 notes and were printed in denominations of six pence, nine pence, one shilling six pence, two shillings six pence, three shillings six pence, three shillings nine pence, four shillings, five shillings, and seven shillings six pence. At the time, the dollar was trading at seven shillings six pence, or ninety pence.

Brearley, Dickinson, Smith and Neil were designated as signers of the second issuance of New Jersey currency.

5.    McCormick, *Experiment in Independence*, 234.

6.    McCormick, Richard, *New Jersey from Colony to State*. New Brunswick, N.J.: Rutgers University Press, 1964, 166.

7.    Ibid., 164.

8.    "William Churchill Houston to William Livingston, February 17, 1785," collection of Massachusetts Historical Society, quoted in McCormick, *Experiment in Independence*, 236.

9.    Ibid., 237-238.

10.   Ibid., 239.

11.   *Votes and Proceedings of the General Assembly of the State of New Jersey, Tenth Session, Second Sitting*, 12-13. Cited in McCormick, *Experiment in Independence*, 239-240.

12.   McCormick, *Experiment in Independence*, 242.

13. Ibid., 244.

14. Ibid., 253n.

15. Bogin, Ruth. *Abraham Clark and the Quest for Equality in the Revolutionary Era, 1774-1794*. Rutherford, Madison, and Teaneck, N. J.: Fairleigh Dickinson University Press. 1982, 132-133. Also McCormick, *Experiment in Independence*, 254-255.

16. Bogin, *Abraham Clark*, 132.

17. McCormick, *Experiment in Independence*, 252-253.

18. Ibid., 255.

19. Glenn, Thomas Allen. *William Churchill Houston 1746-1788*. Norristown, Pa.: Privately printed, 1903.

20. Boyd, Julian P., ed. "The Connecticut-Pennsylvania Territorial Dispute," in *The Papers of Thomas Jefferson. Volume 6. 21 May 1781 to 1 March 1784*, Princeton, N.J.: Princeton University Press, 1952, 477.

21. Haskett, Richard C. *William Paterson, Counselor at Law*. Princeton University, Princeton, N.J., 1952, 210-211.

# Chapter VIII. Virginia vs. New Jersey: Forging a Large-State/Small-State Compromise

1. New York delegate Robert Yates' notes for June 9,1787, in Farrand, Max, ed., *The Records of the Federal Convention of 1787*. New Haven: Yale University Press, 1911, Vol. I, 182.

2. Rossiter, Clinton Lawrence. *1787: The Grand Convention*. New York: Macmillan, 1966, 160-1.

3. Peters, William. *A More Perfect Union*. New York: Crown Publishers Inc., 1987. 17.

4. Rossiter, *1787: The Grand Convention*, 161.

5. Peters, *A More Perfect Union*, 19.

6. "William Livingston to David Brearley, Burlington, May 19, 1787," in Prince, Lustig, Voorhees, and Weiss, ed., *The Papers of William Livingston*, 290-291.

7. Journal of convention secretary William Jackson for May 25, 1787, in Farrand, *Records of the Federal Convention*, Vol. I, 1.

8. Rossiter, *1787: The Grand Convention*, 83-87, 93-96, 101-109.

9.   Ibid., 166-167.

10.  Virginia delegate James Madison's notes for May 29,1787, in Farrand, *Records of the Federal Convention*, Vol. I, 18-19.

11.  New Jersey delegate William Paterson's notes for May 29, 1787, in Farrand, *Records of the Federal Convention*, Vol. I, 27-28.

12.  Madison's notes for May 29, 1787, in Farrand, *Records of the Federal Convention*, Vol. I, 20-22.

13.  Peters, *A More Perfect Union*, 45-46. Also Journal of convention secretary for May 31, 1787, in Farrand, *Records of the Federal Convention*, Vol. I, 46-47.

14.  Lurie, Maxine L. *New Jersey and the Ratification of the United States Constitution: An Exhibition Catalog*. New Brunswick, N.J.: Rutgers University Press, 1976, 13.

15.  Houston's date of departure and Livingston's date of arrival can be determined from the voting records kept by convention secretary William Jackson. Jackson's records show New Jersey participating in the only vote held June 1, which authorized a seven-year term for the executive. New Jersey was unable to cast votes on the seven resolutions considered June 2, the five resolutions decided June 4, or the first three resolutions considered June 5, but was able to participate in the final four votes that day. Jackson's records and Madison's notes for June 5 both note Livingston taking his seat. See Farrand, *Records of the Federal Convention*, Vol. I, 79, 95, 115, 119.

16.  McCormick, *Experiment in Independence*, 256n. Also "Jonathan Dayton to David Brearley, June 7, 1787," in Rutgers University Libraries, Special Collections and University Archives, "Jonathan Dayton Papers, 1783-1819 (inclusive)." Manuscript collection.

17.  Rossiter, *1787: The Grand Convention*, 100.

18.  Peters, *A More Perfect Union*, 53-54. Also journal of the convention secretary for June 8, 1787, in Farrand, *Records of the Federal Convention*, Vol. I, 163.

19.  Yates' notes for June 8, 1787, in Farrand, *Records of the Federal Convention*, Vol. I, 170.

20.  Farrand, *Records of the Federal Convention*, Vol. I, xii.

21.  John Quincy Adams, *Memoirs*, Vol. IV, May 13, 1819, 363-387, in Farrand, *Records of the Federal Convention*, Vol. III, 430-434.

22.  Paterson's notes in preparation for June 9, 1787, speech reprinted and analyzed in Farrand, *Records of the Federal Convention*, Vol. I, 185n, 185-189.

23. Journal of convention secretary for June 9, 1787, in Farrand, *Records of the Federal Convention*, Vol. I, 175.

24. Madison's notes for June 9, 1787, in Farrand, *Records of the Federal Convention*, Vol. I, 176.

25. Yates' notes for June 9, 1787, in Farrand, *Records of the Federal Convention*, Vol. I, 181.

26. Madison's notes for June 9, 1787, in Farrand, *Records of the Federal Convention*, Vol. I, 177.

27. Ibid.

28. Yates' notes for June 9, 1787, in Farrand, *Records of the Federal Convention*, Vol. I, 182.

29. Madison's notes for June 9, 1787, in Farrand, *Records of the Federal Convention*, Vol. I, 177.

30. Massachusetts delegate Rufus King's notes for June 9, 1787, in Farrand, *Records of the Federal Convention*, Vol. I, 184.

31. Madison's notes for June 9, 1787, in Farrand, *Records of the Federal Convention*, Vol. I, 177.

32. Yates' notes for June 9, 1787, in Farrand, *Records of the Federal Convention*, Vol. I, 182.

33. For background on the port and tariff issue, see Richard McCormick's *New Jersey From Colony to State*, New Brunswick, N.J.: Rutgers University Press, 1964, 166.

34. Madison's notes for June 9, 1787, in Farrand, *Records of the Federal Convention*, Vol. I, 178.

35. Ibid.

36. Ibid.

37. King's notes for June 9, 1787, in Farrand, *Records of the Federal Convention*, Vol. I, 184.

38. Yates' notes for June 9, 1787, in Farrand, *Records of the Federal Convention*, Vol. I, 182.

39. Madison's notes for June 9, 1787, in Farrand, *Records of the Federal Convention*, Vol. I, 178.

40. Yates' notes for June 9, 1787, in Farrand, *Records of the Federal Convention*, Vol. I, 182.

41. Madison's notes for June 9, 1787, in Farrand, *Records of the Federal Convention*, Vol. I, 179.

42. Yates' notes for June 9, 1787, in Farrand, *Records of the Federal Convention*, Vol. I, 183.

43. Madison's notes for June 9, 1787, in Farrand, *Records of the Federal Convention*, Vol. I, 180.

44. Ibid.

45. Ibid.

46. "David Brearley to Jonathan Dayton, Philadelphia, June 9, 1787," in Farrand, *Records of the Federal Convention*, Vol. III, 37.

47. Madison's notes for June 11, 1787, in Farrand, *Records of the Federal Convention*, Vol. I, 196.

48. Ibid., 196-197.

49. Ibid., 197-200.

50. Journal of convention secretary for June 11, 1787, in Farrand, *Records of the Federal Convention*, Vol. I, 195.

51. Madison's notes for June 11, 1787, in Farrand, *Records of the Federal Convention*, Vol. I, 201.

52. Yates' notes for June 11, 1787, in Farrand, *Records of the Federal Convention*, Vol. I, 204.

53. Journal of convention secretary for June 11, 1787, in Farrand, *Records of the Federal Convention*, Vol. I, 195.

54. Madison's notes for June 11, 1787, in Farrand, *Records of the Federal Convention*, Vol. I, 201.

55. Journal of convention secretary for June 11, 1787, in Farrand, *Records of the Federal Convention*, Vol. I, 195.

56. Madison's notes for June 11, 1787, in Farrand, *Records of the Federal Convention*, Vol. I, 201.

57. Farrand, *Records of the Federal Convention*, Vol. I, 209-239.

58. Madison's notes for June 14, 1787, in Farrand, *Records of the Federal Convention*, Vol. I, 240.

59. Yates' notes for June 14, 1787, in Farrand, *Records of the Federal Convention*, Vol. I, 240.

60. Rossiter, *1787: The Grand Convention*, 175. Also Farrand, *Records of the Federal Convention*, Vol. I, 242n.

61. Peters, *A More Perfect Union*, 81-82

62. Williams, Robert F. "The New Jersey State Constitution Comes from Ridicule to Respect," in *Rutgers Law Journal*, Vol. 29, No. 4A, Summer 1998, 1038.

63. Journal of convention secretary for June 15, 1787, in Farrand, *Records of the Federal Convention*, Vol. I, 241.

64. Madison's notes for June 15, 1787, in Farrand, *Records of the Federal Convention*, Vol. I, 242-245.

65. King's notes for June 15, 1787, in Farrand, *Records of the Federal Convention*, Vol. I, 247.

66. Fliegel, Jonah. *William Paterson*. Master's thesis, Columbia University, New York City, n.d., 138-144.

67. Ibid., 139.

68. Murrin, Mary R. *To Save This State From Ruin: New Jersey and the Creation of the United States Constitution 1776-1789*. Trenton, N.J.: New Jersey Historical Commission, Department of State, 1987, 56-58.

69. Yates' notes for June 15, 1787, in Farrand, *Records of the Federal Convention*, Vol. I, 246.

70. Ibid.

71. Madison's notes for June 16, 1787, in Farrand, *Records of the Federal Convention*, Vol. I, 249-250.

72. Ibid., 251.

73. Yates' notes for June 16, 1787, in Farrand, *Records of the Federal Convention*, Vol. I, 259.

74. Madison's notes for June 16, 1787, in Farrand, *Records of the Federal Convention*, Vol. I, 251.

75. Ibid., 252-254.

76. Ibid., 255.

77. Farrand, *Records of the Federal Convention*, Vol. I, 281-311.

78. *Convention*, Vol. I, 314-322.

79. Journal of convention secretary for June 19, 1787, in Farrand, *Records of the Federal Convention*, Vol. I, 313.

80. Journal of convention secretary for June 21, 1787, in Farrand, *Records of the Federal Convention*, Vol. I, 353.

81. Papers with Paterson's other notes from the convention. Farrand, *Records of the Federal Convention*, Vol. I, 443.

82 "William Paterson to his wife, Euphemia White, July 2, 1787, Philadelphia" in Rutgers University Libraries, Special Collections and University Archives, "William Paterson Papers, 1766-1898." Manuscript collection.

83. Madison's notes for June 30, 1787, in Farrand, *Records of the Federal Convention*, Vol. I, 481.

84. Ibid.

85.  Journal of convention secretary for June 30, 1787, in Farrand, *Records of the Federal Convention*, Vol. I, 480.

86.  Journal of convention secretary for July 2, 1787, in Farrand, *Records of the Federal Convention*, Vol. I, 509-510.

87.  Rossiter, *1787: The Grand Convention*, 187.

88.  "William Paterson to his wife, Euphemia White, July 2, 1787, Philadelphia" in Rutgers University Libraries, Special Collections and University Archives, "William Paterson Papers, 1766-1898." Manuscript collection.

89.  Madison's notes for July 9, 1787, in Farrand, *Records of the Federal Convention*, Vol. I, 559-560.

90.  Ibid., 561.

91.  Ibid., 562.

92.  Ibid.

93.  Journal of convention secretary for July 9, 1787, in Farrand, *Records of the Federal Convention*, Vol. I, 558.

94.  Paterson's notes on estimated number of free and slave inhabitants in the 13 states, in Farrand, *Records of the Federal Convention*, Vol. I, 572

95.  Brearley's estimate of the number of white and black inhabitants of each state was written on a single sheet of paper. The page was among the Brearley papers turned over to Secretary of State John Quincy Adams in 1819 by Brearley's executor, Joseph Bloomfield. The other side of the paper contained Brearley's estimate of the number of members of Congress to which each state would have been entitled if representation were based upon each state's tax quota as of 1785. Both sides of page printed in Farrand, *Records of the Federal Convention*, Vol. I, 573-574.

96.  Charles C. Pinckney's speech to the South Carolina House of Representatives on a Thursday in January, 1788, in Farrand, *Records of the Federal Convention*, Vol. III, 252-253.

97.  Journal of convention secretary for July 10, 1787, in Farrand, *Records of the Federal Convention*, Vol. I, 563-565

98.  Madison's notes for July 10, 1787, in Farrand, *Records of the Federal Convention*, Vol. I, 566.

99.  "George Washington to Alexander Hamilton, July 10, 1787," in Farrand, *Records of the Federal Convention*, Vol. III, 56-57.

100. Farrand, *Records of the Federal Convention*, Vol. III, Appendix A, LVII-LVIII.

101. "William Paterson to his wife, Euphemia White, July 11, 1787,

Philadelphia" in Rutgers University Libraries, Special Collections and University Archives, "William Paterson Papers, 1766-1898." Manuscript collection.

102. "Jonathan Dayton to William Livingston, Philadelphia, July 13, 1787," in Prince, Lustig, Voorhees, and Weiss, ed., *The Papers of William Livingston*, 293-294.

103. "William Livingston to John Jay, Elizabeth Town, July 19, 1787," in Prince, Lustig, Voorhees, and Weiss, ed., *The Papers of William Livingston*, 301.

104. Journal of convention secretary for July 16, 1787, in Farrand, *Records of the Federal Convention*, Vol. II, 13-15.

105. Madison's notes for July 16, 1787, in Farrand, *Records of the Federal Convention*, Vol. II, 18.

106. Ibid.

107. Ibid.

108. Peters, *A More Perfect Union*, 130.

109. Journal of convention secretary for July 23, 1787, in Farrand, *Records of the Federal Convention*, Vol. II, 84-86.

110. "William Paterson to his wife, Euphemia White, July 17, 1787, Philadelphia" in Rutgers University Libraries, Special Collections and University Archives, "William Paterson Papers, 1766-1898." Manuscript collection.

111. "David Brearley to William Paterson, August 21, 1787," in Rutgers University Libraries, Special Collections and University Archives, "William Paterson Papers, 1766-1898." Manuscript collection.

112. Peters, *A More Perfect Union*, 169.

# Chapter IX. Breaking the Constitutional Deadlock: The Committee on Postponed Matters, the Electoral College, and the Vice-Presidency

1. Rossiter, Clinton Lawrence. *1787: The Grand Convention.* New York: Macmillan, 1966, 218.

2. Madison's notes for August 31, 1787, in Farrand, *Records of the Federal Convention*, Vol. II, 475.

3.  Ibid., 476-479.

4.  Journal of convention secretary for August 31, 1787, in Farrand, *Records of the Federal Convention*, Vol. II, 473.

5.  Berkin, Carol. *A Brilliant Solution: Inventing the American Constitution*, New York: Harcourt, Inc., 2002, 136-137.

6.  Jillson, Calvin C. *Constitution Making: Conflict and Consensus in the Federal Convention of 1787*. New York: Agathon Press Inc., 1988, 169-173.

7.  Journal of convention secretary for September 1, 1787, in Farrand, *Records of the Federal Convention*, Vol. II, 483.

8.  Peters, *A More Perfect Union*, 188.

9.  Maryland delegate James McHenry's notes for September 1, 1787, in Farrand, *Records of the Federal Convention*, Vol. II, 485.

10. Rossiter, *1787: The Grand Convention*, 148.

11. Madison's notes for September 3, 1787, in Farrand, *Records of the Federal Convention*, Vol. II, 489-492.

12. Journal of convention secretary for September 3, 1787, in Farrand, *Records of the Federal Convention*, Vol. II, 487.

13. Madison's notes for September 4, 1787, in Farrand, *Records of the Federal Convention*, Vol. II, 497.

14. Farrand, *Records of the Federal Convention*, Vol. II, 496n-497n.

15. Madison's notes for September 4, 1787, in Farrand, *Records of the Federal Convention*, Vol. II, 497-499.

16. Journal of convention secretary for September 4, 1787, in Farrand, *Records of the Federal Convention*, Vol. II, 493.

17. Peters, *A More Perfect Union*, 189.

18. Solberg, Winton U., ed. *The Constitutional Convention and the Formation of the Union*. 2d ed. Chicago: University of Illinois Press, 1990, 304-305

19. Fliegel, Jonah. *William Paterson*. Master's thesis, Columbia University, New York City, n.d., 51.

20. Madison's notes for September 7, 1787, in Farrand, *Records of the Federal Convention*, Vol. II, 537.

21. Rossiter, *1787: The Grand Convention*, 222.

22. Madison's notes for September 4, 1787, in Farrand, *Records of the Federal Convention*, Vol. II, 499-503.

23. Madison's notes for September 5, 1787, in Farrand, *Records of the Federal Convention*, Vol. II, 508-509.

24. Ibid., 510-513.

25. McHenry's notes for September 5, 1787, in Farrand, *Records of the Federal Convention*, Vol. II, 516.

27. Madison's notes for September 6, 1787, in Farrand, *Records of the Federal Convention*, Vol. II, 521-529.

28. Madison's notes for September 7, 1787, in Farrand, *Records of the Federal Convention*, Vol. II, 535-543.

29. Journal of convention secretary for September 8, 1787, in Farrand, *Records of the Federal Convention*, Vol. II, 543-545.

30. "Jonathan Dayton to Elias Dayton, Philadelphia, September 9, 1787," in Farrand, *Records of the Federal Convention*, Vol. III, 80.

31. Journal of convention secretary and notes by Madison, McHenry and King for September 11-15, 1787, in Farrand, *Records of the Federal Convention*, Vol. III, 555-636.

32. Madison's notes for September 17, 1787, in Farrand, *Records of the Federal Convention*, Vol. III, 641-644.

33. Ibid., 644-645.

34. Ibid., 645-646.

# Chapter X. A Task Not Yet Complete: Steering New Jersey's Ratification Convention

1. *New Jersey Journal*, December 26, 1787, in Jensen, Merrill, ed. *The Documentary History of the Ratification of the Constitution. Volume III. Ratification of the Constitution by the States Delaware New Jersey Georgia Connecticut*. Madison, Wis.: The State Historical Society of Wisconsin, 1978, 194.

2. "Elias Boudinot to William Bradford Jr., Elizabethtown, September 28, 1787," in Jensen, *Documentary History of the Ratification, Vol. III*, 134.

3. "Lambert Cadwalader to George Mitchell, New York, October 8, 1787," in Jensen, *Documentary History of the Ratification, Vol. III,*, 137-138.

4. *Pennsylvania Gazette*, October 10, 1787, in Jensen, *Documentary History of the Ratification, Vol. III*, 140.

5. Jensen, *Documentary History of the Ratification, Vol. III*, 136-137.

6. Ibid., 139-140.

7. Ibid., 133-134.

8. *Trenton Mercury,* November 6, 1787, in Jensen, *Documentary History of the Ratification, Vol. III*, 147.

9. "A Farmer of New Jersey: Observations on Government," November 3, 1787, in Jensen, *Documentary History of the Ratification, Vol. III*, 143-145.

10. "John Stevens Jr. to John Stevens Sr., Hoboken, December 9, 1787," in Jensen, *Documentary History of the Ratification, Vol. III*, 145n-146n.

11. "Wil: Livingston, David Brearley, W. C. Houston, Jona. Dayton to the Legislative Council, Trenton, October 25, 1787," in Prince, Carl E., Mary Lou Lustig, David William Voorhees, and Robert J. Weiss, eds. *The Papers of William Livingston, Vol. 5.* Published for the New Jersey Historical Commission, Department of State, by Rutgers University Press, New Brunswick, N.J., and London, 1988, 303-304.

12. Jensen, *Documentary History of the Ratification, Vol. III*, 167.

13. "William Livingston to Jedidiah Moore, Trenton, November 1, 1787," in Prince, *The Papers of William Livingston, Vol. 5.*, 309-310.

14. *Pennsylvania Journal*, December 18, 1787, in Jensen, *Documentary History of the Ratification, Vol. III*, 153, 154n.

15. Jensen, *Documentary History of the Ratification, Vol. III*, 134.

16. Ibid., 168.

17. Ibid., 162.

18. Ibid., 173.

19. "Diary or Memorandum Book kept by Joseph Lewis of Morristown. From the First of November 1783 to November 26, 1795," *New Jersey Historical Society Proceedings*, Vol. LXI, 1943, 199.

20. "Robert Morris to Peter Wilson, New York, November 22, 1787," in Jensen, *Documentary History of the Ratification, Vol. III*, 174-175.

21. "Robert R. Livingston to John Stevens Sr., New York, December 8, 1787," in Jensen, *Documentary History of the Ratification, Vol. III*, 176.

22. McCormick, Richard. *Experiment in Independence: New Jersey in the Critical Period 1781-1789.* New Brunswick, N.J.: Rutgers University Press, 1950, 266-267.

23. Jensen, *Documentary History of the Ratification, Vol. III*, 173.

24. McCormick, *Experiment in Independence, 267-268.*

25.  Walker, Edwin Robert, et. al. *A History of Trenton 1679-1929: Two Hundred and Fifty Years of a Notable Town with Links in Four Centuries.* Vol. 1. Princeton, N.J.: Princeton University Press, 1929.

26.  Jensen, *Documentary History of the Ratification, Vol. III,* 178, 178n.

27.  Stockton, Samuel Witham, Esq., Convention Secretary. *Minutes of the Convention of the State of New Jersey Holden at Trenton the 11th Day of December 1787.* Trenton, N. J.: Isaac Collins, Printer to the State, 1788. Convention Proceedings for Wednesday, December 12, 1787.

28.  Stockton, *Minutes of the Convention of the State of New Jersey.* Convention Proceedings for Thursday, December 13, 1787.

29.  Jensen, *Documentary History of the Ratification, Vol. III,* 182n.

30.  Stockton, *Minutes of the Convention of the State of New Jersey.* Convention Proceedings for Friday, December 14, Saturday, December 15, and Monday, December 17, 1787.

31.  *Trenton Mercury,* December 25, 1787, in Jensen, *Documentary History of the Ratification, Vol. III,* 193.

32.  *New Jersey Journal,* December 26, 1787, in Jensen, *Documentary History of the Ratification, Vol. III,* 194.

33.  "Unitas," *Pennsylvania Mercury,* January 5, 1788, in Jensen, *Documentary History of the Ratification, Vol. III,* 194-195.

34.  Jensen, *Documentary History of the Ratification, Vol. III,* 195n.

35.  *Trenton Mercury,* December 25, 1787, in Jensen, *Documentary History of the Ratification, Vol. III,* 183n.

36.  Stockton, *Minutes of the Convention of the State of New Jersey.* Convention Proceedings for Tuesday, December 18, 1787.

37.  Ibid. Convention Proceedings for Wednesday, December 19, 1787.

38.  *Trenton Mercury,* December 25, 1787, in Jensen, *Documentary History of the Ratification, Vol. III,* 186.

39.  *Pennsylvania Mercury,* December 28, 1787, in Jensen, *Documentary History of the Ratification, Vol. III,* 186-187.

40.  Stockton, *Minutes of the Convention of the State of New Jersey.* Convention Proceedings for Wednesday, December 19, 1787.

41.  Ibid. Convention Proceedings for Thursday, December 20, 1787.

42.  *Trenton Mercury,* December 25, 1787, in Jensen, *Documentary History of the Ratification, Vol. III,* 190-191.

43.  *Pennsylvania Mercury,* January 5, 1788, in Jensen, *Documentary History of the Ratification, Vol. III,* 193.

44. *Pennsylvania Packet*, December 21, 1787, in Jensen, *Documentary History of the Ratification, Vol. III*, 192-193.

45. *Massachusetts Centinel*, January 5, 1788, in Jensen, *Documentary History of the Ratification, Vol. III*, 193n, 194n.

46. "William Livingston to George Clinton, Elizabeth Town, January 9, 1788," in Prince, *The Papers of William Livingston, Vol. 5.*, 325.

47. "Samuel W. Stockton to John Stevens Sr., Trenton, December 27, 1787," in Jensen, *Documentary History of the Ratification, Vol. III*, 190.

48. "John Stevens Sr. to David Brearley, Hoboken, February 11, 1788," in Jensen, *Documentary History of the Ratification, Vol. III*, 191.

49. Rossiter, Clinton Lawrence. *1787: The Grand Convention*. New York: Macmillan, 1966, 285-289.

50. McCormick, *Experiment in Independence*, 271.

51. "William Livingston to Elijah Clark, February 7, 1788," in McCormick, *Experiment in Independence*, 275.

52. "William Livingston to the Assembly, Trenton, August 29, 1788," in Prince, *The Papers of William Livingston, Vol. 5.*, 354-355.

53. McCormick, *Experiment in Independence*, 274.

54. Ibid., 255.

# Chapter XI. The First Electoral College: A Final Duty, Death 'Much Regretted'

1. "David Brearley to W. Dayton, December 17, 1789," in Monmouth County Historical Association, *Cherry Hall Papers*, David Brearley File.

2. McCormick, *Experiment in Independence,* 288, 288n, 289n.

3. "Proclamation by His Excellency William Livingston, Esq., New Brunswick, [January 13, 1789]," in Prince, *The Papers of William Livingston, Vol. 5*, 372.

4. Peters, *A More Perfect Union*, 197-199.

5. "Electoral Votes for President and Vice President." http://www.nara.gov/fedreg/elctcoll/ecstats.html.

6. Ibid.

7. Walker, Edwin Robert, et. al. *A History of Trenton 1679-1929: Two Hundred and Fifty Years of a Notable Town with Links in Four Centuries.* Vol. 1. Princeton, N.J.: Princeton University Press, 1929.

8. Stryker, William S., *Washington's Reception by the People of New Jersey in 1789.* Trenton, N.J.: Naar, Day & Naar, 1882, 4-6.

9. Lender, Mark Edward, *"This Honorable Court": A History of the United States District Court for the District of New Jersey* (working title). New Brunswick, N.J.: Rutgers University Press, 2005, draft of Chapter 1.

10. Ibid.

11. "Elias Dayton to George Washington, Elizth Town [N.J.], August 17, 1789," in Abbot, W. W., and Dorothy Twohig, eds. *The Papers of George Washington, Confederation Series, Vol. 3,* Charlottesville, Va., and London: University Press of Virginia, 1992-1997, 480-481.

12. Lender, *"This Honorable Court,"* draft of Chapter 1.

13. "David Brearley to Jonathan Dayton, September 24, 1780," Newark Historical Society, quoted in Lender, *"This Honorable Court,"* draft of Chapter 1.

14. Abbot and Twohig, *The Papers of George Washington, Confederation Series, Vol. 4,* 85.

15. Whitehead, John. *The Judicial and Civil History of New Jersey.* Boston: The Boston History Company, Publishers, 1897, 405-406.

16. Lender, *"This Honorable Court,"* draft of Chapter 1.

17. "David Brearley to Jonathan Dayton, November 22, 1789," in McCormick, *Experiment in Independence,* 285.

18. David Brearley letter to a creditor, January 11, 1790, in Monmouth County Historical Association, *Cherry Hall Papers.* Box 1, David Brearley File.

19. "David Brearley to W. Dayton, December 17, 1789," in Monmouth County Historical Association, *Cherry Hall Papers.* Box 1, David Brearley File.

20. Lender, *"This Honorable Court,"* draft of Chapter 1.

21. David Brearley letter to a creditor, January 11, 1790, in Monmouth County Historical Association, *Cherry Hall Papers,* David Brearley File.

22. Marcus, Maeva, ed. *The Documentary History of the Supreme Court of the United States, 1789-1800. Volume Two. The Justices on Circuit*

*1790-1794.* New York: Columbia University Press, 1988, 20.

23.   "The Early Documentary History of the United States District Court for the District of New Jersey." http://pacer.njd.uscourts.gov/njdc/hist1.htm.

24.   Hutchinson, "Allentown," and Tanner, "David Brearley," in *Pictorial History of Lawrence Township,* 224.

25.   Smith, Edward Y., Jr., Earl G. Gieser, George J. Goss, Frank Z. Kovach, and Stanford Lanterman. *History of Freemasonry in New Jersey Commemorating the Two Hundredth Anniversary of the Organization of the Grand Lodge of The Most Ancient and Honorable Society of Free and Accepted Masons for the State of New Jersey 1787-1987.* History Committee, New Jersey Masons, 1987, 5.

26.   Schuyler, Hamilton. *A History of St. Michael's Church.*

27.   "Will of David Brearley, August 31, 1790," in Monmouth County Historical Association, *Cherry Hall Papers,* David Brearley File.

28.   Ibid.

29.   "Inventory of David Brearley's Estate," September 18, 1790, in Monmouth County Historical Association, *Cherry Hall Papers,* David Brearley File.

30.   Brearley, W. H., "Genealogical Chart."

31.   Hutchinson, "Allentown."

# Appendices

1.   Yale Law School's Avalon Project provides on-line access to a comprehensive catalogue of the most important documents in U.S. history. The home page is http://www.yale.edu/lawweb/avalon/. The Articles of Confederation were approved by Congress on November 15, 1777, and took effect after ratification by Maryland on March 1, 1781.

2.   http://www.yale.edu/lawweb/avalon/artconf.htm.

3.   Journal of the House of Delegates of the Commonwealth of Virginia, January 21, 1786, reproduced by the Avalon Project at http://www.yale.edu/lawweb/avalon/const/const03.htm.

4.   McCormick, Experiment in Independence, 253.

5.   The report of the Annapolis Convention was signed by all twelve com-

missioners: Egbert Benson and Alexander Hamilton of New York; Abraham Clark, William Churchill Houston, and James Schureman of New Jersey; Tench Coxe of Pennsylvania; George Read, John Dickinson, and Richard Bassett of Delaware; and Edmund Randolph, James Madison, and St. George Tucker of Virginia. Posted at http://www.yale.edu/lawweb/avalon/amerdoc/annapoli.htm.

6.  Madison's notes for May 29, 1787, in Farrand, *Records of the Federal Convention*, Vol. I, 20-22.

7.  http://www.yale.edu/lawweb/avalon/const/pinckney.htm. Plan quoted from *American Historical Review*, Vol. IX, 741-747.

8.  Madison's notes for June 9, 1787, in Farrand, *Records of the Federal Convention*, Vol. I, 176-177.

9.  Yates' notes for June 9, 1787, in Farrand, *Records of the Federal Convention*, Vol. I, 181-182.

10. King's notes for June 9, 1787, in Farrand, *Records of the Federal Convention*, Vol. I, 184.

11. Strayer, Joseph Reese. The Delegate From New York or Proceedings of the Federal Convention of 1787 From the Notes of John Lansing Jr. Princeton, N.J.: Princeton University Press, 1939, 42-43.

12. Paterson's notes for June 9, 1787, in Farrand, *Records of the Federal Convention*, Vol. I, XXX.

13. "Sherman's Proposals," in Farrand, Records of the Federal Convention, Vol. III, 615-616.

14. "Paterson Resolutions," in Farrand. Records of the Federal Convention, Vol. III, 611-613.

15. Luther Martin's draft of resolutions considered for inclusion in the New Jersey Plan, cited at http://www.yale.edu/lawweb/avalon/const/patextc.htm.

16. Brearley's and Paterson's copies of the New Jersey Plan, cited at http://www.yale.edu/lawweb/avalon/const/patexta.htm.

17. Madison's notes for June 15, 1787, in Farrand, *Records of the Federal Convention*, Vol. I, 242-245.

18. Madison's notes for September 1, 1787, in Farrand, *Records of the Federal Convention*, Vol. II, 484.

19. Madison's notes for September 4, 1787, in Farrand, *Records of the Federal Convention*, Vol. II, 497-499.

20. Madison's notes for September 5, 1787, in Farrand, *Records of the Federal Convention*, Vol. II, 508-509.

21. Constitution of the United States as adopted September 17, 1787.

# Index

(Note: All towns and counties are New Jersey,
unless otherwise noted).

Brearley, Elizabeth Mullen (first wife), 47-51, 80-82, 121

Brearley, Esther (daughter, nicknamed "Hettie" or "Hetty"), 81-82, 122, 126, 247

Brearley, Esther (sister), 31, 43

Brearley, George (son), 247

Brearley, James (cousin), 44

Brearley, James (uncle), 28-29, 39

Brearley, James, of York, 24

Brearley, John (grandfather), 23-31

Brearley, John (uncle), 28-30, 39, 44

Brearley, Joseph (uncle), 28-29

Brearley, Joseph (brother), 31, 41, 43-44, 55, 58-62, 68-70, 74-77, 126

Brearley, Joseph (son), 126,247

Brearley, Louisa (grand-niece) , 49, 76

Brearley, Mary (stepsister, Mary Olden), 25-26, 29

Brearley, Mary (daughter), 82, 126, 247

Brearley, Mary Clark (mother), 30, 43

Brearley, Polly, 89

Brearley, Rachel McClary (sister-in-law), 74, 76

Brearley, Ruth (aunt), 28-29

Brearley, Sarah Wood Biles Brearley (grandmother), 25-26, 28-30, 43

Brearley, William (son), 51, 81-82

Brearley, William Henry, 30-31, 49, 55, 122

Brearley, Zerujah (sister), 31, 44

Brearly, Christopher, 24

Brereleye, Sir John, 24

Brereleye, Richard de, 24

British East India Company, 52

British, 41, 46, 52-55, 65, 68, 70-71, 79-80, 83-86, 91, 94-96, 105, 111-112, 114, 116, 162, 231

Brooklyn Heights, N.Y., 70

Brunswick (New Brunswick), 52, 63, 65, 72, 91, 126, 192, 215, 219, 237, 244-245

Brunswick Gazette, 215

Bucks County, Pa., 23-25

Burgoyne, John, General, 47, 89

Burlington Advertiser, 245

Burlington County Militia, 66

Burlington County, 29, 66, 98, 228, 230

Burlington Court, 109, 179

Bush, George W., 300

Butler, Pierce, 152, 195

Cadwalader,  Lambert, 214

Camp, Caleb, 100

Canada, 59, 62, 65, 70, 75

Canterbury Tales, 24

Cape May County, 220

Carhampton, Earl of (see Luttrell, Henry Lawes)

Carroll, Daniel, 195

Carrollton, Charles, Congressman, 87

Census, U.S., 303

Chadd's Ford, Pa., 83

Chatham, 100

Chaucer, Geoffrey, 24

Chester, Pa., 24, 87, 240

Chew House (see Cliveden)

Christy, Howard Chandler, 150-151

Cincinnati, Society of the, 125, 234-235

Circuit Court, U.S., 241, 245

Circuit Courts, New Jersey, 126

Clark, Abraham, 40, 54, 132-136, 142, 154-155, 217-218,

Clark, Elijah,  235

# About the Author

Donald Scarinci is a Founding Partner of Scarinci & Hollenbeck, LLC, a 55-attorney law firm with offices in Bergen County, New Jersey, and in New York City. He serves as Counsel to the New Jersey State Assembly, and as Corporation Counsel for the City of Union City and the City of Passaic City, two of New Jersey's twenty largest cities. He also served as Counsel to both the New Jersey Congressional and the New Jersey Legislative Redistricting Commissions in 2000.

Mr. Scarinci has published articles in the *Seton Hall Law Review*, the *Seton Hall Legislative Journal*, *New Jersey Heritage*, the *New Jersey Law Journal*, *New Jersey Lawyer*, *Municipal Bond News*, *The Numismatist*, and *The Colonial Newsletter*. He and his wife, Lisa, have two children, Paul and Elizabeth. *David Brearley and the Making of the United States Constitution* is his first book.